THE ONE STORY

A Psychologist Reaches for the Heart of God

DR. JOHN L. COX

Copyright 2022 © John L. Cox

Book Designer, Carroll Moore
Content Editor, Katie Walker Sikkema
Editor, Lindsay Henrichs

Dr. John L. Cox has been a clinical psychologist in private practice since 1989. He is a frequent speaker and conference leader on topics of marriage, parenting, growth, and the One Story of God's redemption. He is also the author of *Setting Parents Free*. Dr. Cox can be found on social media at @johncoxpsych, online at Johncoxpsychology.com, or on his podcast Good Enough Living.

For the One whose name is Faithful and True,
the Lion of Judah, the Lamb who was slain.

> One of the tasks of the saint is to renew language, to sing a new song.
> –Walker Percy

Table of Contents

Preface ix

Introduction 15

Chapter One - The Seeking God of Eden 27

Chapter Two - What God Has Always Wanted 47

Chapter Three - Noah and the Watershed of Grace 67

Chapter Four - Abram and the Blood of God 89

Chapter Five - Abraham and Isaac: The Hope of the Son 113

Chapter Six - Moses I: The God of Flame and Belonging 133

Chapter Seven - Moses II: Who is this Yahweh? 157

Chapter Eight - Moses III: Love and Law 169

Chapter Nine - David and The King of Israel 203

Chapter Ten - The Prophets I: The Heart of God 231

Chapter Eleven - The Prophets II: The Hope of the Redeemer 261

Chapter Twelve - The Teller of all Stories 289

Chapter Thirteen - The Redeemer of the World 301

Chapter Fourteen - Heaven and the Beginning of the Always Story 333

Endnotes and Appendices 363

Acknowledgements 375

Preface

Yes, I'm a clinical psychologist who has written a book about God.

Of course, in my daily life I do more "psychological" things: I do a lot of therapy, mostly with adults like you and me, who are dealing with depression, anxiety, compulsive behaviors, marriage problems, etc. In other words, I live in the trenches. I also travel around the country, speaking on topics like marriage, parenting, or growth. I get to spend my life engaging the hearts of dear people at a depth that is rare for the everyday human. It's a gift to get to do so. I love my job, and I'm actually pretty good at it.

In addition to my work, I'm also a follower of God (often not so good at that part). But my life with him is very important to me. In fact, given the option of studying, speaking, or writing about psychology or God, I would choose him every time! Psychology is my job, but he is my savior and my joy.

A lot of the reason that my heart can feel so full when I think about him is because of something that happened to me about 30 years ago. One day, the Christian Education director of my church asked if she could come to my office and talk to me. She walked in, sat in *my* chair, and handed me a book. It was called *The Christ of the Covenants* by O. Palmer Robertson. She told me that she wanted me to read the book and then teach it at our church. I haven't been the same since. I found there a God and a story that I had never heard before. The book described how every story in the Bible was unfolding a single story of God's plan to save us. And even better, I found in these stories the heart of a God who loved me and sought me from the first book of the Bible to the last. His heart was filled with a passionate pursuit of me and his people. I found *him*. Or rather, he found me.

After that day, and for thirty-something years since, I have read and studied everything I could find that would tell me more of God's covenant story, what I am going to call the *One Story* of his salvation. Again and again, I was shocked at the God I found there. Questions that had puzzled me for years became clearer as I began to see him through the eyes of this overarching story. And *he* became clearer as well. Historically I had often experienced God as frightening, sometimes fighting shame that I didn't live up to his standards. Was he angry at me when I (often) didn't obey him? I even used to find myself sort of skimming the scary, "judgy" parts of the Bible, relieved to get back to the friendly, "gracious" passages. But I needed not fear. I learned that this God whom I was finding was someone who wove a heart of gentleness and protection even into his most powerful demands. His law began to make as much sense to me as his love. With both he had a direction, a story, and that story was about finding me and making me his own.

In addition, all of the seemingly disparate histories and stories of the Bible stopped feeling like a mishmash of "Amorites and Midianites" and became a woven tapestry of God's love and pursuit of his people. They became chapters in his developing odyssey to save us, a story that ended in heaven. And through the lenses of his One Story, heaven became clearer as well. No longer some kind of blurry image of "pearly gate" bliss, now God's eternity with us was clarified into tangible images of real things that he had been promising all along. Heaven made sense. And the Law made sense. The prophesies about Christ made sense. Suddenly, the God of the Old Testament began to remind me more and more of the welcoming Christ of the New. He is one God. And I was discovering his One Story.

As a result, I got something I had always wanted: *I felt closer to him!* I wanted to be with this person, and it overwhelmed me that he so deeply wanted me.

I love stories. I love hearing them and I love telling them. Frankly, (as you are about to discover) I haven't graduated much past the wonder of a wide-eyed child, dazzled at the tales of God's mighty hand. (All I need now is a black felt flannel board!) But apparently God loves stories as well. In Richard Pratt's book, *He Gave Us Stories*, he talks about how God intentionally wants to communicate his heart, not with dry doctrines, but with the richness of stories. Stories speak to our hearts. Stories speak to our souls. Stories speak to the parts of us that feel love and fear and joy.

And this book is going to be full of wonderful stories!

As my C.E. director had requested, I taught the amazing saga of God's redemption at our church and have gone on to teach it in countless places around the country. Now I want to tell his story to you.

The majority of my clientele are Christians, and despite the various struggles that bring them to my office, one thing seems to lurk in the background of most of their lives: their relationships with God can often feel dry or distant. They don't feel as close to God as they wish. They know God loves them, but they don't live filled with the wonder of knowing that the creator of the universe calls them by name. If you struggle with this kind of dryness, you are the ones to whom I write. If you have spent years in the pews and feel strangely bored, I want to relaunch you into a story that will remind you of the wild adventure that belongs to those who know the God of the World. Stories speak to our hearts. They whisper that language of the soul that can be so hard for our right brains to hear. God gave us stories to help us feel his heart. I want to help you reignite the delight that originally brought you to him by retelling his story. I want to help you see his face. I want you to feel joy again.

What a psychologist does is learn about the hearts of others by listening to their stories. Psychologists develop the ability to learn who a person really is by listening to what they teach us and tell us through the tales of their lives. Years ago, as I grew in my ability to understand and listen to my clients on matters of the heart, I found myself more deeply hearing *God's heart* in his stories as well. What does he love? What matters to him? What hurts him the most? My job is understanding hearts. As I heard his story I began to better see and understand his heart!

I want to share that heart with you.

Walk with me through this One Story. Listen in a fresh way to the heart of the God who made you and wants you as his very own. And let your soul feel alive in his love!

This book is the fruit of my reading and listening to many teachers describe the flow of God's salvation and the nature of who he is. I'm indebted to them for many of the ideas offered herein. I don't even remember where all of my references have come from over the past decades, so pardon is begged for those whose knowledge will be used and uncredited. I do know that special thanks is given to my favorite seminary professor, Dr. R.C. Sproul. And woven throughout this book are wonders that I have received from listening to the sermons of Dr. Tim Keller. His insights, wisdom, and biblical perspective have informed this book deeply. Dr. Keller's ministry has given so much to the kingdom at large, and his work has given so much to me as I have written this book. His insights are scattered throughout, and I am grateful.

Also, as I sit with you to tell this One Story, I have reached for multiple translations of the Bible. Rather than sticking to one version, I have found it helpful to draw from what I believe are the most accurate elements of different translations. I've done this in an attempt to best capture what I believe God's heart is trying to communicate to us in our passages. What you are about to read will include passages from the old King James, New American Standard, NIV, ESV as well as my engagements with the original Hebrew and Greek when I really got stumped, all in an attempt to communicate what I believe is the most lucid image of what our God wants to tell us. So to those of you who like one translation and one translation only, *mea culpa!*

Furthermore, the goal of this book is not rigorous biblical exegesis or erudition in the field of "covenant theology." You can find plenty of books that do that. They're widely available. (I think I read most of them.) This book has been written to fill a space left by the scholarly books: that warm place in which the necessity of theological acumen resulted in a loss of the worship, wonder, and delight of knowing and rejoicing in our God – the celebration, the intimacy. This book is simply an attempt to re-embrace the joys of our savior and faith that arch beneath the truths of those scholarly works. I want to reunite our *hearts* with his, not just our brains. So, to those of you who want a book that dwells just on scholarly theology, *mea culpa* again. This is a simple book with a simple heart, hoping to remind you of the one who "first loved you."

I must admit that I always find it daunting to speak or write about God. It feels like a fish being asked to describe the entire ocean. Certainly, that fish has plenty of experience "living, moving, and having its being" in that ocean, but how can it have any concept of what the whole ocean is like? It certainly cannot, and neither can I. But if you ask me to pull up a chair and tell you stories about the "ocean," stories that give us glimpses into the character and heart of our God, I can do that all day! They are my favorite stories.

Though there is no way to capture the infinite, boundless nature of God's heart, he gives us countless pictures of his character in his word. John Calvin once said that, in the Bible, God is really just "lisping" to us. That means "baby talk." In other words, Calvin was telling us that God has to sort of "dumb down" his true nature and heart in order for us to even begin to understand him. If that is true of the very word of God, then what hope can there be for regular ole humans like us in our attempts to describe him? Fortunately, we can "lisp" as well. And lisp I have. In the process, may he and you pardon me for any distortions or misrepresentations of his heart that might here appear. Instead, may we all take the pieces of this work that *do* reflect his glory and allow them to lead our hearts to worship him, glorify him, and enjoy him forever. And perhaps, to use a term rarely applied to "spiritual" works, maybe we'll even have some fun together!

Listen – his story is brimming with wondrous joy!

JLC

Introduction

The God and The Story

What if I told you a wonderful story? Would you like that? Remember, good stories are rarely simple. They aren't easy. Most really interesting stories are complicated. They are often glorious, frightening, and tender, all at the same time. Some of them can leave you confused or frustrated. Most make you pause and think. Now and then, they can be playful and fun. But regardless, all wonderful stories awaken your heart.

If you want a simple, easy story turn back now. But if you want a story that possesses that curious difficulty and strangeness that all great stories have, then perhaps I have a tale for you. And I think you will be glad you listened because this story has a glorious ending.

So, do you want me to tell you a story?

Oh – and by the way – this story is true!

This story is the tale of a God and of a people. It is a story of great danger and terrifying cost. It is a story of sacrifice and blood. And it is a story of safety, warmth, and hope.

It is the story of God's heart for us.

Most people live assuming that the Bible is sort of like that sophomore lit book you had in college – a loose collection of somewhat unrelated stories, poems, and letters that someone collected into a book. But what if all the tales, events, history, and prophecy in God's Word are actually all joining hands to tell us the same wonderful story

– the gradually developing biography that is the story of us and God? What if, despite their variations and differences, the books of the Bible are all ultimately written by the same author telling us the same story; an author who wants to convey wonderful news to his beloved people?

I want to tell you this story, and I want to tell you about the God who wrote it.

The Unfolding Story

Here's the secret: when someone says that "Christ came and died so that you might live," what they are telling you is actually the *end result* of something that developed for centuries. Most contemporary Christians know a lot about how Jesus died on the cross to save us from death and isolation. We understand that our salvation comes by his atoning death; his paying the price for our sins, and his righteousness that is given to us. But Christ's arrival on earth actually comes as a culmination of an epic One Story that started in a garden and took centuries to come to fruition. This wonderful story didn't start in the New Testament. The faith that we embrace, the salvation that Christ accomplished on the cross, actually began all the way back in the book of Genesis.

This story is about the amazing process that's been going on behind the scenes of history since the beginning, a gradually developing rescue operation – God's plan to save us and make us his own. And all of the Bible's stories are actually developing this 'One Story.'

If you think about it, most of the things that God has created *develop*. For some reason, God made most of his creations to begin small and then gradually "grow up" over time, becoming bigger, richer, and more like they should be. Babies are born pretty undeveloped. When they come out of the womb, they really don't have much to offer. But if that baby gets what he needs, he will soon develop. Within eighteen or twenty years, he will become a young adult, able to live, choose, and love in ways that an infant never dreamed.

Our salvation develops in the same way. If you read the Old Testament carefully, you'll observe something. You'll see that God's people are always looking for something, someone. Listen to the Old Testament stories and you'll hear the people in them anticipating a land, a promise, or a special "One" who is expected. They believe they are a part of a work God is already doing. They are participants in God's plan to accomplish something massive during their own days on earth. Maybe they've wrecked the world like Adam and Eve. Maybe, like Abraham, they're wandering toward a promise they don't even understand. Maybe, like Moses and the people of Israel, they are slaves of the most powerful nation on earth. Whatever the case, all of God's Old Testament followers are looking, searching, and anticipating something that is as yet undeveloped.

And they are looking because God comes to Adam and Eve right after the Fall in the Garden of Eden and tells them to look. In other words, God begins promising. They are all expecting something because God has told them to expect something – something wonderful that will develop for God's children as history unfolds.

That something is a salvation, a promised hope – a story.

Snapshots of a Promise

Within the first few pages of this story, moments after his new children first turn their backs on him, God begins promising that he will bring redemption and hope. But his salvation will not come all at once. It will develop a little at a time, almost imperceptibly, but grandly, with a beauty, breathtaking. The whole Bible is the tale of that gradual unfolding of God's wonderful story. Let's indulge ourselves in a preview of what God is going to do.

- God will chase after *Adam and Eve*, immediately addressing the catastrophe that they have brought upon themselves. He promises that a powerful but bruised "seed" will bring them back home. Even at Eden, God is beginning a story that will redeem his people.
- God begins fulfilling that promise to Adam and Eve through his relationship with *Noah*. He tells Noah that somehow the One Story will be about protection and preservation. Even in the midst of worldwide destruction, God is working to build a cradle of safety for his growing promise.
- The One Story continues, and the salvation promise develops meat on its bones in God's mighty dealings with *Abraham*. God tells Abraham that the promised salvation will be by faith, as well as by the miracle birth of a son who will save his people – a miraculous "ram in the bushes" who will be a substitute for his lost children. He also promises Abraham a land, the beginnings of a new "garden," as a home for his people.
- With *Moses*, God deepens his Eden promises and enriches the story even more. Somehow the One Story will involve a dramatic rescue from a powerful foe. For the first time we will see God reaching down with saving power to free his people from bondage and slavery. And once God's people are saved from that enemy, he will teach them through Moses that he wants them to *look like him*. His law will spell out the way God wants his children's hearts to live and love. He wants the members of his family to bear a "family resemblance" to their Father. At Eden he wanted his people to bear his image. In the wilderness, his love and his law will begin working to heal his people and bring them back to his likeness. But even with Moses, it is the same promise being fulfilled – the same story developing.

INTRODUCTION

- In God's relationship with *David*, the One Story develops even more complexity and richness as the promised salvation takes a turn toward royalty. Not only will a special One arrive and bring salvation, but he will also be a king who reigns forever. God had wanted Adam to rule wisely over his creation. In David, he will be working to restore that perfect kingship once more, and ultimately, his promise will bring us the King of kings himself.
- The *prophets* are next, and they will stand as powerful spokesmen for the heart of God. In the prophets, we will hear the subjective personal thoughts of God himself as he develops his One Story. He will speak his heart to us about the promises (and the dangers) of life with him. Also, many of the shadowy, symbolic themes of the One Story will be illuminated by the prophets. Their proclamations will bring deeper clarity to what God has in store for us all.

  Through his prophets, God will also unfold powerful images of *the One who has been promised as redeemer* of his people. We will learn that, while he will be a king, he will also be a suffering servant. He will come as a baby and be like a little lamb, but one day he will rule with a rod of iron. Somehow, this redeemer will be brutally sacrificed to save his people, yet ultimately "of his kingdom there will be no end."

- And finally, with the arrival of *the Christ* in the New Testament, we have the long-awaited announcement of good news. The Promised One has come! Now at last there are "good tidings of great joy, which shall be to all people." And in Jesus we will see the fulfillment of all the shadowy symbols that have been foretold for centuries. In Jesus, the promised Messiah, we will find that God keeps his promises. Though death will briefly cover him, he will emerge gloriously alive to reclaim his people.

But even then, the One Story is not over.
- God promises not just a savior, but a *kingdom* that will last forever. He is not just wanting our personal salvations; he is wanting to *rebuild his original creation* completely! And that restoration is continuous. Even today, we are still living the One Story. We are further along in its progression than men like Abraham and Moses. We know more of the story than they did and have seen more fulfillment. But we are still living in "the waiting" before the promise is fully realized – just like our Old Testament fathers did. The One Story is still not fully complete, and won't be until God brings ultimate, glorious resolution to his people and his creation – when all things are made new. Until he does so, we, like the creation, continue to "groan" as Paul says in Romans 8, longing for the restoration of God's perfect world.

From ancient times until the present, the One Story remains the same. From its earliest whisper to Adam to its formal inception with Abraham, it's the same story. From its development with Moses to its richness in David, the same One Story plays out, all working to fulfill God's unprecedented promise to bring us back home. Through the kings – the same promise. Through the prophets – the same promise. And in Christ, it is the same promise, fulfilled.

And today, it's the same promise that we believe.
The same hope. The same One Story.
Join me as we follow its trail.

INTRODUCTION

The Heart of God

His story is breathtaking. The woven pieces of his promise form a tapestry of love. And it only gets better. The other treasure that we will discover together is the *God who writes this story*. As we watch it unfold, I want us to look together and find his *heart*.

When I began exploring the One Story of the Bible, I was initially motivated out of my desire to understand God's salvation and the way it unfolded throughout scripture. But as I read and studied, what I found was not just a story (much less a doctrine or a theology). What was knocking me out of my chair was the heart of God himself.

As a therapist and a speaker, people often talk to me about their experiences of God. They run the gamut. Some people experience him as angry and full of disappointment at their "idols" or lack of commitment. Others portray him as just a big meek teddy bear. Sometimes people see him as benevolent, but really just sort of "putting up" with them because of Jesus. Unfortunately (and I get this one a lot), many Christians ache because they feel so far from him. They say things like, "My relationship with God just feels flat, even rote or boring. I want to feel close to him again, but I don't even know how."

Whatever your experience is, I want to help you find God's true heart again. God wants to be known by you, really known. Part of that is because he doesn't like being misunderstood any more than you do. But mostly it is because he knows that if we ever truly saw him, the wonder of who he really is would reach down into our souls and give us something to finally satisfy our deepest thirst.

Here's the wonder: the One Story is not just the tale of God's unfolding salvation; it is also a beacon designed to help us find his true heart for us. In other words, in the background of all of his stories is the heart of the God who writes them. They are singing his desire for us, longing to show us who he really is. Understanding the flow of his salvation story is wondrous, but finding God's heart in these stories is even richer. I want us to find him together.

Our hearts need to know this God

Recently, I was having lunch with a friend of mine who was lamenting the fact that he spent such little time with God. He confessed how he often felt bored and disinterested in his faith. I appreciated his honesty. Many of us can feel this way.

Then he asked me if I had any thoughts as to why this was the case. "Why do you think that I am struggling so much in my relationship with God?"

"Well," I replied, "I believe the reason that you (and all of us) struggle with feeling closer to God is that we obviously must not have any idea of what he is like. What he is *really* like. Because if we did, I believe we would find him irresistible."

I related to him an experience I had years earlier when I took my teenage daughter to a Bruce Springsteen concert. I wanted to introduce her to the wonder that "the Boss" can create. That night, as he flipped the crowd of thousands into a frenzy of joy; as he had us all singing along with him to *Thunder Road* and *Jungleland*, a question hit me: how is it that this man, one of God's creations, can create such absolute ecstasy and joy? And if one of God's image-bearers can create this much wonder – then what must the *creator himself be like?* If being with Bruce Springsteen created this much explosive delight, why are we not all completely intoxicated when we get to be with the very *author* of delight himself?! If God is truly this amazing, then why do we get bored in church?

The only answer I have come up with is that we must not actually live aware of what God is really like. We must not live conscious of his wonder. Because I believe if we were, we would never be able to get enough.

My friend is a painter. I told him, "I love your paintings. You know that I own several. But if given the option to have lunch with you or one of your paintings, which do you think I would find more interesting?" The creation cannot be better than the creator. And we will do anything to engage God's creation – skiing, sailing, sunsets, a full moon. If these small shadows of who he is so enchant us, what must *he* be like? "You just got back from skiing in Vail." I added. "It was beautiful; I saw your pictures. But what would it be like to be with the person who *invented* Vail, Colorado?"

My friend said he had never thought of God like that. Like most of us, he considered God part of his "spiritual" life, someone to whom we are supposed to worship and pray, but who is frankly rather dry, distant, and ephemeral.

But what if who God is is better than anything we know? After all, his heart is the source of all the things we love. I believe that the biggest lie in the universe (the first lie, in fact) is that being close to our God would not be the most delightful, wonderful thing we could possibly experience. Let's find him again!

The God we do not expect

So, what *is* he like? Who will we find as we listen to this story? I think you will find him captivating. He is brilliant, forceful, and sometimes even funny. In his stories, we will see mankind creating all sorts of disastrous problems, and then we will watch as God responds with creative, powerful, and even agonizing solutions. And his solutions are rarely what you might expect. He is wise and clever and shrewd.

We will often see God engage the foolishness and hurtfulness of mankind with justice and rebuke. Remember that when *we* see injustice and wrongdoing in our world, we are frequently offended and angry. Should we be surprised that he is as well? But he doesn't just react out of vindictiveness or revenge as we often do. Instead, he carefully sculpts his response in such a way as to bring the best new peace and life. We will see him do this repeatedly. This is what he's like.

When he encounters our failings and broken needfulness, he isn't irritated and annoyed. He is soft and gentle, responding with an unexpected patience as he sees who we can *become*, even though we are so often broken and fallen. He is "slow to anger and abounding in lovingkindness." (Psalm 103:8) But he *does* respond. He is not a lame softie. He is relentless power.

Love seems to govern his heart, and he longs for the warmest relationship with us. He even sings songs about it! He has swirled in the overflowing love of the Trinity for eternity, and he created us so that we can share in that love. So much so, that he will see him put aside what he cherishes most in order to have us with him. Even to the point of watching his own son die so that we can be his.

He is deeply warm and tender. He promises us that even if a mother can forget her nursing child, he will not forget us. But when his holiness is violated, he responds with blistering justice and wrath. Yet as we will see throughout his story, the most noteworthy thing about him is that when his wrath and justice most endanger his beloved children, his heart is such that he turns that vengeance upon himself so that he can protect us. Somehow, he is someone who would die for you.

When I hear his stories and witness what he is like, he breaks my heart; he makes me laugh; he frightens me to death; and he makes me feel like I could conquer the world – all at the same time. I believe that you will find this person likewise as compelling. He is wise and loving and overwhelmingly strong. And mostly, he wants you. He wants joy for you. He is joy!

God wants to be known. And in Hebrew culture, the word "know" doesn't mean having a cognitive knowledge or understanding, like, "I know how to update my iPhone." Hebrew "knowing" implies a deep abiding, connected intimacy, reflected in statements such as "Adam *knew* his wife Eve, and she conceived." (That is some seriously intimate knowing!)

God wants us to see him and be so very close to him. It is my prayer that as we look at his stories, we will not only see his salvation promise unfold, but that we will get a deeper and richer sense of what our God is like. What better way to get to know someone than to hear stories about them, and God's story tells us who he is. He is wonderful and alive, and safe and scary. He has fathomless love, and frightening righteousness. He would do anything to have you, and he wants you to do anything to have him back.

Welcome to the One Story. Let's listen to it together in all its chapters. Let's marvel as we see God's redemption unfold through centuries of promise. And let's find together the God of that story. His stories are a centuries-long song proclaiming his true heart for us.

I want us to hear his music.

And he wants us to sing along.

Chapter One

The Seeking God of Eden

When I was growing up, there was an old man with a long white beard who was quite a fixture at our church. His name was Mr. Lemon, but as kids we called him "Moses." He later became one of my favorite people, and whenever I saw him in the halls at church I would stop and listen to his commentary on life.

One day when he was quite old, I passed him in the hall as he hobbled by on a cane. Playfully, I put my thumbs in the pockets of my pants and started sort of rocking and dancing down the hall (kind of like those old *Keep on Truckin'* T-shirts in the 70's). As I did, I musically intoned, "Mistah Lemonnnn, lookin' gooood!"

He didn't stop. He didn't turn around. He just kept hobbling. And I heard him say to me over his shoulder in his creaky old voice, "Look again!"

Well, if you think you know when God began saving us, then I'm about to invite you to "look again!"

People often contrast what they consider the "wrath-filled" God of the Old Testament with the gracious arms of Jesus in the New. They talk about how the Old Testament is filled with all that "law and judgement." They think, "Thank goodness that God put all that harsh treatment aside and became the 'nice God of salvation' in the New Testament."

Well, if we *look again*, we will find that God's merciful story of redemption actually begins long before most of us realize. In fact, our first installment of the One Story is about how God responded with staggering love all the way back at the beginning – to Adam and Eve in the Garden of Eden.

Let's join the scene in mid-story.

Adam and Eve have sinned and turned from God. As we peek into the garden, we find God's children frightened and afraid. And then they hear something that scares them even more. They hear the sound of God walking in the garden in the cool of the day. I imagine that in those early days of Eden, this was a little ritual they shared, like how we often walk down to the beach at sunset when on vacation (it's the best time of the day!). As we'll discuss later, this togetherness was something God deeply wanted. A major reason that he created us was to walk at his side. He wanted to be with us.

Well, what had once been the best time of the day for Adam, Eve, and God has now changed. Something heartbreaking has happened. We read about it in Genesis 3:8-13.

Adam and Eve hear God's footsteps in the Garden and instead of running to greet him, they hide from him.

God calls to his children and says, "Where are you?"

Adam replies, frightened, "I heard the sound of you in the garden, and I was afraid, because I was naked, so I hid myself."

God responds, "Who told you that you were naked? Have you eaten of the Tree that I told you was off limits? The one I said would kill you?"

Even more frightened now, Adam panics, pointing the finger at his wife. "The woman you gave me, she gave me the fruit and I ate."

Then God turns to Eve and says, "What is this that you have done?"

Eve finally replies almost pitifully, saying, "Yes, I ate of the Tree. The Serpent tricked me."

And this is how our One Story begins: with frightening accusations answered with terrified blame and finger pointing. We have walked into a world of fear and shame and loneliness.

But it wasn't always this way.

Three chapters earlier things were actually pretty great. God was busy. Like the old gospel preacher said, "The Lord is a busy, *busy* man!!" And what God was busy doing was creating a perfect world for his children, an amazing world. A world that involved deep blessing: intimacy with him and each other; rich, powerful work; soothing rest and peace. All of which was in provision for the deepest needs of his creatures. (We'll talk more about that perfect world God created in the next chapter.)

But there was a catch to that lovely set up. In order to be such a blessed creature, you had to *stay a creature*.

In other words, creatures don't make the rules. Creatures can't just take what they want. Creatures don't get to sit in the big chair. Only God, whose creatures are under him, gets to do these things.

We're creatures, not God. Get it?

So when God calls Adam and Eve to obey him and not eat of the Tree, he's commanding them to remain in their position as creatures under him. He is saying in essence, "If you wait on me, I will provide for you. You will have everything you could ever need. But if you take matters into your own hands, you will lose me and everything else."

Well, we all know what happens next. Along came a spider and sat down beside her, and into our story lands the Serpent. And what is the Serpent's message? His thinking is just the opposite of God's way. It's not, "If you live under God you will receive." The Serpent's message is "If you wait on God you will go *without*."

The Serpent tells Eve that what God really wants to do is to deprive her. "He will not provide for you if you submit to him. You must take!

Take what is yours!"

Now, I expect that the Serpent's message sounds pretty familiar to you. I'm thinking you've heard it before. This is the way he thinks and the lie he tells. And it has defined the destruction of our relationships and our lives since the beginning of time. Satan says, "If you follow God you will go without, so step away from him and take what you want."

It's actually a deviously smart plan if you think about it, and you can see it still working all around us. If one's goal is to alienate people from God, one should first portray his wonderful Way as a list of scary laws. Then characterize the power that God uses to restrain harmful evil as the actions of a judgmental, petty deity. Pretty soon you've created the image of someone whom *no one* would like: a big scary God who wants to hurt people if they don't do what he says – and a list of laws that are oppressive and diminishing. It is a brilliant plan to distort and destroy the truth about God's heart, and it has worked for millennia! We all have fallen for it. It is the Lie.

In this story, Adam and Eve fall for it as well. They believe the distorted words of the Serpent and they break the way that God created things to work. They violate God's plan for them, his protection of them. They ruin it all.

In addition to the fact that this will completely screw up their lives, there is a bigger problem: this act also happens to be cosmic treason. Adam and Eve have turned their backs on the King and have joined Satan's camp. And even though God has only given them one commandment (not even ten), this crime comes with a death sentence and the world hangs in the balance.

What is going to happen?

The One Story Begins

As we begin our journey into God's One Story, I want to look at this Eden event from a little bit different perspective than how it's usually told. Often, when people look at this story in scripture, they focus on all the nasty things that are about to happen. And honestly, there's a lot of bad stuff that's about to unfold.

There will be curses: man's work will become laborious and painful. Even worse than that, the man and the woman will ultimately die. Woman will be hit at the level of her relationships with her children and her husband; instead of safety and significance, she will have loneliness and heartbreak. And to top it all off, they're both under the condemnation of God – eternally!

This is the bleak part of our story. These curses are all part of that "death" that God promised would happen if they left him. The garden of joy and life is now a bleak, lonely, dangerous place.

But if you go to church very much, you've probably heard a lot about the dark part of this story: the sin, the death, and the curses. I know I have. I'm a Presbyterian!

So as we begin watching our One Story unfold, I want to shift our focus a bit. Yes, there are curses and condemnations that will hang dreadfully over this story. But also, here in Genesis 3, we are going to encounter the loving heart of God in a dazzling way. God is beginning his One Story, and in this first chapter of his tale we're going to see some of the most marvelous and gracious things that God ever does!

So, I want us to look at the *good* things that are about to happen after the Fall. And that's not just because I have such a sunny disposition. It's because realistically, this encounter between Adam, Eve, and God is packed with loving, gracious gifts from God to them – and to us. We're going to see here the beginning heralds of our salvation. Somehow, God is going to respond to all of this death by bringing life!

We will see five manifestations of God's pursuing heart as he responds to the Eden disaster. Let's spend the rest of the chapter looking at them.

1. The Seeking God

One of the most beautiful events in the whole Bible happens immediately after Adam and Eve break off their relationship with God. They have eaten the fruit; I imagine the Serpent is off somewhere celebrating his victory, and Adam and Eve have become flooded with shame and dread. Their hearts are reeling with that horrible realization we have all felt at some point: "What have I done?" And all they know to do is to hide.

But what does God do?
He looks for them!

Maybe the sweetest words in all of scripture. (Gen. 3:9)
He says, "Where are you?"

Think about this situation for a second. Here's God, he's the wronged party here. He's created a perfect world. He's created beloved children with whom he wants to walk, and they immediately turn from him. But what is God's response?

He comes after them!

Now, I don't know about you, but when someone has hurt me, it's not *moi's* job to come back and ask to talk. Not a chance. What do we do when someone wrongs us? Let's say you have a group of friends with whom you always go on vacation. But this year you don't hear from them. Then you start getting texts and seeing Instagram pictures from their trip *without you* – selfies from restaurants! "Nothing like a fun vacation with friends!" they say, grinning into their phones.

What do you do? What do you feel?

Do you fly out to their vacation spot, knock on their hotel room door, and say, "Hey, what's going on, guys? I want to be with y'all!"

No, *we write 'em off!* And the next time we see them, our voice has that little edge of coldness and hurt. In other words, "This is on you! I ain't fixing it."

By contrast, here's God, and all he has done is create a very good world for his beloved children and they immediately betray him. But instead of blowing up the world, which would have been his right, he comes looking for them. "Where are you?"

And we will see this all through the history of the Bible, throughout our One Story. We will listen to him in the prophets and hear a relentlessly pursuing lover and husband, seeking his bride, wounded by her infidelity. When he says, "These people honor me with their lips, but their hearts are far from me," (Isa. 29:13) that's not just a statement of judgment, it's a statement of sorrow and longing. He's saying, "I want you back!"

The most natural thing in the world about being human is that when we're hurt, we want to hurt back, withdraw, retaliate. In my work, I watch people destroy their lives and their relationships with this kind of "get even" philosophy. God doesn't do this. He looks for us.

Let's not miss what we can learn about his heart here. If you are like me, you sometimes struggle with those feelings of shame that whisper scary doubts and fears into your heart. Does God really want me? Are my failings and my sin too much for him? Our minds can know that we are saved by his tender grace, but our hearts can wonder, "Do you love me, God, even as mean and insecure and petty as I am?"

Well, here's our answer, my friends! *He comes after us!* Before we can even ask; even while we're still hiding in the bushes – God wants us, seeks us, and desires us.

He calls to us, "Where are you?"

The problem of the Tree

Unfortunately, Adam's answer to God's question doesn't offer us a lot of encouragement here. God says, "Where are you?" and Adam says, "I heard the sound of you in the Garden," (which must have been an interesting sound), "and I was afraid because I was naked, so I hid myself." (Gen. 3:10) Instead of running out to join their loving father, Adam and Eve are naked, afraid, and hiding. They are flooded with the blistering shame and fear that makes us run from love. Notice that they don't run *to* God: "Lord, we have really messed up. Only you could possibly make this right!" They run *away* from him. Shame always does this to us. We run from the very love that is our only hope.

So now in the garden, love feels gone, so Adam is gone too. He's hiding. They both are!

Now, God knew his children would not be self-condemning in their created state. In other words, they would not know about fear, shame, and judgment unless something had happened. After all, if you don't have the "knowledge of good and evil" you can't judge, right? Yourself, or anyone else.

In fact, I think if you had asked Adam before the Fall, "Is Eve a 'good' wife?" I think he would have looked at you a little confused. (He doesn't know how to judge yet, remember?) "I'm not exactly sure what you mean," he might say. "She's Eve. She loves me. I love her."

Then Adam might add, "Wait a minute! I've got an idea! I bet God can answer your question. He is always calling things 'good,' or 'very good' or 'not good.' Why don't you ask him? *He* is the only righteous judge! *Not me!*"

Can you see the realistic problem with the Tree, not just the "obedience" problem? (We make this stuff too religious sometimes.) The ability to have an experiential knowledge of good and evil, in other words, the ability to judge, is something God wanted to protect us from. He knew it would kill us to have it.

Doesn't it kill you? How much does it crush our lives? Don't you struggle because you judge yourself to be inadequate? Haven't you been hurt because someone close to you judges or criticizes you? Don't you sometimes fear God's condemnation? All of these things happen because you and those around you have the "knowledge of good and evil," the terrible curse of judgment. *Don't you wish you didn't have it?* Of course a loving father would want to insulate his children from it, to make it off limits. He knew it would kill us to have it. And he was right!

One of the most common themes that I deal with in my office is shame. We all have a deep, innate sense that we are not good enough, not worthy of love, not wanted by other people. Or, on the flip side, we are critical and judgmental of others. This shame and condemnation is at the root of so much of our depression, anxiety, and relational struggles. Judgment and shame are innate parts of who we are as broken humans in this broken world. Shame creates isolation, and like Adam and Eve, we want to hide. And guess where our shame and pain will never heal – in hiding, in isolation, running away from God and each other.

We now live with an existential knowledge of good and evil, and the chasm of difference between the two. We are haunted by the shame, guilt, and judgment this knowledge produces.

So, like Adam and Eve, if we're judging and feeling judged, God knows something is wrong.

God responds to Adam, "Who told you you were naked?" In other words, "How did you become aware of vulnerability and shame unless you learned of condemnation and judgment from the Tree?"

At this point, Adam does what any self-respecting husband would do: he blames his wife! In fact, he blames and judges God, as well. He actually judges them *both* – at the same time – in one sentence! (Which, I'm thinking is pretty good for your first day as a sinner. Kind of like hitting a double play as a rookie in the big leagues!) Adam says, "The *woman* whom *you* gave to be with me, she gave me the fruit, and I ate." (Gen. 3:12)

Judgment and condemnation seem to now reign in this world. Adam blames God and Eve. Eve blames the Serpent. And though God has come searching for his children after they have left him, their hearts are poisoned with shame and selfishness. God's Way has been wrecked and, as is always the case when we drink poison, death and heartache are about to come.

But this is the One Story, and as we will learn, God does not encounter darkness without forging a dawning of light. Judgment is about to come, but at the same time, we are going to see God jumpstart our salvation. We are about to witness the beginning of God's plan to bring us home!

And it starts when God curses the Serpent.

2. *God Takes his Children Back.*

A pretty big cosmic shift took place about ten verses earlier when Adam and Eve sinned by eating from the Tree. But in the upcoming interaction between God and the Serpent, there is going to be another shift that will shake all of history. Because the very words that are about to pronounce a curse, are also going to be the same words that will inaugurate our redemption. In fact, these words are so important, that theologians have given this proclamation a name. It is called the *protoevangelium*. I know that's a serious ten-dollar word, but look at it – root word, "proto." A prototype is a kind of first version of something, right? So, this is the first version of the *"evangelium,"* the gospel!

In other words, our God is such, that even in his first blush upon encountering our betrayal of him, he is already promising a salvation. In the protoevangelium, God is already formulating a prototype for his rescue plan. Here God declares,

> And I will put enmity between you and the woman,
> And between your seed and her seed;
> He shall bruise you on the head,
> And you shall bruise him on the heel."
> – Genesis 3:15

In this quatrain of salvation, God plants the seeds of his One Story. Let's dig a little deeper and take a look at the treasures that he has tucked inside for us.

The gift of hatred

Notice the first thing that God says he will do as he curses the Serpent. He says that he will "put enmity" between the seed of the woman and the seed of the serpent. (The Hebrew word here is *zera*, meaning offspring or descendant.) What does God mean when he says this, and why might it be important?

Think about it like this: What is the current status of the relationship between the woman and the Serpent in our story? I mean, if you have God's way over here, and Satan's way over there, who is the woman (and all of her offspring, us) with?

See, at this point in history, Eve and all of her children (us, again) are galactic traitors. We're friends of the Serpent – allies, compadres. There's a camaraderie between us. We've chosen sides – the Serpent's. We're the guys in the black hats now.

But God does this wonderful thing. He gives us his second beautiful gift. He declares that *he* will initiate a change in relational status between us and the Serpent. He declares that no longer will there be friendship between his people and Satan. There will be enmity, hatred, deep-seated ill will. And not only will there be enmity, there will be enmity and hatred that is present by the very act and design of God himself: "I will *put* enmity."

In essence, he's saying to the Serpent, "You can't have them, they're mine!"

What an act of grace! God says, "I will personally destroy your affection for the evil one. I will make you enemies!"

My friends, don't you experience this? Don't you have areas of brokenness and sin in your life, and you *hate* them? I hear this from my clients (and my own heart) all the time. Don't you wish you didn't act in the hurtful, cutting ways that you do? Isn't your heart broken and defeated sometimes at how much you can still be controlled by your critical heart or your anger or fear?

If you do, then this passage invites us to take heart. When we are repelled by our sinfulness, it proves that God's promise to "put enmity" worked! He kept his word that he would make us hate the way of the Serpent. His promise is so effective in fact that Paul can later talk about this miracle when he writes Romans 7. Remember what he says there about his sin? He says, "For the thing I wish I do, I do not do. In fact I do the very thing I" …what?…

I "*hate.*"

Get it? If you struggle like Paul and I do, hating the way you live and the choices you make, it means the spirit of God is alive in you, pouring "enmity" on that sin. Now, even our discouragement about our brokenness and sin can point us to his love, pulling us back to him and our need for our savior.

What a precious gift we have from our beloved Father. After all, he could have just "given us over" to our sinfulness like he does to the unrepentant in Romans 1:24. He could have said, "If this is what you want, then have at it!" But instead, he stands between us and the Serpent. He gives us the gift of hating our sin.

3. The First Christmas Story

So how is God going to make this cosmic change in loyalties happen? How is he going to put us "at enmity" with the Serpent and woo our hearts to long for him again?

He tells us in the next part of the Serpent's curse. And to understand his plan, I'm going to ask you to pay more attention to *grammar* than you probably ordinarily do. But bear with me, I was an English major; you're in competent hands.

Notice that in the first few lines of the curse to the Serpent, the word "seed" or "offspring" refers to a *group of people*:

"I will put enmity between you and the woman. Between your *seed* and her *seed*."

When God talks about the "seed of the woman" here he means us, the community of people who are his, the ones whom the Serpent has stolen, the multitude of people who are Us.

But then, like a shocking chord change in music or the unexpected hook at the end of a movie, the next line changes our focus entirely. Suddenly, the antecedent of the word "seed" shifts from *plural to singular* – from speaking about a *group* to referring to an *individual, a person* – and hope dawns again on planet earth! God says,

He shall bruise you on the head,
And you shall bruise *him* on the heel.

The pronoun changes to *He!*

God is telling us that in order for the seed/*group* to be saved, there will have to be a Seed/*Individual* who will come; someone who will do battle with the Serpent. And the Serpent will wound him, but God promises that ultimately this Seed/Warrior will crush the Serpent and bring his children home.

In other words, this really *is* the "pre-evangelism." God is already promising a redeemer, someone to destroy the destroyer. And that Seed is Christ, already promised, here, three chapters into the Bible.

Here in the protoevangelium, we are witnessing the original headwaters of the One Story – themes that will later fill the Word of God from beginning to end. God is laying the groundwork here for a restoration that will one day redeem his people and his creation: A champion will crush our greatest enemy! (see *Appendix 1.a* for a "post credits scene" from this promise.)

4. *The Covering of God*

He looks for us. He puts enmity between us and our mortal enemy. He promises Christ. But God still isn't finished loving us here.

Remember the first emotional fallout of the Sin? The first effect that the Fall had on Adam and Eve? That shame, that humiliating self-consciousness? It used to be safe to be "naked and not ashamed," but as a direct consequence of eating of the Tree, Adam and Eve wanted to hide. They felt exposed, humiliated, ashamed.

So what did they do? They hid from one another, they hid from God, and they made themselves coverings out of fig leaves. "Then the eyes of both were opened, and they knew that they were naked. And they sewed fig leaves together and made themselves loincloths." (Gen. 3:7)

Great plan, right? I like this plan! I mean, have you ever touched a fig leaf? They are prickly and fuzzy and ... we're not even gonna go there! (No one ever said that sin makes you smart.) Bottom line, Adam and Eve frantically (and pitifully) attempt to hide and cover themselves in their shame.

Now, I don't know about you, but if I were God and my rebellious children had hurt and betrayed me like this, and then they came walking out of the bushes covering themselves in such a ridiculous manner, I think my response would have been to snatch those leaves off and say, "Oh, no you don't! You sowed this life of shame and now you're going to reap it!"

But God doesn't do this.

Instead, what is God's response to them?

He sees they've destroyed his world. He sees that they have hurt him. He sees they're hiding from him in their shame in this ludicrous way.

And the loving father makes his children better clothes!

We are told, "The LORD God made garments of skin for Adam and his wife and clothed them." (Gen. 3:21)

Look at what he is doing here! Instead of exposing them to a full blast of judgment and shame, he's already saying to them, "Let me protect you. Come back to me. Let me cover your shame for you. You want to hide? Hide in me!"

What could be more comforting to hear? We all live with fear and shame. We want to hide from each other, from God, even from ourselves. I don't want you to see my badness. I want you to think I'm ten feet tall, good-looking, and bulletproof! But God says that all of our shame and badness is safe and covered by him. The only place we need to hide is in his arms.

But I've got to ask a question at this point:
Where did he get the animal skins?

Do we think about the fact that in order to cover Adam and Eve's shame, there already had to be a shedding of blood in the Garden of Eden?
Someone else had to die to cover them.

I'm convicted by how easily and quickly I run back to God and in essence say, "Hey, God, will you forgive me again? Yep, I've done it again, Lord. You've got a lot of that forgiveness stuff, right?"
And I forget this cost that sits just behind the scenes.
He covers his children – but with the blood of another.
My shame is covered, but someone else paid for that.
Ultimately, he will.
It will be his blood.

5. God's Strangest Gift

But our Father is still not finished loving us here. There is more blessing yet to come here in our first story. And in some ways, it is one of the strangest gifts that God ever gives.
Because, you see, there was another tree.
The story takes a chilling turn in Genesis 3:22 as God sort of says to *himself,* "Behold, the man has become like one of us, knowing good and evil. And now, lest he stretch out his hand and take also from the Tree of Life and eat, and live forever…"
It's almost like he doesn't even finish the sentence. Like if you

realize you don't see your three-year-old, and the back door is open, and the back door leads to the swimming pool…you don't finish your sentence, you just drop and run.

God immediately reacts as well.

The next thing we are told is that "he drove the man out, and east of the Garden of Eden he stationed the cherubim and the flaming sword which turned in every direction to guard the way to the Tree of Life." (Gen. 3:23-24)

What does this mean? What's happening here? Why does God react with such urgency? People speculate, but one commentator said the following, and I love it. But you're going to have to stretch a little with me here.

Think about it. There is broken relationship. God's perfect way of creation is destroyed. Adam and Eve and their offspring are now imprisoned in a world that Paul will later say "groans." They (we) live in a world where death destroys and shame isolates. They are cut off in a world apart from God.

So, what's the worst thing that could ever happen at this point?

God has already figured it out and taken action. Can you see it yet?

The worst thing that could ever happen in this story would be for Adam and Eve, in their sinful state, to take and eat of the Tree of Life and *never die!* Think about it. They would be condemned to live *forever* in a world in which they have destroyed God's Way. If they were to eat of the Tree of Life, they would be forever separated from him, forever imprisoning themselves (and us) in a life without their Heavenly Father.

So God gives this strangely gracious gift.

He makes sure that they could never get to the Tree of Life and live forever.

He makes sure that they could die.

Death haunts us. It's an obscenity. The loss of those we love and the looming specter of our own death cast a constant darkness. God hates it, too. We are told that death will be the last enemy that will be defeated, and I believe that God will rejoice with us on that day at the end of the world.

But in this story, even at the world's beginning, God begins to beat death at its own game. He defangs it. He assures that though death is the ultimate enemy, it can do its work and set us free to be with him as we were intended.

Because of God's unfolding redemption, death is no longer the end of our story. It is an interlude, a doorway, leading us into a wonderful eternal future. Because of him, now when we die, our bodies aren't buried. There's a sense in which you could say they are "planted!" "Unless a grain of wheat falls to the ground ..." (John 12:24) Perhaps this is one of the reasons that, "precious in the sight of the LORD is the death of his faithful ones." (Psalm 116:15) Because that enemy, death, is the very gateway that brings us home to him.

God protects us from many dangers in this Eden story, but here he protects us from the most horrifying danger of all: the danger of living imprisoned on earth, forever separated from his loving presence. His solution is horrifying but brilliant if you think about it. Get to know him!

The Guardian to Eden

So we can't go back to Eden now. We are excluded from God's presence. The place where God dwells was sealed on that day and protected by guardian cherubim with flaming swords, cherubim who will not let anyone in.

But as we are learning, the God of the One Story is not a God of closed doors and hopeless endings. Indeed, Eden is guarded by impenetrable cherubim. But it is guarded by cherubim just like the ones we see somewhere else in scripture.

The Holy of Holies was the most sacred chamber in the temple of Israel. It contained the Ark of the Covenant, the altar, and the holy presence of God himself. Like Eden, it was the place where God dwelt. It was so sacred that it was separated from the rest of the temple by a barrier, a veil, a vast curtain that stood like a wall between the people and the most holy place.

A barrier to anyone who would enter back to where God was.

A barrier to Eden, if you will.

And upon this veil lay one of the most beautiful and divine twists of irony in scripture. Upon this veil lay an image of our hope.

Do you know what the veil looked like? It's described in Exodus 26, a passage in which God instructs the artisans of Israel on his design for the great curtain. He wanted the veil to be 40-feet-tall, purple in color, and held up with loops of gold. And get this: God also wanted the veil to be embroidered with *cherubim!* Cherubim just like the ones who guarded the entrance back to Eden, the place where God once walked freely with Adam and Eve. Cherubim guarded the entrance to the Holy of Holies, the place where God's holy presence dwelt.

So, we've lost our access to him. We are shut out from the presence of God by cherubim angels that you do not want to mess with!

But remember this story I've been telling you. God came to us. He looked for us. He worked to make us enemies with Satan. He covered our shame, and he promised a Seed to save us!

And, my friends, that Seed does come, and he does battle with the Serpent. And he is bruised.

And he is nailed to a cross – without covering.

And the God who looks for us does not look for him.

In fact, the Seed pleads for God to come to him, "Why have you forsaken me?" But God does not respond.

But through his humiliation and shame, this rejected one crushes the Serpent.

And what happens when he does?

When the promised Seed dies, that veil of cherubim in the Holy of Holies rips from top to bottom! It is torn apart! The guards are gone; the barrier is no more. And who takes their place as guardian to the presence of God? The Seed himself!

And suddenly our eyes are no longer filled with images of guardian cherubim blocking God's people from coming close to him. Our vision can now rush forward in history to a young woman, Mary, encountering two angels in the tomb of Jesus, the Seed of the woman. And these are not guardian cherubim, but bright heralds of glory. And their response to Mary is not to draw swords or to keep her away.

They simply say, "Why are you looking for the living among the dead?" (Luke 24:5)

Because now, cherubim don't stand in the doorway to Eden. Jesus the Christ does. And there is no longer any reason to look for the living among the dead, for death has been defeated. Christ is alive and now we will be too! The barriers are broken down. And he welcomes his children home.

All because God began his One Story by seeking us at Eden.

Read and hear the truth that God wants you this badly!

Why? I do not know. But this story in Genesis is just a taste of what he is willing to do to have you back.

Welcome to the One Story!

Chapter Two

What God Has Always Wanted

As we saw in the fallout from the Garden of Eden, God is already hard at work redeeming his people. In fact, you can't talk to Christians about their faith for very long without someone talking about God's "redemption." We believe that in Christ, God is redeeming us from spiritual death and bringing us to himself – all the time! This is our delight as his children, to be his and to be made into his glorious image.

But here's the part I want you to get: God is passionate about saving us and forgiving our sins, but he also wants to do much, much more than that. *Remarkably, God wants to do more than just save us and bring us to heaven. He wants to redeem <u>all</u> of creation!* He wants to make something new out of something damaged. He wants a fully restored Kingdom, and he wants us in it with him!

So what does that look like? If God's story is about the redemption of all things, then what needs redeeming? What kind of hope is his One Story pointing toward? If we are going to spend a whole book talking about his redemption story, it might be a good idea to understand what it is that needs redeeming in the first place.

I love "backstory" movies. (Like, how did Bruce Wayne become Batman?!) Well, there's a backstory to God's redemption. To really understand our One Story, we have to go back to the beginning and learn what it is that he is working to rebuild. Let's pause our tale momentarily and do a little homework so we can understand what God is up to in the rest of our One Story. Then we'll get back to the action.

The Eden Plan

Let's begin with something obvious: When God created everything, he could have done it in any way that he wanted, right?

So what did he want? How did he want things to be?

Well, he describes the way he wanted creation in the first couple of chapters of Genesis. I'm going to call that original model, that Way that God wanted things to be, the *Eden Plan*. Theologians throughout history have called it more sophisticated things like the "Covenant of Works," "the Created Order," or the "Covenant of Creation." Whatever you call it, God had a plan when he created the world. He had a Way, a model. And it was wonderful.

Let's look at it.

We get our first glimpse of the Eden Plan as it unfolds during God's dance of creation. The story begins of course, in Genesis 1, with the song that describes God at work creating. And notice it *is* a song. If you look at the way the passage is set out on the page, it's in lyrical form and it has a musical style, a sort of repetition. Each part flows with a refrain something like this: "God said 'Let there be light', and there was light. And God saw that the light was good, and there was evening and morning, of the first day." (Gen. 1:3-31)

And this pattern runs throughout the whole chapter.

The Old Testament is full of these kinds of songs. It's how ancient people remembered their stories. It's how they worshiped. There's Moses's song at the Red Sea, and Hannah's song in the book of 1 Samuel. Old Testament people worshiped in song and God sings one of them as he makes the world. And it's not so much a song about *how* the world was created as it is a song about *who* did the creating and what he originally wanted that creation to look like.

So what is the form that God originally wanted for his world? What is the Eden Plan? The Song of Creation reveals five things God wanted:

1. A people who were like him, "in his image."
2. A people who worked and ruled in his creation.
3. A people who lived in abiding relationship with him and each other.
4. A people who rested in him and in his Sabbath.
5. A people who submitted to him and his Way.

These five parts of God's Eden Design will be important to us throughout our One Story. If you are going to walk this journey with me, you need to understand this: *God still wants what he wanted in the Eden Plan.* The Eden Plan will not be some left over model, forgotten in the book of Genesis; God still wants these things today. He will always want these things. I believe that even heaven will reflect his original plan. This is what he is redeeming. Restoring these things is what the One Story is about!

So you might want to get out your highlighter and notebook, because we're going to look at what God originally wanted. I want to ground you in what you were created for and where God is taking you before we get back to watching him work. Let's look more closely at what God has always wanted.

1. A people who are like him in his image.

> *So God created man in his own image, in the image of God he created him; male and female he created them.*
> *– Genesis 1:27*

THE ONE STORY

If you were the king of an ancient civilization (before the days of TV news and internet), there were countless members of your kingdom living in outlying regions of your land who would probably live and die and never actually *see* you. And that's a problem. Because one day when it is time for these citizens to pay their taxes or to send their sons off to fight in your wars, they are going to start wondering, "Wait a minute, who is this king who keeps demanding so much of me? I've never even seen him! Have you?"

Well, to solve that problem, many rulers would erect a statue of themselves in the town square of remote villages. That statue was called an "image." And it said, in effect, "Look at me and you will see the king."

It is not coincidental therefore, that God describes his mark placed on mankind as his "image." We were created to be his image-bearers, reflections of his likeness. Within the Eden Design, God meant for *us* to be able to say, "Look at me and you will see the king."

But what exactly does it mean to bear God's image?

One way to explain it is this: The image of God simply means that we share in God's attributes and characteristics – only to a lesser degree.

In other words, God *is* love. We can be loving. He's omnipotent (all powerful). We are "potent" (we have some power). He is omniscient (he knows everything). We are "sentient" (we can know and think pretty well – sometimes).

But mostly this image-likeness applies to issues of the heart.

Like God, we can have hearts that are powerful and loving, submissive and creative. People who bear God's image can forgive those who wound them. We can give up things we wish for in order to care for others. We can be warm and gentle, noble and courageous, like our Heavenly Father. God wanted humans who understood love and power, self-sacrifice and humility. He wanted us to be bright images of his wonder.

We often turn the idea of being holy, or being in God's image, into some sort of an unpleasant "act nice and go to Sunday school" sort of thing. I believe that if we think that way, we miss something wonderful about God and about us. *Righteousness and reflecting God's image are not about being "good." They are about living richly in the ways that God created us to function. Being in his image is designed to bring us the greatest joy!* He is Life, and he wants us to share that life and *fully live!*

My job as a psychologist is about helping people function in a healthy way. And the longer I've been in practice, the more I have seen that bearing God's image is simply *healthy functioning*. His "image" is the model for what makes life work for humans.

Think about it in reverse and you'll understand better what I mean. What is it like for you when you *don't* reflect his character? In our broken, fallen world, God's image is distorted and fragmented in every one of us. We are a mess! Don't you feel this? Aren't you dissatisfied with what you are like? Don't you long to be more spontaneous, more thoughtful, more creative? Don't you wish you could better stand up to difficult people; be more patient, less critical, less insecure? Are you burdened by depression or anxiety or the out-of-control choices that you make? I am, and I know that you are, too (because the fact that we are is the reason I have a job!).

One thing that we all have in common is that we walk through life seeing the ways we live or feel, and we long to be better than we are, stronger and more loving than we are. And when we feel those longings, we are experiencing the ache of *not living in God's image*; not being in a place where we are complete.

Imagine what it would have been like to be Adam, back before he and Eve wrecked the world, back to when he lived fully in God's image. He reflected the very character of God in everything he did. All the capacities of his heart and character worked the way they were supposed to. He didn't wake up and feel that dread about the day that we often feel. When he looked at his wife, his heart felt no distance or resentment. And as he listened for God's arrival in the cool of each day, his heart always lept within him. He was what Man was supposed to be: powerful and alive and creative.

God spends the rest of the Bible calling us back to living out of that image. He wants us to be whole again. This is what lies behind his call for our obedience and righteousness throughout scripture. His desire for holiness and wholeness in our hearts is echoing his creation of us at the beginning. His One Story will call us to be "conformed to the *image* of his Son, that he might be the firstborn among many brethren." (Rom 8:29) He wants us to be joyful and complete. He wants us to be like him again.

When the people in my office grow, it is a lovely thing to behold. They become stronger and more patient. They develop a sort of gravity and substance. I feel it from them when it happens. They are able to connect with others in relationships and they are more confident about making decisions, even in the face of possible failure. Sometimes they even end up intimidating me with the power and love they wield. What's happening is that they are more and more reflecting the image of God.

C.S. Lewis talks about these kinds of people in *Mere Christianity:*

> They will not be very like the idea of 'religious people' which you have formed from your general reading. They will not draw attention to themselves. You tend to think that you are being kind to them when they

are really being kind to you. They love you more than other men do, but they need you less. ... When you have recognized one of them, you will recognize the next one much more easily. And I strongly suspect (but how should I know?) that they recognize one another immediately and infallibly, across every barrier of color, sex, class, age, and even of creeds. In that way, to become holy is rather like joining a secret society. To put it at its very lowest, it must be great *fun*. [1]

Throughout the rest of the Bible, you will hear God calling us to more and more reflect his image in righteousness, obedience, and a heart of love. When you hear this, realize that this is not a new idea. God has wanted this since the beginning. He has always wanted his "image-bearers." This is one of the reasons it makes no sense to talk about being a Christian and yet not to care about the condition of your heart. It's like being a bird who has had his broken wings healed, and then says he doesn't want to fly. He's missing the point! God wants to give us back the chance to be who we *are*. So when he calls us to bear his image, he is not pulling us backwards into some kind of staunch, stuffy "goodness." Instead, he is opening the door to real life and wholeness as a human and saying, "Step through."

He has always wanted this for us. And we will see him at work in our One Story, "beginning a good work in you and not stopping until it is complete." (Phil. 1:6) And once you feel it awakening in you, you will never stop wanting more.

2. A people who work and rule his creation.

> *And God blessed them; and God said to them, "Be fruitful and multiply, and fill the earth, and subdue it; and rule over the fish of the sea and over the birds of the sky, and over every living thing that moves on the earth.*
> *– Genesis. 1:28*

In the Eden Plan, God called Adam to subdue the earth, rule the planet, and name the animals. (It's actually the first commandment in scripture, if you think about it!)

In God's original Eden Design, he wanted us to enjoy rich, wonderful work. Though God was the creator who formed the whole world, he immediately gave Adam the role of subduing it and ruling it. That's what the job of "naming the animals" meant. In ancient Hebrew culture, when you named someone or something, you were establishing your authority over them. That's why God is always re-naming people in the Bible, such as changing Abram's name to Abraham, or Jesus changing Simon's name to Peter.

When God gives Adam the job of naming the animals, he is saying, "I created everything, but you are now my executive vice-president. You are to work, subdue, and take dominion over this creation."

"But wait a minute," you say. "I thought the garden of Eden was fun, but now you're telling me that God put Adam to work? That doesn't sound like the 'paradise' we are always told existed in Eden."

Good observation! But remember that all work as we know it now is cursed because of the Fall. It's a burden. In our current world, we don't know what good work felt like. Work is broken. But work as God originally created it would have been great – rewarding; delightful even!

You may not realize it, but you have an index for this. Think about the things you love to do, the fun things you do well, and how you feel doing them. You're at a college ball game and your team scores. You get on the scale, and you've lost 10 pounds! You finally get up on water skis. That's what work was supposed to feel like. Those times when you work, you subdue, and you *score!* That's what work felt like to Adam! (We'll talk about this more in the heaven chapter. It's gonna be awesome!)

Within the Eden Plan, God wanted to give his people the gift of wonderful, challenging work that filled their souls with satisfaction and joy. Then his people could share with him in the joy of creating.

He still calls us to work, and will do so throughout the One Story. Sometimes we are the eyes and hands of Christ, giving to those who are struggling. Sometimes we are learning and speaking his heart to one another like I wish to do in this book. Or maybe we are just living out the professions to which he has called us: being accountants, rockstars, moms, cowboys, or even psychologists, and doing so as his representatives. God makes no distinction between "sacred" and "secular" work. Martin Luther talked about how the work of a milkmaid honored God as much as the work of the "spiritual estates." He could say that because he knew that when we do noble work as God's people, we are fulfilling the first commandment ever given: to subdue the earth for the Creator with powerful work. As Eric Liddell says in the movie, *Chariots of Fire*, "God made me fast, and when I run, I feel his pleasure."

For the rest of the Bible God will talk about how he wants us to work to further his kingdom. Now you can see that this is not a new idea. The kingdom of God is at hand and we get to work, helping to achieve it in all of its richness!

3. A people in abiding relationship with God and each other.

And the man and his wife were both naked and were not ashamed.
—Genesis 2:25

Relationship with each other

Psychologists love describing relationships. We look at individuals, families, and couples and ask, "What are the dynamics going on here?" "What is this marriage like?" "How can I understand this relationship?" Genesis 2 does a great job of describing the kind of relationships that God wanted for his people within the Eden Plan. The first psychological description of a relationship comes in Genesis 2:25. We are told that the man and the woman were "naked and not ashamed."

Despite how it sounds, this passage is not describing the first nudist colony. It is describing a *relational status*. It's saying that Adam and Eve were able to be really who they were, truly themselves, fully known by each other, and the result was that they were *loved*.

Try that on for a second. Isn't that what we want?

Adam and Eve were able to share their hearts, and it was welcomed. They were able to voice a need, and it was met. Perhaps they even could speak a complaint, and it was received. No blaming. No shaming. No loneliness. This was a good plan!

Don't we all live with a dilemma every day? What if people really knew what I was like? What would they think? Should I hide who I am so others will love me, or risk losing their love by being really who I am? This is the ultimate relational dilemma: Can I be me and still be loved, even with my ugly showing? This is why we are all such good spin-doctors. Deep inside all of us lurks this question: What if people really saw me?

Within God's Eden Design, Adam and Eve didn't have to worry about this question. *Within God's original Way, they were fully known and fully who they were, and the result was greater intimacy, greater harmony.*

God deeply wants to restore us to this kind of safety. Making our love for each other warm, tender, and wise again is another one of his passions throughout the One Story. This is why Jesus will say that the second greatest commandment is to love each other even as we love ourselves. (Matt. 22:39) This is why John will tell us, "Beloved, if God so loved us, we also ought to love one another. (1 John 4:11) God has always wanted to give us a world in which we could be "naked and not ashamed." When his Way is fully restored in heaven, this kind of intimacy and safety with one another will be the water in which we swim. Until then, God still wants us to live our lives seeking and abiding in this kind of love for each other.

Relationship with God

God also wanted Adam and Eve to have a deep intimacy and closeness with *him*. Do you ever wonder why God created everything in the first place? Why did he do this? What did he want? One thing he makes clear is that *a primary reason he created all of creation and all of us is that he wanted to love us and be loved by us.* He wanted intimate, abiding relationship with his children. God didn't create his people to just be obedient little robots. He wanted image-bearers with whom he could "walk in the cool of the day."

And in the Eden Design, God *initiated this closeness with us!*

Do you ever feel like you're dropping the ball with your personal time with God? (Welcome to the club!) Well, Adam and Eve didn't have that problem. They never reflected on whether they should be spending more time with God. God came looking for *them!*

As we said in our introduction, God wants to be known. He wants us to spend our lives dazzled by the depth of his heart. And I believe that if you ever truly experienced even a drop of what he is really like, you would never want anything else. Whatever the richness and wonder of heaven, nothing about it will compare to simply being in his presence. Forget your "streets of gold." Once you see his face, you will want nothing else. Wondrous belonging with God, the softest, safest intimacy with one another, this is what God wanted his children to have when he created life and relationship. And he still wants this. You will hear these themes in the rest of his Bible.

Now when you hear him say, "Love the Lord your God with all your heart and your neighbor as yourself," you can know that that is not a new commandment. In fact, it actually began as an *invitation* – an invitation to not be alone. It is not good for us to be alone, and his One Story is about redeeming our lives so that we will never have to be alone again.

4. *A people who rest in him and his Sabbath.*

> *And by the seventh day God completed his work which he had done; and he rested on the seventh day from all his work which he had done. Then God blessed the seventh day and sanctified it, because in it he rested from all his work which God had created and made.*
>
> *– Genesis 2: 2-3*

I have to confess something: before I began to learn what God's One Story was about, I never really understood why "keeping the sabbath" made it into the Ten Commandments. I mean, if you're going to list the top ten things to command, I can think of about 15 distasteful habits that seem more worthy of rebuke than "acting up on Sundays."

The reason I thought that way was because I was still thinking like a "religious" person rather than thinking like a follower of the King. Everything else God has created so far in the Eden Plan has been brilliantly designed to give us wonderful things. And then he elects to rest on the seventh day and calls us to do so as well.

Why would God want this and why is it such a fundamental part of his design for his people?

Think about it like this. Have you ever had a real hardship to go through, and then there comes a time when it's over? Or have you ever worked exhaustingly for days and days, and then it's Friday afternoon? Or have you had your extended family come to visit for the holidays, and then they get in their car, and they *leave?* Maybe you've been afraid of the outcome of a medical test or a committee's decision – and then it's resolved. It's over. You are done. At last, you can let down.

If you think about it, our hearts are constantly oriented toward an anticipation of "rest." We experience work or disappointment or suffering, and we long for them to be over or accomplished. We long for rest. And when we get it, it's the best thing in the world! We are finally at peace again.

The Old Testament is full of images of a time when peace is established; a time when wars are over; a time when debts are paid, and the people are finally at rest. The Hebrews called this time *shalom,* meaning peace. Hanging in the background of their culture was an ongoing longing for the "shalom of Israel." They even named their capital city after it, "Jeru – shalom," the City of Peace.

Built into the Eden Plan was God's recognition that he wanted his people to rest. He wanted our hearts to be at peace. How often my clients say things to me like "I feel like my mind never stops;" "I'm just emotionally exhausted;" or even "Sometimes I wish for death, because it would just be easier."

When I was in graduate school in California, I had a client who was marginally schizophrenic, and as a result, lived in a constant state of internal turmoil and disruption. Sometimes during his sessions with me he would just fall asleep on my couch. I asked my supervisor about how I should respond. "He lives in so much mental chaos," he said, "your sessions with him may be the only real rest he ever gets." From then on, I just let him sleep whenever he wished.

I used to wonder why Sabbath rest was included within the top ten of God's commandments. I now hear it daily among the most frequent things people long for. Of course, God would call us to it. He knows we need it. He calls us to rest because he loves us.

As we tell God's One Story, we will also find a marvelous *ultimate* implication of sabbath. He promises us that arching beyond the pain, sorrow, and ordeal of history, his completion will be flooded with wondrous rest. His story is about a promised Messiah who will come, not just to bring salvation, but to bring with him an ultimate sabbath, a peace deeply longed for by his people. The pain will be over, the hardship will end, our troubled hearts and racing minds will finally settle. God wants this for you. It's what Revelation 21 is talking about when the Redeemer who sits on the throne promises that on that day there will finally be "no more crying or mourning or pain, the old things have passed away. Behold, I am making all things new."

"The Sabbath is here," he will say. "The Rest has come."

So keeping the Sabbath holy is not just about "abstaining." It is a call for us to begin *now* partaking in the sweetness of God's rest. The Sabbath is an opportunity for us to go ahead and start enjoying the appetizer in anticipation of that ultimate meal. I want to invite your heart to welcome the Sabbath day and say, "How can I get a picture today of the rest that is to come? How can I get a sense today of that place where God will ultimately hold me, that place where this tiny, dim shadow-reality will melt away and I will finally stand immersed in joy inconceivable?"

So sabbath is not a burden. It's more like Lucy's experience in C. S. Lewis's *The Lion, the Witch and the Wardrobe,* when she first hears Aslan's name. She says a feeling comes over her like "that feeling you get when you wake up and you realize it's the first day of summer vacation." [2]

That is rest. That is the way God wanted things to be when he made them. He still wants that way. And he is redeeming the world to be that way again.

5. A people who submit to him and his Way.

> *And the LORD God commanded the man, saying, "From any tree of the garden you may eat freely; but from the tree of the knowledge of good and evil you shall not eat, for in the day that you eat from it you shall surely die."*
> *– Genesis 2:16-17*

The problem

If you want to get dirty, you have to get in the dirt. If you want to get rained on, you have to stand under a precipitating cloud. And if you want to have the provision that God wishes to shower upon you, you have to stand *under God.*

It is clear from reading about God's Eden Plan that he wanted to give wonderful things to his children. He even *anticipated* their needs. Notice that Adam did not come to God saying, "Lord, I'm lonely." God came to *him* and said in essence, "It's not good for you to be alone. Let me give someone to you, to love you and be with you." (Gen. 2:18)

In the Eden Design, God was in a position to give his children everything they needed most. But as we said, there was one catch: if you hope to be such a blessed creature, you have to stay a *creature*. You have to remain *under God*, honoring him rather than turning from him to make your own rules. In other words, if you want the things that come from God, you have to be *with God*. (If you think about it, God's Way is often more about *reality* than it is *morality*!)

So, this is a lovely set up, right? God is big. We are small. It's a marriage made in heaven (literally). But then the problems started. When Adam and Eve ate of the tree from which God had said not to eat, they basically stepped out of the position of being "creatures" and declared, "I'm the boss now! No God for me! We are going to do what we want and take what we take." In other words, they, like we often do, turned their back on the Giver of Gifts. And then we all wonder why the goodies stopped. We wonder why work is now burdensome; why life is frightening; why our relationships are so painful. But we shouldn't wonder. It's like disowning your family and then wondering why you didn't get invited to Thanksgiving dinner!

Within the Eden Design, God was the sovereign creator and sustainer of his universe, and his people lived under him. Then Adam and Eve immediately wrecked this setup. So now we are needful, hungry, lonely, frightened creatures who desperately need to be cared for. Yet we are creatures who also just happen to have turned our backs on our only hope for provision. This is a very big problem.

So what needs to happen? Well, for the rest of scripture you will hear God calling us to come back to something he calls "waiting upon the Lord." (Is. 40:31, Psalm 27:14) He will call us to lay down our grandiose attempts to *take*, and instead be humble and submit to his will and his way. This is why, centuries later, Jesus will tell us that the "meek will inherit the earth." (Matt. 5:5) It's the reason why the Kingdom of Heaven belongs to the "poor in spirit." (Matt. 5:3) It is why Paul glorifies in his infirmities, "that the power of Christ might rest on him." (2 Cor. 12:9) It is why the Children's Catechism asks the question, "Why do I need Christ as king?" and invites us to answer beautifully, "Because I am weak, and I am helpless."

Over and over again God tells us that the only way that life works is when we are willing to step back into that place where we are small, and he is big. In other words, we will only thrive when we honor him as God, when we submit to his will.

Of course, we all resist this, and we are in good company. Adam and Eve take from the tree on their own terms. Abraham uses Hagar to provide a child rather than waiting on God to fulfill his promise through Sarah. The children of Israel, hungry in the wilderness, grumble and demand to be cared for. None of us like obeying, and none of us like to be small. But the good news is that if we are small, we get everything God offers. He says if you are humble, he will lift you up. But if you try to be big, you get a piece of fruit and nothing else. You get absolutely nothing else.

In fact, you die.

The solution

The death that Adam and Eve created had disastrous consequences. The most profound of which was that Adam and Eve and all their children found themselves under eternal condemnation. They owed an unpayable debt for their betrayal of the King. God's children left him, and the penalty for such treason was death. And as God throws Adam and Eve out of the Garden, this rebellion against him just hangs, pregnant with darkness and danger, for the rest of the Bible. *How can the lost people of God ever be restored to him? Will anyone ever turn and come back to live in submission to the Father?*

The rest of the Old Testament almost feels like it's asking this question softly but urgently in the background. Will anyone obey God? Will anyone bend the knee? As we hear the stories, they almost invite us to wonder, will *this* person live under God's way and honor him? How 'bout *this* person? Or that person?

And the answer keeps being "No."

We see Abraham and think, "Wow, Abraham is really a true man of faith. Surely, he will follow God." But Abraham fails God repeatedly. Then there are the stories of Moses. Surely the Lawgiver himself will follow God perfectly! The answer again is no. We have David and Solomon, and even the prophets. Repeatedly, no one fulfills God's requirement. The answer is always "No."

Until finally, someone says "Yes."

Despite all we have done to prevent God from being the Gift Giver, he has one last gift up his sleeve. There is no one who can come and live rightly before him, so God comes and does it himself in our place.

Our first hint that Jesus is a different kind of man takes place not in a garden but in a wilderness. (Matt. 4:1-11) The Son of God is not surrounded by countless wonderful trees from which he may eat, like Adam. He is surrounded by starvation and thirst. And in that wilderness, the Serpent of Eden reappears and taunts him to not wait on God. "Turn the stones to bread! Take the throne now for the kingdoms of the world!" And something unheard of happens:

The man refuses.

The man goes hungry.

The man waits upon the Lord.

And a few years after that, in another garden, Jesus is presented with another choice of whether to live under God's Way or not. In the Garden of Gethsemane, the man Paul calls the "second Adam" does the opposite of what the first Adam did. Instead of saying, "Not *thy* will but *mine*," Jesus says, "Not *my* will but *thine*." (Luke 22:42)

When the "Seed of the Woman" does this, the world changes. As the second person of the Trinity himself, God incarnate, stoops down from his holy position as King of the Universe and submits himself humbly to the Father, he realigns the Eden Design at last. At last God's man submits again to the will of the Father.

But Jesus's story is different from Adam's, tragically and beautifully different. God promised Adam that if he obeyed him, his reward would be blessing and richness of life. But Jesus is promised something horrifyingly different. For Jesus in his garden, his submission to God will not result in life. His "reward" for obedience will be that he will be cast out of God's Way altogether. For him to submit to God's Way doesn't mean that he will live, it means that he will die. God says to Jesus in essence, "What you will receive for your obedience is that you will be despised and forsaken – a man of sorrows, acquainted with grief." (Isa. 53:3)

Christ is willing to submit every day of his life to the point of death, even death on a cross, that we might be given the precious gift of living back under the glorious Way that God offered at the beginning. And because of him, we now have the chance to begin living under the Eden Plan once more.

This is what the redemption of the Eden Plan is pointing toward. This is why God has done all of this. He wants his people back. He wants his garden. He wants Life!

Thanks be to God, he hasn't changed his mind.

Remember this chapter!

The reason I have told you so much about what God wanted at Eden is because you will need to understand it all if you are going to make sense of the rest of the One Story. *God still wants what he's always wanted.* The work we will see him accomplish throughout his story is not arbitrary and it is not about "religion." His redemptive work is focused on restoring this beautiful perfect Way: a people in his image; a people who relate in a loving way to him and to each other; a people who work in his kingdom; a people who rest in his sabbath, and a people who submit to his way. He has always wanted these things and he still wants them. Throughout the rest of the One Story, he will be rebuilding this wonderful world. One day he will call it the Kingdom of God. And ultimately, he will breathe life into it by providing a bright and holy One who will finally gather his lost children together in a garden that will never end. The One Story is the chronicle of how he will bring about this glorious restoration.

In our next story, the tale of Noah's flood, God is going to build a platform upon which to launch his plan to breathe life back into all that he has always wanted. It's going to be a flood of redemption!

Chapter Three

Noah and the Watershed of Grace

I think that you will find our next story to be a surprising one. We are all so familiar with the story of Noah that it's almost become trite and fabled. Most people reflect on this story almost as they would a children's book or a fairytale: *Goldilocks and the Three Bears, Hansel and Gretel,* and the story of "Noah and the Ark." Think about it: the story of Noah is more often taught in children's Sunday schools than in serious spiritual dialogue. I mean, how many other stories of God's redemptive power do we decorate our babies' rooms with? Didn't your kids have Noah's Ark bumper pads or baby mobiles? (I vote we dress our children in other weighty stories of God's powerful redemption. How about the story of David at the threshing floor of Arruna the Jebusite? I want to see that one on a set of footie pajamas!)

But the Noah event is not a children's story. God's beautiful promise to Adam and Eve that he would send his Seed, the Christ, happened just a few chapters ago in Genesis 3, and the formal inauguration of God's relationship with his people is soon to come with Abraham. But something has to happen in the meantime.

In the story of Noah, God is going to create a rich, wonderful *context* in which he will guard and protect his people in preparation for the coming of the Savior. God will make a promise here that's going to radically alter the structure of how he will deal with us from here on out. *With Noah, God's love and his wrath are going to meet!*

The Fall Gets Worse

The hope for the future that God promised at Eden doesn't necessarily mean that things went cleanly afterwards. The thorns, thistles, and death that our forefathers reaped began to destroy their world. We see this immediately in the story of Cain and Abel. Cain kills his brother, and Genesis 4 follows the line of Cain as it degenerates, each generation becoming more wicked and destructive than the one before it. The story carries us all the way down to Genesis 4:24, where we are told about a descendant of Cain named Lamech, who has stooped so low that he is making up "gangsta rap" style songs, celebrating all the people he's killed! This lineage is essentially the "seed of the Serpent" that we heard about in the protoevangelium, and they are becoming more and more dangerous, further and further from reflecting God's image.

Meanwhile, what are the people of God doing? They are looking for the Seed who was promised. They're looking for that One. You see, they listened to the promise God was making in the protoevangelium. God said he was going to send an individual to restore his Way. An Offspring. A Seed. And Adam and Eve took him seriously.

After the death of Abel, Adam and Eve have another child. Eve names him Seth, declaring that, "God has appointed me another offspring in place of Abel, whom Cain killed." (Gen. 4:25) The literal Hebrew word here for "offspring" is the same one used in Genesis 3, *zera* or "seed." Poignantly, Eve is hoping maybe this is that One whom God promised years before in the garden. Maybe this is the Seed who will bring healing from the destruction that they have caused. One can almost feel the burden of her sorrow for what her choices have cost herself and her children.

Genesis 5 then follows the line of Seth all the way down to the birth of Noah. In Genesis 5:28-29, we meet Noah's father who is also named Lamech. Lamech names his son Noah saying something amazing that echoes the longings of Eve, "this *one* shall give us rest from our work and from the toil of our hands arising from the ground which the Lord has cursed."

Which "one" do you think he's talking about? Which curse do you think he's remembering?

Like Eve, Lamech remembered the curses of the Fall. Apparently, the people of God lived with an ongoing awareness of the curses and promises of Eden and were anticipating the Seed who would come and redeem them. Lamech believed that Noah would somehow be this One. Because, after all, the name Noah means "rest."

We are going find that Lamech's hopes for Noah were more on target than he ever expected and yet will be realized differently than he ever imagined.

The God of Wrath

As our story develops, things go from worse to "worser" with the state of degenerate man. By Genesis 6, the decline of mankind seems to have reached a sort of a nasty culmination in God's eyes. Genesis 6:5 tells us, "The LORD saw that the wickedness of man was great in the earth, and that every intent of the thoughts of his heart were only evil continually. And the LORD was sorry that he had made man on the earth, and he was grieved in his heart." (Gen. 6:5-6)

God sees an overwhelming flood of destructiveness and harm across all of mankind, and we are told that this depth of wickedness "grieved" him. Poetically, the word "grieved" here parallels the words that God used in describing his curse to Adam, that Adam's life and work would be filled with burden, sorrow, and pain; that life would "grieve" him. God hurts over the state of man. The pain that they create wounds him deeply.

At this point in our story, all of mankind is lost in wickedness and destruction. God, who is holy and repelled by such darkness, must act. God says, "I will blot out man whom I have created from the face of the land, man and animals and creeping things and birds of the heavens, for I am sorry that I have made them." (Gen. 6:7) God determines that since the life and love that he desired to create have been completely lost on earth, he will visit the planet violently and with justice. God is about to destroy every living thing!

This is a problem for us

We've talked a good bit so far about the dazzling benevolence and grace of our God. We have looked at his lovingkindness and said, "This is who he is!"

Well, *this* is who he is as well! He is just, and he is dangerous.

Aren't we all delighted with the warm, surprising mercy and grace of God? Aren't we overwhelmed sometimes at his sacrifice on our behalf? I know that I am. And I also know that I am less comfortable with this "righteous" God, this God of judgment. How do we make sense of a God who would destroy all of his creation? Is this the God we worship, someone who would regret his choice of creating man and respond by killing us all?

Let's begin by remembering that God's decision to destroy the earth is not some kind of divine temper tantrum. God is not Zeus, who, irritated at mankind, decides to smite them with thunderbolts. What is happening here is God is responding to *total evil and destructiveness*. What God calls "evil," you and I call violence, injustice, betrayal, murder, violation. God is intervening against a world that is described as "only evil continually." He has heard the cries of the victims. He has seen how much his beautiful world has been violated. And though his

One Story plan of salvation is waiting in the wings, he refuses to sit aside and watch evil, harm, and destruction go unchecked. It offends everything in him (even more than seeing such things would offend us). Everything good and righteous about him demands that he not stand by and watch deep harm and cruelty. So he intends to wipe out everything.

We cannot sanitize this. God's holiness demands that such evil be destroyed. But if you are like me, this story still makes you uncomfortable. If God is like this, we have a problem.

But here is the good news (and the point of the Noah story):

God has this problem, too.

God's problem

This may come as a surprise to you, but all of this wrath and destruction causes "problems" for God, too. Actually, he has the same problem with *himself* that we often have with him. It is vital that we understand this.

Ever since Adam and Eve turned from him, God has had two parts of his will that he must make sense of. *His question has been this: how can he be both the God who loves us and draws us close, and yet also be the God who responds with righteous vengeance against evil?* How can he make sense of bringing justice against cruelty and wrongdoing, while also making room to love and preserve his people?

This was a huge problem. After all, the reason God created everything in the first place was because he wanted a *people*, remember? He wanted us to look like him and walk with him at his side. But he cannot sit idly by while our destructiveness and cruelty harm the weak and violate his holiness. He cannot see selfishness, brutality, and destructiveness and just turn away.

But, if he responds only with justice, he will never have a people.

He would live obliterating us with righteous wrath.

On the other hand, if he responds with only gentleness and love, he violates everything holy about himself. If God is who he says he is, he cannot turn a blind eye on sin. It violates his very being.

Do you see his problem?

If you want to understand God and why he created his plan of redemption, you must understand this. Here's how Paul expresses it in Romans: How can God be both "just and the justifier?" (Rom. 3:26) How can he draw us close, and yet still be holy and righteous?

Good news. This just happens to be the problem that he plans to address in the story of Noah.

Justice, but ....

Here is how God begins solving this problem: Yes, his justice will come to put an end to the people who are "only evil continually." Everyone will get justice in this story. Everyone will die. Everyone, that is, except one man. One man who does not get a "just" response. One man, Noah.

At the end of this passage that is filled with despair and judgment, we somehow are given this message of hope: "But Noah found favor in the eyes of the LORD. These are the records of the generations of Noah. Noah was a righteous man, blameless in his time. Noah walked with God." (Gen. 6:8-9)

For some reason, in the midst of this global death sentence, God decides to spare some of the race of man. Beautifully, the structure of this passage in the original Hebrew makes it clear that Noah is not spared *because* he was righteous and blameless. People often believe that perhaps Noah was the one "righteous" man who walked the earth, and that therefore, God looked down upon him and spared him. That is not what's happening here. Our first introduction to Noah is the announcement that God simply comes to him and "favors" him.

Why? Who knows? Why has God favored you?

I don't want you to miss this. Noah was saved because God favored him, just as God comes to us, "while we were yet sinners." (Rom. 5:8)

Then the phrase, "These are the records of the generations of Noah," begins a new section in the Hebrew, it begins a new story, Noah's story. In other words, only now that we've established that God favors Noah, can we talk about how the result of that is that Noah is righteous. In God's deep mercy, Noah is saved by the same loving gracious heart of God that saves you and me. In the Noah story, we are seeing how God comes to his people with his gracious love throughout the Bible, even during dark times of judgment such as these.

So here we begin to see those two aspects of God's heart meet. In the midst of God's terrifying judgment, his gracious hand is extended. He is the God of both loving grace and ruthless justice. At the same time that he is closing the door on man's destructiveness, he is reaching out and opening a door of salvation. He is both of these things. And for the whole of scripture, you will see him operating out of both of these sides of his personality: his abiding love *and* his intolerant heart toward destructiveness and sin.

The rest of our Noah story is going to tell us how God will bring these two sides of his heart into harmony, and in so doing, redeem the world. Indeed, in him, "Mercy and truth will meet together; peace and righteousness will kiss." (Psalm 85:10)

The Blessings of Protection

In the midst of the coming judgment, God now turns his attention toward his favored Noah. Though this story is often called "Noah and the Ark," you may notice that Noah actually has no speaking lines. It should be called "God and the Ark," because this whole story is about God and his creation of a newfound protection for his people. Noah is just along for the ride.

So how does God respond to Noah, whom he loves and favors? First, he's going to tell Noah his plans.

The warning

God comes to Noah and says, "The end of all flesh is before me, for the earth is filled with violence because of them, and behold, I'm going to destroy them with the whole earth." (Gen. 6:13)

Though I imagine that an announcement of global destruction may not be on your top list of "gracious things" you want to hear from God, this warning is actually an act of mercy, not only for Noah but for the rest of the world. Usually in the Old Testament, if God wants to destroy a group of people, there's not a lot of small talk. He just destroys them. But here, in spite of the out-of-control evil that runs rampant on the earth, God *warns* Noah. And this warning is a gift to all men. We will find out later that it will take Noah and his sons 120 years to build the Ark. Peter actually references this in 1 Peter 3:20. He talks about how the preparation of the Ark was an act of patience on God's behalf, an allowance for the people who were doomed to destruction to come back to God. It's as if God is saying, "Watch this man build a giant boat for the next 120 years and wonder why! Come back from your destructiveness before it's too late."

Even in the midst of favoring Noah, God is still reaching out to all of mankind.

The boat

Next, God is going to "put some teeth" into his promise to protect Noah. He wants Noah to build a boat, an ark. And he's going to tell him exactly how he wants it done. He tells Noah to make an ark of gopher wood. God says it is to be 450 foot long (equal in length to one and a half football fields), 75 feet wide and 45 feet high. It is to have rooms inside and be covered with tar and pitch to keep it watertight. In addition, God tells Noah to put a window near the top of the Ark, to set a door in its side, and to make it with "lower, second, and third decks." (Gen. 6:16) (As a lifelong sailor, I love this first ever use of nautical terminology!)

By Genesis 7, we get some fine print on the Ark plan. God tells Noah to bring animals with him on the Ark, two of each *unclean* animal. We all know this, right? But here's a little surprise: he also says take of every *clean* animal *seven by seven*! (Looks like we are going to have to change some children's Sunday school songs!)

Finally, Noah and his family enter the Ark, and as the floodgates of the sky and the depths of the earth open up to begin overwhelming God's creation, we are given one last beautiful moment: We are told that *God himself* closes the door of the Ark behind them. (Gen 7:16)

As the judgment unfolds, the rain and upheavals of water continue for 40 days and 40 nights until water covers every mountain. And in verses 21 and 22, we are told that every creature that lived on the earth died.

The background questions in the Noah story are these: Who is God really? How will he respond to lost people? With wrath? With love? The Noah event begins to answer this question. *Somehow, he is the God who brings a flood of wrath on sin as well as the tender savior who tucks his children inside the safest place with his own hand.* Again, in this story, the wrathful God of judgment meets the tender God of protective love. He is about to show us how.

The Breaking of Dawn

A Covenant

Imagine with me this silent planet, covered with water, completely blue now if seen from space. And upon it floats a speck, a lone lifeboat amidst the abyss of death. The echoes of countless lost lives have subsided, and there is nothing left of God's original vast creation but a small family, huddled in a boat. The splendor of Genesis 1 and 2 has been brought to ruin, and only a small remnant remains.

No wonder God grieved.

But just as silently, something else happens in the background, something that will change our lives forever.

We are told in Genesis 8:1 that "God *remembered* Noah and the beasts that were in the Ark and caused a wind to pass over the earth and the water subsided."

God remembered Noah. The word "remember" is a technical term in the Old Testament. It is the language of biblical promise. It is the language of *covenant.* You see, something else happened back in Genesis 6 when God was building his protection for Noah. Obviously, he guided Noah in the design of the Ark, a vessel to surround and protect him from the flood. But God also built another protection for Noah (and for all of us) that would shield the old patriarch with a safety far greater than planks of gopher wood. God came to Noah and made a "covenant."

In the Old Testament, when God speaks of a covenant, he is referring to a solemn vow that he makes to his people. He is committing himself with undying promise to the person he covenants with. God says to Noah in Genesis 6, "But I will establish my covenant with you, and you shall enter the Ark – you and your sons and your sons' wives with you." (Gen. 6:18)

A world of promise

We are on a journey together to understand God's One Story. It is the story of God's endeavor to provide, protect, and redeem his people. But it is going to take centuries for that redemption to be fully realized. Until then, this will be a journey of *promise*, of *covenant*. Until his One Story of redemption is completed, God lives with promises to his people! He is the *promising God*.

Remember how God came to Adam and Eve in the Garden? His curses to the Serpent in the protoevangelium were actually *promises* to us! God promised he would send a seed to save his people. Later in our story, he will come to Abraham with promises. Centuries later, God will come to Moses and David with even richer promises. And Jesus will bring the greatest promise of all.

Here with Noah, God tells him that not only will he get an ark for safety, he will get a promise, too: a *covenant of safety* that will surround him and all of his family. There will be death all around, and though Noah's family will be protected safely inside an ark, they will most deeply be protected inside God's covenant promise.

A God who remembers

And now as Noah and his family float alone upon the waters, we are told that God "remembers" this covenant promise. In other words, God is about to act to hold himself accountable to the promises that he has made. He is coming through on his commitment. We will hear him remember his people and his promises over and over again in our story, and I want hearing him do so to begin thrilling your heart.

Why? Because if you are like me, you go through spells of feeling like God is far away. Everyone else seems to be basking in the glow of heavenly blessing, but your life feels full of hurt and loneliness. Has God forgotten you? Do his promises to you not matter to him anymore? A client recently told me that she was angry at God, jealous of how he seemed to flood her friends with blessing and warmth while she lived in ongoing suffering. She wondered if God had just scratched her off his list, ignoring her pain. Something in us can want to just shake God sometimes and say, "Have you forgotten I exist?" However, though I often don't understand why God allows so much pain in our lives, I know that somehow his heart never leaves ours.

This is why I smile every time I hear the Bible tell us about how God *remembers* his covenant; how he *remembers* his people. These phrases remind and comfort us that God himself is *holding himself* accountable to never forget us!

Some of us have accountability partners, individuals in our lives who keep us honest and true to our commitments. How would you like to have God himself hold you accountable!? Well, God does. He is accountable to the highest standard of honesty and faithfulness imaginable: his own heart. Sometimes his presence can feel hard to touch, but he never forgets you. I promise. And in the midst of this worldwide destruction of the Noah story, God *remembers* his promises to Noah. He is about to begin restoring Noah and the earth, and as he does, the spark of our One Story is going to burst into flame.

The Downpour of Preservation

God begins rolling back his wheels of justice by closing the floodgates, and by the seventh month of the year, the Ark rests on the mountains of Ararat. (Gen. 8:2-4)

By the tenth month, the tops of the mountains can be seen, and Noah is optimistic enough to send out a raven to scout the land (which doesn't really help very much). Then in Genesis 8:8, he sends out three doves consecutively. The first one returns, apparently having had trouble finding any place to survive. Dove number two comes back with an olive leaf (rumors of good things). And dove number three doesn't return at all (apparently having found something more interesting than the Ark to do).

And after approximately a year afloat, Noah and his family finally exit the Ark. (Gen. 8:18)

Now, as God's people walk back out of the Ark and step upon dry land, we need to really tune in. Just as the protoevangelium announced an eternal shift in the way that God would relate to his people, the events that are about to occur here with Noah are going to change our relationship with our heavenly Father at a cosmic level. God is about to step down from his role as ruthless judge of sin and put on the loving hat of redeemer and preserver of his people.

He's going to initiate *three things*, and all of them are going to be about *re-establishing and protecting* his people. In fact, theologians will later call these promises the "Covenant of Preservation," or the "Covenant of Peace." Because what God wants to do here is to make sure that the kind of destruction we just witnessed never happens again.

At least not to his people.

"Plan A – Again

We watched in Genesis chapters 1 and 2 as God very consciously and deliberately created a world according to the way that he wanted it. But now we've seen him destroy that world. Has God changed his mind? Does he no longer want a world and a people? Does he no longer see creation as "good?" If you are Noah and his family, surely you are asking these questions by now.

God immediately answers them as Noah exits the Ark.

In Genesis 8:22, God says,

> While the Earth remains,
> Seedtime and harvest,
> And cold and heat,
> And summer and winter,
> And day and night
> Shall not cease.
> And God blessed Noah and his sons and
> said be fruitful and multiply and fill the Earth.

Do you hear him? He's answering our questions, and doing so by echoing his own words from creation! He's telling us that, despite how the whole world turned away from him and reaped destruction, he wants to try again – with us – with his world! He still wants his people. He hasn't given up on his plan!

He's talking about "seedtime and harvest," "sun and moon," "day and night," "be fruitful and multiply?" What does this sound like? These all echo the themes of creation, the Eden Design. We often read right through this passage and don't realize the beautiful news that it announces.

God still wants his world!

He still wants his people!

His intervention against the destructiveness of mankind was not inflicted in order to destroy all creation. It was designed to preserve it! Can I get a "Hallelujah!"

And if this sounds like good news to you, just think of how good it would have sounded to Noah!

Protection from a dangerous world

God wants his world and his people, but as we've seen, mankind seems deviously adept at sidestepping God's desire and instead creating a world of malicious chaos and pain. So if God wants to protect his new creation, he's going to need to tweak things a bit this time around. We must understand this or God's next statements will seem rather cryptic.

God says to Noah, "And for your lifeblood I will surely demand an accounting. I will demand an accounting from every animal. And from each man, too, I will demand an accounting for the life of his fellow man. Whoever sheds the blood of man, by man shall his blood be shed; for in the image of God has God made man." (Gen 9:4-6)

What's God saying here?

Here's a principle that every psychologist knows: if you are dealing with out-of-control people, you must create powerful limits to contain their destructiveness – or else! God knows this as well. So, as he begins to open the curtain on this "second chance" earth, he lays down some restraints on the kinds of dangers that lay in wait for man. Coming out of the chaos and destruction before the flood, God is saying, "From here on, we are going to create more boundaries to limit the destructiveness that is possible on earth." He declares a reestablishment of man's dominion over creation and institutes the most severe punishment possible if man kills man. (Because man being in God's image is a holy thing, of immeasurable value.) In other words, if there's any hope of preventing the kinds of destruction we saw in Genesis 6, we gotta get some rules in this place!

We will talk later in the Moses story about how, though we often resist rules and law, spiritually and psychologically the structure they bring is an enormous blessing. Just like with children, limits create order in the midst of chaos – and this world has been chaotic. So here, God begins a new level of protecting man from the danger of beasts and the danger of other men.

But this doesn't even scratch the surface of the real protection that man needs.

Protection from something far more dangerous

God works in Genesis 9:4-8 to give mankind protection from the dangers of animals and evil men. But the real point of the covenant with Noah involves God's protecting us from something far more dangerous than animals or murderers. It's actually the first thing God addressed when Noah emerged from the Ark.

Think about it like this: God's decision to flood the earth was the result of a particular policy he had regarding responding to evil and to the men who perpetrate it. Specifically, this: See wickedness and blot it out, primarily by blotting *sinful man* out. As God saw the destruction wrought by evil and injustice on the earth, his response was to obliterate man in righteous wrath.

Well, in the next few lines redemptive history is going to be made. God is about to establish a new way of dealing with man and his evil. In this Covenant of Preservation, God is not just going to protect mankind from animals or evil men. God is going to protect us from something far more dangerous.

God is going to protect us from *himself*.

Here's how it unfolded:

The first thing that Noah does when he and his family step out of the Ark is to take one of every clean animal, build an altar, and make a sacrifice to God, specifically, he offers a "burnt offering." (Gen. 8:20)

The burnt offering was an extravagant sacrifice. The sacrificial animal was killed and completely consumed by fire on the altar. No part of the sacrifice was left for the penitent. All of it was given to God. God does not demand this sacrifice from Noah; it just flows out of the man's heart. Noah, like any of us who really see the unimaginable gift of God's grace, responds with overflowing thankfulness; flaming, sacrificial gratitude for God's preservation. This sacrifice is a statement of Noah's heart. A recognition, like Peter says in 1 Peter 3, that the voyage of the Ark was almost like a "baptism," carrying the convicted sinner safely through the danger of judgment. (1 Peter 3: 20-21)

And then it happens. God responds to Noah's sacrifice – and a beautiful turning point in his dealings with mankind is forged.

We are told in Genesis 8:21 that God smells the soothing aroma of the sacrifice and responds by saying, "I will never again curse the ground because of man, for the intention of man's heart is evil from his youth. Neither will I ever again strike down every living creature as I have done."

What is God saying here? Commentators tell us that God is essentially proclaiming, "I cannot allow men to live being so harmful to me and to each other. But since man's heart is evil from his youth, I know that he will continue to be destructive. However, my solution to this problem cannot just be ongoing judgment and wrath. All that does is destroy the dear people whom I have created to be my children, the ones with whom I desire to walk in the cool of the day. I want more than judgment. There has to be another way."

This proclamation from God declares that he is no longer going to relate to man just from a position of judgment.

God is about to unveil his new way.

And he's going to do it by showing us his *bow*.

The Disarmament of God

One of the things we'll see as we follow the One Story is that many of God's landmark covenant promises are marked by a special *sign*. Under our covenant as modern Christians, the New Covenant instituted by Christ, we celebrate the signs of baptism and the Lord's Supper. Under Abraham, the covenant sign will be circumcision. Similarly, the covenant that God makes with Noah has a sign, and it is vital that we see it because, hidden in this covenant sign is the secret message of how God is going to protect us all.

So what is the sign of this covenant with Noah? You guys have been to Sunday School, right? You know what it is.

It is the covenant sign of the *rainbow!*

Fast forward to Genesis 9:12. God says, "This is the sign of the covenant I am making between me and you and every living creature that is with you, for all successive generations; I set my bow in the cloud, and it shall be for a sign of the covenant between me and the earth. And it shall come about, when I bring a cloud over the earth, that the bow shall be seen in the cloud." (Gen. 9:12-14)

To solidify his promise to protect us, God gives us the rainbow.

Unfortunately, like many of God's overwhelming gifts, our culture has taken this precious symbol and turned it into things it was never intended to mean. Be it by leprechauns promising gold, people pushing alternative lifestyles, or those who just want to sell *Skittles*, we are told to "embrace the rainbow." But this sign of the rainbow is not sweet or trivial. It is a picture of the new way God is going to handle the problem of man's destructiveness.

If not with wrath, then how?

Meredith Kline is an Old Testament scholar and archaeologist who has unpacked this image in the ancient language. He tells us that the Hebrew word that God uses here when he talks about the rainbow is the word *qeset*. And to the ancient listener, God is not talking about a rainbow. To their ears, they hear God, the bringer of wrath and justice saying, "My bow, the one you see in the sky – my *qeset* – doesn't means rainbow. It means *battle bow!*"

God is saying to Noah and to us, "I have made a radical change. You know that justice that I have held over you? You know that righteousness that demanded that I destroy the earth? Well, I am going to drop my weapons against you. My battle bow, I now hang in the sky. It is no longer in my hands; it is no longer bent towards you."

This is God's watershed. Remember that unfathomable destruction that God unleashed on the earth? It was disturbing to even contemplate. Here God is proclaiming that there will be a new way that he will respond to our evil. He will lay down his destructive wrath. He will hang up his battle bow. From now on, when you see a rainbow, remember that it is proclaiming from the heavens that though God is the God of justice, he is also the God of long-suffering grace. Because he loves you, he hangs his battle bow of wrath in the sky and promises not to use it. Instead, he will bend his knee and bring his children to his heart.

See his promise and let your hearts be filled with his mercy.

God declares that he will never ever again act with such vengence toward his people.

However, he *will* do so toward someone else in our place.

The covenant with Noah is God's promise to no longer inflict that kind of blistering wrath *on man*. But that doesn't mean he will not bring that judgment against *one man*. The only other time that we will see God act with the kind of rampant vengeance that we witnessed at the Noah flood, is on the day he unleashes it again against his beloved Son, the one who is shattered by the wrath that we deserve.

Centuries after Noah, the promised Seed comes, and on that day, God finally lifts his battle bow again, and brings it to bear upon Jesus. On that day we finally see again the vengeance that destroyed the world. God releases the piercing arrow of his battle bow against one who was not shielded, not protected from God's wrath – and he sacrificed him with it – for us.

Isaiah tells us about that day when he says that the Seed, our Jesus, was "stricken, smitten by God, and afflicted … he was *pierced* through for our transgressions; he was crushed for our iniquities; and the punishment for our well-being fell up on him, and by his wounds we are healed." (Isa. 53:4-5)

In the sacrificial death of Jesus, God finally solves his problem. He is the just God and the loving God, both. His love will surround his people for the rest of the One Story, and his wrath will wait for Calvary to at last appear again. Now we see he is both "just and the justifier." (Rom. 3:26)

With Noah he creates a "safe zone," a "Covenant of Preservation" for his people, allowing time for his redemption story to develop.

In the meantime, we are safe. We are at peace with God.

The floods have finally stopped.

Isaiah 54 is like a commentary on the Noah story, applying it to future generations. This is what the story means to us as modern-day Christians. As we end this chapter of the One Story, listen to him now as he speaks to you.

> You will not be put to shame.
> Neither feel humiliated, for you will not be disgraced.
> You will forget the shame of your youth
> And the reproach of your widowhood
> you will remember no more,
> For your husband is your maker,
> whose name is Yahweh of Hosts.
> And your redeemer is the holy one of Israel,
> who is called God of all the Earth.
> For a brief moment I forsook you,
> but with great compassion I will gather you.
> In an outburst of anger,
> I hid my face from you for a moment.
> But with everlasting kindness
> I will have compassion on you,
> says Yahweh, your Redeemer.
> For this is like the days of Noah to me.
> When I swore that the waters of Noah
> should not flood the Earth again,
> So I have sworn that I will not be angry with you
> nor rebuke you.
> For the mountains may be removed and the hills may shake,
> but my lovingkindness will not be removed from you.
> And My Covenant of Peace will not be shaken,
> says Yahweh
>   – who has compassion on you.

So you see, Noah's father was right. Noah *was* a picture of the One. Like Noah, Christ gathers us to himself, safe in his ark; rest from the curse. Death is all around, but we are safe in him.

Chapter Four

Abram and The Blood of God

When we last saw the planet Earth, it was still drying out from its diluvial nightmare. Noah and his family stumbled out of the Ark and were met by a God who dropped his weapons. God had postponed his role as judge of the earth. As we said, Noah himself had no actual speaking lines in the story. The only character who spoke was God, and when he did, it was to himself. And what he spoke was a vow of peace and preservation. No longer would he lead with his hand of judgment; the battle bow is hung up; the weapons are shelved. There is going to be another way. And we are about to see it in action.

As we pick up our story after Noah, we are immediately confronted with a renewed rise of despicable evil. By Genesis 11, a few generations after the flood, man who is "wicked from his youth," is back at it again, engaging in the same kind of behavior that had caused God to bring the flood in the first place. What are they doing? These guys are building a *tower!*

They say, "Come let us build for ourselves a city and a tower whose top will reach into heaven and let us make for ourselves a name lest we be scattered abroad on the face of the whole earth." (Gen. 11:4)

Now, why are we getting so uptight about a tower? I mean, there aren't any "thou shall not build a tower" commandments in the Bible. Why would this act be considered rebellion against God?

The problem is not *what* they are building, it's *why* they are building it. Their reason for building the tower, according to verse 4, is "to make a name for ourselves." A phrase that literally means that they are seeking to make their names eternal. In other words, these guys are trying to become *gods themselves*. Their intention is clarified by the name the tower later receives, Babel. In the original language, Babel translates as "heaven's gate." In essence, these mutinous builders are saying, "Let us go up to heaven *ourselves,* and seat *ourselves* there. We will be gods, like God himself."

In my line of work this is called a "grandiose psychotic delusion." In the Bible, it's called idolatry, self-idolatry. Mankind is wanting to dethrone God and take the crown for themselves.

So before you know it, man is revolting against God – again. And as a result, we have a set up for the same kind of destruction we saw with the flood. Man is forsaking God. He's even wanting to *be* God. And judgment should come.

But there is no death. The Babel tower is a destruction–worthy set up, but there's no annihilation of the earth this time. Why?

Because the Noah Promise was for real!

God said to Noah that his way with us would no longer be destruction. And three chapters later, we see man practicing all of his same wicked shenanigans again. But God keeps his promise. Instead of death and retribution as we saw with Noah, God does two things. He sets obstacles and limits on the tower builders (confusing their language, frustrating their strength, and scattering them across the earth).

And, secondly, he lights the fires of his restoration.

How? He is about to begin the story of Abram.

A New Family and a New Story

The One Story is about God's rebuilding of his relationship with his people. He wants us back. Immediately after Adam and Eve betrayed him, he began promising this restoration. With Noah he created a "preservation" and safety for us all. But we are still early in his story, and God really hasn't actually begun any legit restoration of his world yet.

He is about to. He's about to build a new family. He's going to create a new people who are his very own. And from this new family, God will form his innumerable beloved children. They will be his new image-bearers. They will walk with him in a land that is God's new 'garden.' They will live and work in his kingdom. And from them, their own redeemer, the Seed of the Woman, will come.

So out of the line of Adam and Eve's son, Seth, he favors Noah. And from the line of Noah's son, Shem, God reaches down into a pagan metropolis called Ur of the Chaldeans, and chooses a man named Abram.

This man, Abram, will be the beginning of God's new family. And that family will be the home from which God will recreate his beloved people. We are about to meet the father of us all!

Abram meets God

Quite out of the blue, God comes to Abram and tells him that he wants him to leave everything he knows and follow him.

God says,

> "Go forth from your country,
> And from your relatives
> And from your father's house,
> To the land which I will show you;
> And I will make you a great nation,
> And I will bless you,

And make your name great;
And so you shall be a blessing;
And I will bless those who bless you,
And the one who curses you I will curse.
And in you all the families of the earth shall be blessed."

— Genesis 12:1-3

God calls Abram to leave his home of security and luxury and begin an extraordinary new life. He is calling Abram to join the One Story. God is saying, "Leave your nation, leave your home, and I will make *you* a home – a home for a nation of people. Ever since Eden, my desire has been to have a people. Now you will start my new redeemed family by following me. Certainly, I will bless you, but *everyone* will be blessed by you!"

By the way, are you beginning to see a pattern here? Every time we have a new installment to our One Story, God is the one doing the initiating. If we are going to pursue his heart in our story, we mustn't miss this. Maybe it's Adam and Eve who have just wrecked the universe; maybe it's Noah who is trying to "walk with God" in a world that is falling apart; or maybe it's Abram, minding his own business, living his glitzy life in Ur. But God comes to them! (And I love that on the heels of the Babel guys wishing to "make their names great," God comes to Abram and says, "*I* will make your name great. *I* will call my own man out, and *I* will make him eternal because he will be my very own.")

This is who God is! There is no story without his creating it. There is no relationship unless he initiates it. He keeps appearing, reaching out his hand to draw his people close.

ABRAM AND THE BLOOD OF GOD

Abram does what God calls him to do. He leaves home with his wife, his nephew Lot, and all of his belongings (he was very wealthy), and he goes out to meet God.

On his journey, Abram will have many adventures (three of which we are about to discuss). But at the end of Abram's sojourn will lay the greatest adventure of all. God has not just called Abram in order to give him a land or a family. God has called this man to be the *father of our faith*. And when Abram finally reaches his destination, he is going to receive an extraordinary gift: God is going to make a covenant with him.

We saw God establish a covenant with Noah, a promise of safety and salvation. But that was just a precursor, an appetizer in anticipation of the main course. Very soon, we are going to see God come to Abram and establish *the* covenant, the *Covenant of Grace itself*, the very covenant that makes you a Christian. Yes, it happens right here in Genesis with Abram!

But before we get to the main event, let's browse a couple of cool "Old Testament-style" adventures that Abram has along the way.

Failing

Things don't always go ideally for Abram as he wanders with his family. Despite the reminders that he is ultimately our spiritual father, we are also given the gift of seeing some of his failures. For example, during his journey, Abram will have an unpleasant run-in with the pharaoh of Egypt who seems to find Abram's wife, Sarai, quite appealing. Despite being the father of our faith, Abram does not handle this situation in Egypt with faithfulness or reliance upon God. Instead, he botches it with cowardice and deceit.

I find it comforting that God includes this story as he unfolds his covenant journey with Abram. Even Abram dropped the ball! I look forward to the joyful storytelling that I believe we will celebrate in heaven. I believe that we will get to talk with Abraham or Moses or David and poke fun with one another at the ways in which we were so small and God was so big.

I'll probably say, "You won't believe how I let him down over and over. And you won't believe how beautifully he responded to me!" And Abraham will say, "That's nothin'! He put stories about how *I* failed him in the Bible! That's right, you can read about my screwups in 700 languages!"

Faithful

But Abram is faithful as well. One story that's meaningful to me takes place when Abram's and Lot's flocks get overcrowded as they are grazing. Abram demonstrates a deep faith in God's promises by letting Lot choose the preferred grazing land. Abram implies, "God's going to take care of me and give me the land I need. You may pick first, Lot." (Gen. 13:8-9)

Interestingly enough, Lot chooses to settle in the "city," saying it looks like "the garden of the Lord." This is an obvious reference to Eden. Remember, God evicted mankind from the garden, but has begun the One Story to bring his faithful back to himself. However, for the rest of history, mankind will be inclined to try to create his own way back to "Eden" apart from God – to "take and eat" on our own terms. Every time we sin or try to take our own way, we are seeking the "passing pleasures of sin" instead of waiting on God to restore us to the joy that only exists in him. Lot's choice of the "city" is an attempt to take the immediate pleasure that lies in front of him instead of trusting in God.

The only problem is, the city Lot chooses is *Sodom and Gomorrah*! Lot often made poor choices.

Abram's choice, on the other hand, is the way of God; the way of wandering and obedience; the way of faith. God responds to Abram's faith here by visiting him again with more promises of "offspring" and land. He tells Abram that not only will he have a legacy, but it will be as many as the dust of the earth. "So that if one can count the dust of the earth, your offspring also can be counted." (Gen. 13:16)

A visitor

Abram's final adventure before he has his covenant encounter with God involves a very special visit from a mysterious, shadowy figure named Melchizedek. We need to stop again and listen in on this encounter in Genesis 14:18-20.

Wearing a weighty mantle of symbolism, Melchizedek is described as the "King of Salem," which is a reference to being a king in Jerusalem, but also to a more mystical role as the "King of Peace." Melchizedek is also called the Priest of *El Elyon*, of God Most High. And in a very interesting ancient Middle Eastern gesture, Abram honors Melchizedek by paying him a tithe, implying that even Abram, the father of our faith, considered Melchizedek exalted above him. Oh, and one more thing: Melchizedek blesses Abram by bringing *bread and wine!*

So put on your New Testament thinking caps for a moment. Who does this character remind you of? The "King of Peace," the priest of God Most High, reigning in Jerusalem, offering bread and wine to those who are needful; someone to whom even Abram – the father of all – pays a tithe in deference?

Melchizedek is beautiful a pre-figuring of Christ himself!

Hebrews chapter 7 richly unpacks this whole image of Melchizedek and his parallels with Jesus, giving us a gift that reaches back to our heritage in the Old Testament. Even here, in the context of this story about the origins of our faith, we are shown how the very *perfecter* of our faith was already making a veiled surprise appearance. It was almost as if the promised Seed couldn't wait to get here and be with us!

The God who Comforts our Fears

As Abram journeyed, he encountered many challenges and dangers. There were the problems with Lot in Sodom, the difficulty with the pharaoh in Egypt, the spooky visit by Melchizedek, and Abram's daring rescue of Lot from a group of marauding armies. In the context of all of these adventures, God comes back to speak to Abram again. This time simply to speak to his *fears and doubts*. He says,

> Do not fear Abram.
> I am a shield to you, your very great reward.
> – Genesis 15:1

Some translations of this passage read, "I am a shield to you, your rewards shall be very great." But the Hebrew is written differently. The phrase is a *parallelism*, an *appositive*, a statement in which one phrase repeats the meaning of the other and reinforces it. God is saying, "Abram, I am your shield, *and* I am your reward. I am everything you need in the light of all this danger. I will be the one who protects you and brings you blessing."

I love that God initiates this comfort, that he knows our fears and cares about them. I talk with people all the time who need permission to express their doubts to God. Can we tell God that we are struggling to trust him, even that we may be angry at him for seeming to forget us? We are often afraid of angering God if we express our fears or doubts to him. But what he wants with us is a real relationship, remember?

He wants our honesty. He wants our heart. Even our doubting hearts. (Besides, it's not like he doesn't already know!) In this story, God speaks to Abram, but he also speaks to all of us. "I hear your doubts and fears, and I want to comfort you." In fact, again in this story God shows up first! He initiates comfort to his doubting friend, Abram. He says to Abram and to us, "Not only do I know your fear, but my longing is to comfort you. I will be your shield and your reward."

Even patriarchs doubt

This is the best news in the world, right?

But how does Abram respond to this blessed announcement, this personal encouragement from God himself? Does he say, "Oh Wow, Lord, what a wonderful relief! I feel all better now. Thanks for being my comforting God!"?

No. Instead, suddenly Abram starts carrying on about something seemingly unrelated to notions of danger and fear. He responds to God's comfort by saying, "Oh Lord, what will thou give me since I'm childless? And the heir of my house is Eliezer of Damascus. Since I have no offspring to me, a servant in my household is my heir." (Gen. 15:3)

It's almost like, once God opens the door to the topic of Abram's fears, all of the patriarch's concerns start spewing out! Abram starts speaking the depth of his of his doubt, especially regarding his fear of never having a son. This makes sense if we put ourselves in Abram's shoes. He has left the safety of his home and lit out for the unknown territories. All he has had to go on have been God's promises. But central to God's commitment has been the vow that Abram would one day be the father of a great nation. So in the context of all of Abram's difficult adventures, he has begun to wonder whether God is going to actually show up with the payoff. In other words, how is

Abram going to have a lineage, a hope, a future, if he still doesn't even have *a son?*

In essence, Abram is saying, "God, you keep talking about "reward." You keep talking about great "land and descendants like the dust of the earth," but to be honest, at the rate things are going, I'm still gonna die off without any heir at all. What's the point of that? You keep making promises to me, but the only heir I have is Eliezer of Damascus!" (And you have to admit, that does sound kind of pitiful. How would you like your only heir to be some guy named Eliezer of Damascus?)

It seems that, even though Abram hears all of God's promises, he is still fearful and full of doubt. There are no numberless descendants. So far, there is not even one!

Cosmic comfort

God is going to respond to Abram and his fears, but not with reassurances about Eliezer of Damascus, or protection from pharaohs or marauding armies.

Instead, God is going to talk to Abram about the stars!

This is God's response to Abram's fear:

> And He took him outside and said, "Now look toward the heavens, and count the stars, if you are able to count them."
> And He said to him, "So shall your descendants be."
> – Genesis 15:5

As we look in upon this campfire scene, it is as if Abram's eyes are looking down at the fire, discouraged and hopeless. But then God sort of puts his arm around him and says, "I know you're afraid, my dear one. And I know you can't believe that I'm going to take care of you.

But let me show you something: look up at the stars! Count them, if you even dare try. That's how big my fulfillment of this promise will be. This is how great your reward will be. You won't even be able to wrap your mind around it!"

I love when God shifts into "Cosmic Comforter" mode. He does so often, bringing hope and reassurance of his promises by pointing us to the vastness of his universe. He reminds us to resist looking down in despair at our circumstances and instead to look up at him, remembering his power! With Noah he said, "While the earth remains, seedtime and harvest, cold and heat, summer and winter, day and night, shall not cease." (Gen. 8:22) Through Isaiah he says to us, "For the mountains may depart and the hills be removed, but my steadfast love shall not depart from you." (Isa. 54:10) Through David in the Psalms God tells us that his love is as high as the heavens, and his righteousness is like the mountains. His judgments are as deep as the sea. (Psalm 36:5-6)

In other words, God is saying to Abram (and to us), "You want to know how safe you are in my arms? My love is bigger than all the seasons or mountains or oceans or stars! You cannot swim it, lest you become lost in the sea of my love. You cannot climb it, for its heights are too high. And when you have finished counting the stars, only on that day, might my heart for you fail."

"Look at the stars!"

And Abram gets it. He believes.

The Promise of All Hope

Frankly, I'm ready to stand for the benediction at this point. God has promised an offspring and a land, and Abram has believed him. Now, Abram stands together with his God beneath the numberless stars, eyes fixed on his heavenly Father. Let's close in prayer!

But God's response in this scene is far from over. He is about to take everything to a completely different level. And it's important for us to stay alert to what happens here, because in this event, the means by which God will ultimately connect himself to all of his people will be born.

We're about to learn about *faith!*

Faith and righteousness

In Genesis 15:6, we are told that Abram believed God and his promises, and the result was something quite remarkable.

We are told that because Abram believed, God "reckoned it to him as *righteousness*." (Gen. 15:6)

Now, if I were reading this story for the first time, God's response here would seem a little out of left field to me. I thought we were talking about offspring and land, doubt and comfort. Who said anything about righteousness? Yet somehow, God seems to turn Abram's act of believing his promises into something that actually sounds like *salvation!* Because Abram believes God, he is given the undeserved gift (that's what "reckoned" means) of being regarded by God as righteous and pure. What's going on here?

Old Testament scholars explain it like this: Certainly, Abram is believing God's promise to provide an "offspring," a "seed." But scholars tell us that Abram is believing God for much more than that. They tell us that Abram is not just believing in God's provision of an heir. He is also believing in God's provision of *the* heir!

Remember God's promise to Adam and Eve that he would send an "offspring," a "seed," to crush the Serpent? Remember how the great figures of the Bible continued to anticipate this Promised One? Well, in this "faith under the stars" event, what is happening at the deepest level is that Abram is believing that God will provide that Seed, that One, that Heir: the one who will redeem us all.

God is saying to him, "Yes, Abram, not only will I provide for you a son, but through that son the *redeemer himself* will come."

And Abram gets this, and he believes it, and that faith is his salvation, just as it is ours. Just as we look backwards in faith to the Redeemer, Abram looked forwards in time to that same Son; not just the son of Abram, but the Son of God! As that Son will say to the pharisees centuries later, "Your father Abraham rejoiced to see my day. And he saw it and was glad." (John 8:56)

Here, we are seeing faith in its beautiful role of bridging the broken relationship between God and the people he loves. Abram believes God. And our heavenly Father uses that faith to scoop Abram (and all of us) into his arms!

And he is about to respond to Abram's faith by changing the world.

The Promise

Our relationship with God is founded on the arrival and work of Jesus the Christ on planet earth. But our theme throughout this book is that this holy rescue didn't just appear one Christmas day with angels proclaiming hymns to shepherds on a starry night. We have been saying that the advent of Christ was promised and foreshadowed millennia before it occurred, beginning with the protoevangelium of Eden. Then we saw the hope of our salvation guarded and protected by God's promise to Noah and to the world. But now, in this part of our One Story, the promise of our salvation is about to make formal landfall on the beaches of God's world. God is about to promise our salvation, *your* salvation, and do so in a way that will leave no question as to his aggressive commitment to making us his own. With Abram, he is about to make a binding covenant promise to save us all.

When I was in seminary, my favorite professor was Dr. R. C. Sproul. One day after class, a group of us were following him out of the theological studies building, collected around him, stumbling over one another like starry-eyed disciples. As Sproul walked, he moved with his characteristic lumbering gait, as if he could just as well have been a blue-collar steel worker from his native Pittsburg as one of the world's premier theologians. We left the building, walking beneath the big oaks that dotted the campus of Reformed Theological Seminary, peppering him with "erudite" questions. Then one of my buddies asked a question I judged to be silly and unsophisticated. He said, "Hey Dr. Sproul, what's your favorite Bible verse?"

Sproul never stopped walking, yet responded immediately and, as always, enigmatically.

"That's easy," he said. "It's Genesis 15:17, 'When the sun had gone down and it was dark, behold, a smoking fire pot and a flaming torch passed between the pieces.'"

We looked at each other, confused.

Then he stopped walking and turned to us. Pushing his glasses up over his coarse, graying hair, and piercing us with his steely eyes, he said, "Now, gentlemen, in addition to the rest of your assignments, I want you all to come back tomorrow and explain to me *why* that is my favorite verse."

We all looked at our curious friend with that expression of annoyance that you give the kid in grade school who reminds the teacher that she has forgotten to assign any homework for the weekend. "Thanks a lot, pal."

But that night, I figured out what the passage meant. And when I did, there was no longer any confusion as to why it was Sproul's favorite part of scripture.

I'm about to explain it to you, but be warned – things are going to start sounding weird. Yet what God is about to do will be the ultimate reassurance for Abram and for us. And it will change the universe forever.

The blood of God

Following Abram's act of trusting faith, God says to him, "Bring me a heifer, a goat, and a ram, each three years old, along with a dove and a young pigeon." (Gen. 15:9)

Abram brings all of these animals. And then, without further instruction, our father in the faith proceeds to kill them all, hack them in half and arrange the pieces on the ground opposite each other.

Then he waits. The sun begins to set, and darkness starts to envelop him as he bats away the vultures. Then he falls into a deep sleep, and a dark dread oppresses his heart. In the midst of that darkness, God comes to Abram in a dream and renews his pledges to him and his promised offspring. But as the sun fully sets and darkness falls, a bizarre, frightening event takes place. We are told that "a smoking fire pot with a blazing torch appeared and passed between the pieces. On that day the LORD made a covenant with Abram." (Gen. 15:17-18)

Spooky Old Testament stuff if you've ever heard it, huh? Darkness, terror, flames, animals hacked in half – vultures and smoke!

What is going on here?

God tells Abram to bring these animals, and Abram doesn't even flinch. He goes and retrieves the animals and then immediately begins hacking them into pieces! What's that about? God didn't tell him to cut them in half. Abram just does it. So, what does Abram know that we don't know?

Tim Keller talks about this so well in one of his sermons that I'm going to borrow some of his thinking to explain this event. As soon as God told Abram to go get the animals, Abram knew what God was doing. He knew God was about to make a *covenant* with him, a solemn, binding contract – one of those ever-binding promises we saw God make with Adam and with Noah. But here, God is going to take it up a notch. He is going to commit himself faithfully to Abram, and he's going to do so using the customs of Abram's own culture.

The ancient ceremony of promise

The cutting of animals as a means of solidifying a covenant promise was a familiar part of life in the oral, story-telling culture of the ancient Near East. It seems strange and foreign to us because we don't live in an oral culture as Abram did. We live in a written culture. In our world, if we want to make the most binding form of agreement, what do we do? We call lawyers; we draw up contracts; we sign papers; we put those little stickies on them that say, "Sign here," and we complete the contract in writing. When we sign, we are in essence saying, "I commit to this, and I'm willing to pay a penalty if I fail to follow through with my promise. I hereby make myself accountable to you." And when we see someone else sign like that, something in us can relax and say, "Okay, now I know I can believe you."

Well, Abram didn't live in a written culture; he lived in an ancient, oral, story-telling culture. The way they made contracts in their day was not to write them down but rather to *ritually act them out*. It was called a "suzerainty covenant," and it was the gravest form of promise.

One of the reasons that a suzerainty covenant packed such gravity was that the participants did not just agree to a penalty if they violated the contract (cross my heart and hope to die), they literally acted out that penalty! We can hear God talk about such a covenant that was broken in Jeremiah 34. Hear this and feel the weight of this kind of promise: He says, "The men who violated my covenant and did not fulfill the terms of the covenant they made before me, *I will treat like the calf they cut in two and walked between its pieces. … their dead* bodies will be food for the birds of the air and the beasts of the earth." (Jer. 34:18-20)

So can you guess now what's going on in Genesis 15?

The way you made the most binding promise in those days was to cut an animal in half and walk between the pieces. And what you were doing was *ritually identifying* with the pieces. You were acting out the consequences, the penalty, of breaking the contract.

In essence, you would be saying, "If I don't do all the things I am promising today, may *this* be done to me."

Pretty effective motivation, huh? Next time you're getting work done on your house by some unreliable contractor, you might want to offer this as an alternative to his feeble promise. Maybe that would get him to finally show up!

The suzerainty treaty was a favorite among kings in this culture who wanted to dreadfully establish a relationship with servants and vassals. It made it very clear to them how seriously the king was taking this agreement. In fact, this was such a familiar way of making agreements in those days, that the verb used to make a covenant was not "make" a covenant, or to "commit to" a covenant. The verb, in Hebrew, was *kata berit* – to "cut" a covenant.

So Abram is probably getting pretty excited here. He's been wondering and fretting. He feels vulnerable and scared, and he needs guarantees. And Abram now sees that God is about to pledge himself with the most binding promise of his day. He is probably thinking, "Fabulous! We are finally gonna 'get this thing in writing!'" So he busily gathers these animals and starts hacking them up. This is best news possible for Abram.

But God is about to take the good news far beyond what Abram expects.

There are two things that God is going to do in verses 17 and 18 that are earthshaking. And by the end of this experience, we're not going to hear any more doubts from ole Abe. No more whining, "How can I know your promises are for real?"

Who makes the promise

The first amazing thing about this covenant cutting event is *who* passes between the pieces.

Genesis 15:17 tells us, "When the sun had set and darkness had fallen, a smoking fire pot and a blazing torch appeared and passed between the pieces."

Here is Dr. Sproul's favorite passage, and we're about to find out why he got so excited about it! This passage had me stumped as I sat in the seminary library that night. That is, until I crossed-referenced the original Hebrew words that are used in the phrase, "a smoking fire pot and blazing torch." I discovered that another possible translation of this could be "a billowing smoke and a fiery blaze."

Now, your turn! Does this sound like anything else you've heard of in the Old Testament? These are the same images that are used to describe Mt. Sinai when God comes down upon it to visit Moses. The mountain was wrapped in smoke and surrounded by fire. (Ex. 19:18) These are also the same words used to describe God's constant pillar of presence before the children of Israel in the wilderness – a pillar of cloud by day and a pillar of fire by night. (Ex. 13:22) This phrase even parallels the image of God's glory that later fills the temple in Isaiah 6.

So what has appeared here?

These are the emblems of God's actual Glory Presence. It's the same presence of God we see over and over again in the Old Testament.

In other words, *God himself* walks through the covenant pieces! And God himself is evoking upon *himself* the maledictions of this covenant if he breaks his word! He is committing to his promise, and he is swearing to be "hacked in two" if he falters.

Here, with the cut-up animals, God is essentially saying to Abram, "Abram, you want to know how you can trust me? You want to know how you can *know*? If I don't bless you, if I don't save you, if I don't provide for you, then may I be cut up like these animals, cut into pieces and die. That's how much you can know! This is how much you can trust me to never leave you! I swear to my own death that I will be your savior!"

What we're witnessing here in Genesis 15 is God's vow to fulfill every one of his promises to Abram. And more than that, his vow to save Abram eternally, to reckon him righteous – and even more so, his vow to save *all of Abram's children, – Us!*

God is promising a salvation, just as he did in the protoevangelium in Eden. Only this time he swears to his own death that he will make that salvation a glorious reality.

Our salvation *will* be accomplished!

The Christian's hope

You know those times in the middle of the night (those times when scary things feel the scariest)? Those are the times when we can feel those nagging doubts: "Am I really a Christian?" "Does God really love me?"

You have these kinds of fears too, right? The same kind that Abram and I have? We can worry that Christ's blood won't be enough for us; that maybe we didn't quite have enough faith. Perhaps there was that one really bad sin that won't be covered by his blood. If so, God's covenant promise to Abram in Genesis 15 whispers comfort to our fears. Because this act of God says if we are forsaken, then *God will be, too.*

This covenant that God "cut" with Abram says that if God doesn't fulfill his promise to save us, the Sovereign of the Universe himself will be chopped up into pieces and scattered for the birds to eat. He gives us his word! He bets his life on it!

This is the promise that makes you a Christian; this is why we trace our faith back to Abram. Because on this night, God vows to bring our redemption.

And this is why we can sleep well at night, free of those dark fears. Because somewhere in that scary darkness, the smoking fire pot and the blazing torch still move back and forth forever on our behalf, promising God's faithfulness to us always.

Who keeps the promise

The first astounding part of this story is who it is who passes through the pieces: God himself. The other amazing part is who *doesn't* pass through.

Remember we said that when a great king wanted to make a covenant with a vassal or a servant, he'd cut the animals as a promissory act? Well, don't think for a minute that it was the *king* who would walk through the pieces. It was the vassal! Sometimes if the king was really nice, he might walk through as well, but more often than not, the vassal was on his own. In other words, historically, it was the vassal who would be the one to take the vow, pledging his death if the covenant was broken, not the king.

But in this covenant that God makes with Abram, not only does the vassal (Abram) not go through alone, the vassal does not go through *at all!* He's asleep, remember? Out cold!

The passage says, "It came about when the sun had set, it was very dark, and behold there appeared a smoking fire pot and the blazing torch which passed between the pieces. *On that day the LORD made a covenant with Abram.*" (Gen. 15:17-18)

End of discussion, close in prayer, finished, done!
In this covenant, *only the king goes through!*

What is God saying here to Abram? And what is God saying to us?

He is proclaiming, "You can trust me about my promise here because this is not your promise to me, this is my promise to you. No failure that you can conjure will keep you from me. And no lack of faithfulness on my part will get in the way of this blessing. The cost of the covenant and the vow to fulfill this promise falls on me and me alone."

Throughout history, men have been making up religions that define what we must do to be close to God. They say you have to come up with something; you have to do something; you have to try really hard at something for God to be pleased with you. They make *us* go through the animal pieces in some way. "Religion" says that if we do these things then we can know that we are right with God.

But this covenant promises that God will do it all. He swears to his own death that he will be faithful to save us.

And in the most horrible paradox, he is indeed absolutely faithful – yet despite his faithfulness, he is still the one to die, in the person of Christ on the cross at Calvary. We are the ones who chronically break our covenant with him, but he is the one who pays.

The gift for us all

The best part of this whole story is that God's solemn promise is not just a commitment to Abram. This is not just a personal interaction between the two of them. We can watch and listen and be moved by this powerful event that Abram experiences. Beautiful Old Testament faith at work, right? But this promise doesn't just cover Abram in redemptive hope. It reaches forward to us as well. Remember, God has not just been promising this salvation to Abram; he has been promising it to all of Abram's *children!*

God says, "I give this to you and *to all of your descendants!*"

God doesn't just make this promise to the father of our faith. God makes this promise to Abram and to *all of his countless offspring!* That is us, my friends. We are the children of Abram.

>Remember the stars of the sky?
>Remember the sands of the sea?
>Remember the countless the children of Abram?
>That is *us*.
>We are his offspring.
>We are his children.
>We are children of that Covenant.

In Romans 4, Paul talks a lot about the faith of Abram. He even uses the words of Genesis 15 as he reminds us that when Abram believed, it was "reckoned to him as righteousness."

But then the Romans passage goes on as Paul adds a stunning phrase that opens God's arms and gathers *all of us* into this amazing story. Paul says, "Now, not for his (Abram's) sake only was it written that it was reckoned to him, but for *our sake also* – to whom it *will be reckoned* – as those who believe in Him, who raised Christ Jesus from the dead." (Rom. 4:22-24)

"For our sake also!" This is our promise, too!

"It will be reckoned!" This is our hope, as well!

In this passage, Paul is ringing a bell of glory that this covenant of salvation is not just for Abram but for us too! Like Abram, our righteousness before God *will be reckoned,* declared, gifted, and celebrated – because of this covenant promise!

Dear friends, God is far more committed to your heart, your wholeness, and your salvation than you could ever be. He graphically demonstrates that here with Abram. He promises to his own death that he will be our God. And what he promises, he always fulfills.

Hear this story and know it's not just Abram's story.

This story is for us, Abram's children.

It is our story –
> The sands of the sea;
> The stars of the sky;
> We are the children of the promise.
> Praise him, praise him, all ye little children.

Chapter Five

Abraham and Isaac: The Hope of the Son

In our last chapter, we watched as God formally promised Abram that he would establish and fulfill the One Story of salvation. God swore that he would bless Abram and save him. He promised that he would provide for him an offspring and thereby provide for us all. And on that day, Abram believed God's promises, and it was "reckoned to him as righteousness." By that act of faith, Abram became our spiritual father.

But when we last left our old friend, Abram still didn't have a son. And that is a big problem, because if there's not an offspring, our One Story falls apart. There's no Seed. There's no Savior. The story is *over*.

For the One Story to continue, God has to actually make good on his promise. There needs to be child for Abram, and ultimately, a greater child for us all.

Let's look at the story of the son, Isaac, both his arrival and near departure. Here we will be given both a wonderfully joyful story and a very difficult story as we see God's promise further unfold.

The Promised Son

Abram's plan

Concerned that God may be dragging his feet in the provision of an heir, Abram and Sarai decide to try what might be referred to as the "Hagar method" for dealing with infertility. Sarai offers Abram the use of her Egyptian servant, Hagar, to conceive a child.

As strange as this may seem to us, it was regarded as a legitimate way to produce an heir in their culture. But this is not the way that God has intended to fulfill his promise to Abram. In Galatians 4, Paul refers to this errant attempt by Abram as a birth "according to the flesh," as opposed to living in faithful hope that God would do as he promised. (Gal. 4:29)

Nevertheless, in Genesis 16:15 we are told that "Hagar bore Abram a son, and Abram called the name of his son Ishmael."

God's response

God apparently does not like Abram and Sarai taking matters into their own hands. This is *God's* promise to fulfill, and they are essentially jury-rigging a humanly created solution to their problem. So God intervenes and responds.

In Genesis 17:1-2 he makes his first move. He speaks to Abram anew and says, "I am God Almighty (in Hebrew, *El Shaddai*); walk before me and be blameless, and *I* (not you and Hagar) will establish my covenant between me and you, and I will multiply you exceedingly."

God has many names in Scripture. *Elohim* essentially means "Lord." *El Elyon* means God Most High. And in our Moses story, we will receive God's most personal name. But here, God uses his name *El Shaddai*. It means "God Almighty," "the Overpowerer," "the one who will not be thwarted." It is as if God roars back at Abram saying, "Your lame attempt to fulfill my promise is puny and minuscule. The Overpowerer will accomplish what he has promised!"

In response to this, Abram appropriately falls on his face.

God continues. "Behold, my covenant is with you, and you shall be the father of a multitude of nations." In fact, he says, "No longer shall your name be Abram, but your name shall be called, Abraham (which means "father of many"), for I will make you the father of a multitude of nations." (Gen. 17:5)

Essentially, God comes back to him and says, "Okay Abram, I know you're worried. I know that you are going outside the box here to try to make my promises come true. But stop! *I'm* going to do this. *I* will multiply you exceedingly. You will be a father of many nations. In fact, not only are you going to be a father, but your identity, your new name, will define you as that father of many, the father I have promised that you will be."

As we said earlier, when you named someone within Hebrew culture, you were establishing your authority over them. So as God changes Abram's name, he is reasserting his authority over this situation, reminding Abram who's the boss, but he's also deepening his promise – even Abraham's *name* will mean "father." Regardless, Abraham must submit to God's timing regarding the coming of the child.

A forever song

Next, God is going to give us a special treat. Remember the earth-shaking covenant ceremony from the last chapter? God walked the deadly covenant pieces to promise himself to Abram. Well, as our story continues, God revisits that promise, but this time, he flavors it with more intimate, personal notes of relationship. He is the Lord of power and authority, but what God ultimately longs for with his people is our hearts.

Consequently, in Genesis 17:7, God reaffirms his covenant promise, saying, "I will establish my covenant as an everlasting covenant between me and you and your descendants after you for the generations to come ..."and then adds, "to be your God and the God of your descendants after you."

And this is the first time you hear God begin to hint at what will be his redemptive theme song for the rest of scripture: *we will be his, and he will be ours.* We'll hear him sing this promise from this passage in Genesis, all the way to the book of Revelation. In its fullest form, it will go something like this: *"I will be your God and you will be my people, and I will dwell among you."* (Gen. 17:7, Ex. 6:7, Ex. 29:45, Lev. 26:12, Eze. 11:20, 2 Cor. 6:16, Rev. 21:3 – to name a few!)

If you want one little phrase to capture what the One Story is all about, why God is working so hard to save his children, here is your answer. Over and over again he will pledge his longing to belong to us, and we to him. This is his dream of being with us forever. "I want to be *your* God and I want you to be *my* people, and I want to be *with* you."

This dwelling with his people is God's passion. If you think about it, the word "with" is God's favorite preposition. Look it up! He's constantly saying it. When we walk through the valley of the shadow of death, he is *with* us. (Ps. 23:4) Immanuel means God *with* us. Jesus says, "And lo, I will be *with* you always, even until the end of the age." (Matt. 28:20)

"With" is God's favorite way to be!

If we skip forward to the end of the Bible and listen to what God is proclaiming in Revelation as all things are made new, he is still singing this same song. Go ahead and learn it now so you can join in with him on that day. He sings, "I will be your God, you will be my people…" And then up an octave as he draws the story to completion, he says,

> Behold, the tabernacle of God is among men, and he shall dwell among them, and they shall be his people, and God himself shall be among them, and he shall wipe away every tear from their eyes; and there shall no longer be any

death; there shall no longer be any mourning, or crying, or pain; the first things have passed away" And he who sits on the throne says, "Behold, I am making all things new!
– Revelation 21:3-5

The One Story is not just a plan to save ethereal souls. It is a precious plan for restoring loving belonging with our heavenly Father. The broken relationship will be healed, and he will dwell among us. He unfolds this promise to Abraham, and he will one day sing it with all of us!

A helpful reminder

After pledging his faithfulness to Abraham and reminding him that God's plan is still at work, the Lord continues to make his "anti-Hagar" point. He does so by reaffirming his covenant promise to Abraham with a *covenant sign*. As he did with Noah in the sign of the bow, God wants to solidify his promise to Abraham with a tangible symbol of his faithfulness. In Genesis 17, God gives him a sign, the sign of circumcision.

God knows that the spiritual realities of our relationship with him can sometimes feel elusive to us, so he gives us concrete symbols to help us in our frailty. Tangible, physical reminders like baptism and rainbows help us hold onto his goodness. They are tangible pictures of intangible realities.

The gift of receiving the Lord's Supper always blows me away. Though I can know of Christ's death for me, when I worship with his other children at church, I get to receive the gift of having one of his pastors look me in the eye as he hands me a piece of bread. Then he says to me, "John, this is the body of Christ, broken for you." My eyes always well with tears as I tangibly taste his sacrifice for me. I bring the cup of dark red wine to my lips, and I taste the love of one who spilt his blood and gave his life that I might stand before him on a Sunday morning, joyful and free. How is it that I am invited to his table? How could he love me like this!? God's covenant signs rip through the shallow veil of our physical world and enable us to touch the mystery and majesty of his spiritual truth.

The sign of the Abrahamic Covenant, honored for centuries by all of God's Hebrew children, will be circumcision. It will tangibly remind his people for ages that God keeps his promises. (I also wonder if God wasn't sending Abraham a little ironic message here as well, given the reproductive location of this covenant sign.)

God's plan

Finally, in response to the Hagar debacle, God is going to get more explicit about the real heir, the true offspring of the promise. This is where the story gets a little fun, I think.

He says to the patriarch, "As for Sarai your wife, you shall not call her name Sarai, but Sarah shall be her name." (Again, asserting his authority, but also deep blessing, because the name, Sarah means "Princess.")

"And I will bless her, and indeed I will give you a son by *her*. Then I will bless her, and she shall be a mother of nations; kings of peoples shall come from her." (Gen. 17:15-16)

God says he's going to accomplish this birth through ninety-year-old Sarah. To my understanding this is the first time he has made that explicit. So far, he hasn't actually said how he was going to provide the heir. Now he says it's going to be through Abraham's very own (quite aged) wife.

And what is Abraham's reaction of holy reverence to this news? What does the great patriarch do? We are told that "Abraham fell on his face and laughed, and said in his heart 'Will a child be born to a man 100 years old? And will Sarah who is 90 years old bear a child?'" (Gen. 17:17)

Abraham is saying, "Right! Look, Lord. I'm like, 100 years old, and my wife is 90! You want me to believe that she's going to bear a child? I'm at the century mark here. This can't work!"

Like Mr. Lemon said, "Look again!"

He also adds another comment in verse 18 that I love. He says, "Oh, that Ishmael might live before thee." In other words, "Hey Lord, let it go, come on! Ishmael's fine. It's not that big a deal. At least he's not Eliezer of Damascus!"

But God says, "No, Sarah your wife shall bear you a son and you shall call his name Isaac. And I will establish my Covenant with *him* for an everlasting Covenant for his descendants." (Gen. 17:19)

The laughter of God

In further response to Abraham's skepticism, God decides to make a personal house call. We are told in Genesis 18:2 that Abraham receives a visit from "three men." Abraham welcomes them, feeds them, and entertains them in a polite, deferential, Bedouin sort of a way. And "they" say to him, "Where is Sarah your wife?" Abraham says, "She's at home in the tent." And they (God) say to him, "I will surely return to you this time next year and behold Sarah your wife will have a son."

At this point, the scriptures are surely a valid reflection of typical gender behavior, because we are told in verse 10, that as Abraham meets with the three mysterious strangers, "Sarah was listening at the tent door which was behind him." (It's a woman thing, right?) And we are told that Sarah "laughed to herself, saying, 'After I am old (literal Hebrew, "worn out") shall I have pleasure and I shall bear a child?'"

God responds to Abraham, "Why does Sarah laugh? saying, 'Shall I indeed bear a child when I'm so old?' Is anything too difficult for the LORD? I will return to you at the appointed time next year, and Sarah will have a son." Sarah denied it however, and lied, saying, 'I didn't laugh,' because she was afraid. And God said 'No, you did laugh.'" (Gen. 18:13-15)

By chapter 21, however, we are told that God fulfills his promise. The passage says that, "The LORD took note of Sarah as he had said, and the LORD did for Sarah as he had promised, and Sarah conceived and bore a son to Abraham in his old age at the appointed time of which God had spoken to him. And Abraham called the name of the son who Sarah bore him, Isaac.... And Abraham was 100 years old when Isaac was born to him. Sarah said 'God has made laughter for me. Everyone who hears will laugh with me.'" (Gen. 21:1-6)

Laughter is indeed the theme of this story. Even the name Isaac is a teasing, loving jab from God. Abraham and Sarah's reactions to God's promise of a child was to laugh. The Hebrew word for their reaction of laughter is *tishaq*, meaning "they laughed." But God is faithful, and God is loving, and he provides a miracle baby, a foreshadowing of the One, the Seed of the woman who is sent to crush the Serpent. So let their reaction be laughter! In God's providence, the baby's name will be *Ishaq*, (Isaac) which means "he laughs." The "he" referred to here of course, is *God himself!*

So who gets the last laugh of joy in this story? Every time they call little *Ishaq* in from play or home to dinner, delighting in the blessings of their ever so patient Father, they will be reminded of how their faithful, loving God laughed at their faithlessness and doubt. Through this child the world will be blessed. And now we all can laugh.

If you read scripture with any sort of awareness, you will hear God's sense of humor throughout. He loves to mock. Delightfully, he mocks Abraham and Sarah in their laughter. But he also mocks evil with forgiveness. He mocks our "strength" with Christ's "weakness." He mocks our shame and humiliation with Christ's victory. And ultimately, he will mock all of our deaths with the laughter of a Christ who will finally welcome us into his powerful arms.

This is God at work. This is his heart. He brings the child of the promise into the arms of Abraham and Sarah and then laughs with us all in the joy that child will ultimately bring to all of Abraham's children.

The Sacrifice of the Son

That was the fun story. Now it's time for the not-so-fun story. I want to look at this narrative in some detail because it is filled with the power and danger that seem to always lie at the core of God's One Story. However, were it not for how this story ends and what this story means, I would not like it at all. I think it's a troubling story. It bothers me. But let's look at it. It's God's story after all.

The command and the test

We are told in Genesis 22:1, that "after these things, God came to test Abraham." The word "test" refers to a trial designed to try or to prove. And the nature of this proving? He wants Abraham to take that cherished, promised child, you know, the one that we've been hoping for for so long; the one whose life was supposed to bring laughter and hope, and he wants Abraham to sacrifice that child to God. God says, "Take now your son, your only son whom you love, Isaac. And go to the land of Moriah, and offer him there as a burnt offering on one of the mountains of which I will tell you." (Gen. 22:2)

Suddenly, in the midst of the beauty of fulfilled promises, God comes and demands something horrifying. After years of provision and faithfulness, it somehow sounds as if God is turning on Abraham. He wants Abraham's Isaac! And notice that God is very specific here. If he had just come and said, "Abraham, I want you to kill your son," I'm sure the old patriarch would have marched right over to ole *Ishmael's* tent, tapped on the door, and announced, "Boy, we're going on a little camping trip. Pack your things!" But God is very specific here. He says in essence, "Take your son, your *only* son (you know the one I mean), the one you *love*, Isaac. And sacrifice him to me as a burnt offering."

Think about this for a second. Here's Abraham; he's followed God for more than 25 years by now. He's left his home and wandered, living only on God's promises, promises that God has repeatedly vowed he would fulfill. He's probably thought about the beautiful legacy that God has foretold as he laid out at night, trying to count the stars, and clinging to his hope in *El Shaddai*. And now he has finally held this child of promise in his arms; likely even laughed in wonder and joy – this child, the redemption of us all, his little boy, Isaac.

And now God wants him to kill him.

And he doesn't just want him to just kill him. He wants Abraham to sacrifice him as a *burnt offering*. This is the same kind of sacrifice that Noah made in gratitude for God's preservation. Remember that this sacrifice was unique in that unlike many sacrifices of that day, with a burnt offering, the object of sacrifice was completely consumed, everything was given. Furthermore, a burnt offering involved not only killing the sacrifice, but skinning it, and cutting it into pieces, cleaning out the entrails, and then burning the body.

I told you this was a tough story.

But notice, by verse 3, Abraham immediately begins doing what God commanded. We are told that, "Abraham rose early in the morning, saddled his donkey, and took two of his young men with him, and Isaac his son. He then split wood for the burnt offering, arose and went to the place that God had told him." In other words, Abraham immediately gets busy obeying this call that God makes to him.

How do we make sense of this? I mean, doesn't God's request here seem a bit unusual to you? Doesn't it sort of seem like an odd, if not horrifying, demand for God to call Abraham to kill his child?! Does God at any other time send anybody out to kill a family member? Are we to believe that Abraham is okay with this? Does he believe that God would really want a father to kill his only son? Yet Abraham immediately sets about doing this horrific thing that God calls him to do. What's going on here?

As we approach this story, I want to slow us down. We can get so used to hearing these stories, that we can just sort of read them as "Bible stories," and forget about what is really happening to these people. But if we are to fully receive the gift that I believe God has hidden in this baffling, disturbing story, we will need to look deeply into it.

The firstborn

First, we've got to understand the "law of the firstborn." Obviously, for God to ask Abraham to murder someone would be wrong. But the thing that God demands here is not homicide. God asks for something else, something very specific. He asks for something that Abraham would have been horrified at, but would have at least understood. God asks for a sacrifice. He asks Abraham for a burnt offering of the firstborn.

In our 21st century individualistic society we can struggle with understanding the ancient theme of the primacy of the firstborn, the "law of primogenitor." Within many cultures of the ancient Middle East, the firstborn essentially possessed everything in the family and represented everyone in his household, both in terms of possessions as well as debts.

This was a belief among God's people as well. God says something regarding this principle in scripture that Abraham would have already known: that the most precious "fruits" of life belonged to him, *that the first fruits of harvest and the firstborn child were owed to God in honor and service to him as God Almighty.* This is one reason why God was pleased with Abel's offering way back in Genesis 4. His first fruits and "best portions" of his flock were presented to God. (Gen. 4:4)

God will make this even more overt after his rescue of the firstborn of Israel during Passover. In the Mosaic Law, God will spell out how the firstborn of his people are owed to him as a debt of atonement for the family. (Ex. 13:2, Num. 8:17) God makes it clear that the life of the firstborn, be they "of man or of beast," belong to him. This was a given for the people of that day; their first fruits, their first cattle, and their firstborn children were all forfeit. They belonged to God alone. It had always been that way.

However, despite his claim on the life of the firstborn, God has thus far operated with restraint. He has never actually called in the debt he maintains. Instead, he has asked for substitutes or ransoms in some other way. He makes overt provision for a ransom for the firstborn in Numbers 3: five shekels a head to pay the Levites in the payment of the life of the firstborn. (Num. 3:46-47) In other words, so far, God has not demanded the life that was rightfully his. But now with Abraham, could something unthinkable be happening? Could God be saying, "I'm going to take you up on what is owed to me?" Is he calling Abraham to offer up his son, (his firstborn son, the one he loves), as a sacrifice to God? Is God finally calling in that debt?

The journey

Let's go back to the story. We are told that, "Abraham rose early in the morning, saddled his donkey, and took two of his young men with him, and Isaac his son. And he split the wood for the burnt offering and arose and went to the place of which God had told him." (Gen. 22:3)

Now imagine this picture. Like I said, we often don't treat people in the Bible like they're real people. Let Abraham be real for a moment as we look into this story. Think about this experience for him.

Why do you think Abraham rose up early in the morning? Well, wouldn't you? Have you ever had a really difficult, scary day ahead? A surgery or the funeral of a family member? If you wake up early, can *you* go back to sleep? You awaken disturbed, frightened. What this day holds is already overwhelming you.

Then we are told that Abraham saddles his donkey and cuts the wood for the sacrifice. Abraham was one of the richest men in the ancient Near East. If he had wanted a donkey prepared, he had butlers or chauffeurs to do that kind of stuff for him! He probably hadn't chopped wood in 75 of his last 100 years much less saddled his own donkey. So why would he do this?

You can't delegate a task this grave, this horrific, to servants. This was something Abraham had to do himself. God calls him to this horrible task, and certainly he, himself, must cut the wood for the altar to burn his son's body. He must saddle his own donkey to make this trip.

They set off on the journey, only to give us another disturbing image: "On the *third day* Abraham raised his eyes and saw the place from a distance" (v. 4)

They had to travel *three days* to get to the place of sacrifice!

We've all had to wait days for a doctor's report. They do the biopsy on Thursday, and you can't learn the results until Monday. You know how long that weekend feels. This journey is as if God asked you to drive to Anchorage, Alaska with your child sitting in the car next to you as the hours drag by. Three days to get to this place that God sends them, Moriah.

Incidentally, when they get there, Abraham says to his servants, "Stay here with the donkey, and I and the lad will go yonder, and *we will worship and return to you.*" (Gen. 22:5) What do you make of that? Sounds like the first ray of hope in the story! Abraham somehow suspects he will come back with his son.

The altar

Now, as they get ready to climb the mountain, the narrative changes. Moses, who wrote the book of Genesis, obviously sees this as the most important part of the story, because the action slows way down. He wants to get our hearts into this story. He wants us to know every detail.

He tells us that Abraham and Isaac leave the servants and begin their journey up the mountain. Abraham gives the wood to his son to carry, and Abraham himself carries the fire and the knife.

So far in our story we have been imagining the subjective experience of Abraham by reading the narrative of his story. But as Abraham and Isaac begin their way up the mountain, we are given a peak into their hearts, even into their conversation. The writer records that as they walk, Isaac looks up at his dad and in essence says, "Father, I'm confused. I know we are heading up to make a sacrifice, and I've seen you do those before. But haven't we forgotten something? I mean we've got the fire, the wood, and the knife, but there's no lamb!" (Gen. 22:7)

We have said that we want to make these stories personal. Apparently, Moses does as well. I am silenced every time I read this question from Isaac. And I am silenced that Moses would include it. What would we expect Abraham to say at this point? "Well, son, it's you. I'm going to kill you."

Abraham does answer him. He answers him in a way that shows us why Moses *did include* Isaac's heartbreaking question. Abraham says, "God will provide for himself the lamb for the burnt offering, my son." The Hebrew word here is "to see to." He says, "Son, God will *see to* that. (Gen. 22:8)

He is saying, "I don't know the answer, Isaac, but I do know God, and he will take care of us." Hebrew's chapter 11 takes us even deeper into Abraham's heart. The writer of Hebrews tells us that Abraham believed that God would at minimum raise Isaac from the dead. He knew that God had promised this child, and that somehow God would work this out. He doesn't know how, but he knows the God of the Covenant. And he remembers that God has promised to *his own death* that he would not betray his beloved Abraham. God will see to this.

Back to the story. "They came to the place that God had told him, and Abraham built the altar there and arranged the wood, and bound his son, and laid him on the altar on top of the wood." (Gen. 22:9) Mercifully, Moses does not provide us with details about this interaction. What did Abraham say to his son as he tied his hands and feet? Like I said, if it wasn't for the ending of this story, I would not like this story at all. Somehow, Abraham binds his son, and puts him on the altar, and takes the knife, and raises it, preparing to destroy his child.

The salvation

Then suddenly, we are told, the angel of the LORD (the voice of God himself) calls from heaven and says "Abraham! Abraham! Do not stretch out your hand against the boy! Do nothing to him. For now I know that you fear God, since you have not withheld your son, your only son, from me." (Gen. 22:12)

Then, Abraham looks up and sees a ram caught in the thicket by its horns. Understanding this infinite gift, he immediately goes and takes the ram and offers *it* up for a burnt offering in the place of his son.

Then God spoke to Abraham a second time from heaven and said,

> By myself I have sworn, because you have done this thing and have not withheld your son, your only son, indeed I will greatly bless you and I will greatly multiply your seed as the stars of the heavens and as the sand which is on the seashore and your seed shall possess their enemies and in your seed all the nations of the earth shall be blessed because you have obeyed my voice.
> – Genesis 22:15-18

And this story of horror suddenly becomes a story of grace and love and redemption and safety.

Abraham named that place "Yahweh will see to it," using the same phrase that he had used to answer little Isaac's question as they had climbed that terrifying mountain earlier in the day. Indeed, God did see to it.

ABRAHAM AND ISAAC: THE HOPE OF THE SON

<u>*Our*</u> *salvation*

Seeing the miraculous resolution of this story moves my heart to joyful worship. I feel rich gratitude for a sacrifice prevented and provided; a life saved. But if my joy at the salvation of Isaac was where my heart remained, I would be missing something of grave importance and deep wonder.

I began this story by telling you that I did not like it; that it disturbed me. It still does. It should. The fact that Abraham and Isaac are able to walk back down Mount Moriah together after the sacrifice of a ram does not change the fact that this story is brutally heartbreaking. This story is still troubling because it doesn't end here. This story is far from over.

Our hearts can lift in relief at God's salvation of Abraham's son with the provision of the ram, but as any student of the Bible knows, the death of Abraham's son, Isaac, could not have really paid the price for the sins of his family, or even himself, primogenitor or not. And certainly, the ram in the bushes did not ultimately pay for their offenses against God. As Hebrews 10:4 says, "It is impossible for the blood of bulls and goats to atone for sin."

But God is appeased here. The requirement of a sacrifice seems to somehow have been met. What has happened? What is the rest of this story?

Well, the place where God sent Abraham, the place called Moriah, was later settled, and became a major city of the Jebusites. And when the children of Israel entered Canaan and took over the land, it ultimately became their capital city. It was called Jerusalem.

And the hills around this city, the place God sent Abraham and his son, were ultimately the same hills around Jerusalem: Mt. Zion, the Mount of Olives, and Mt. Moriah. And among these hills was one that was called the Skull, *Golgotha* in Hebrew.

It was the hill that we call Calvary.

And this story is not really over until centuries later, when God took *his* son, his only son, (you know the one – the one whom he loved), and walked him up those same hills, and put him on the altar, and bound him there, and raised the knife.

But this time there was no last-minute rescue; no ram in the bushes.

And he killed him there.

He pierced him.

He crushed him. For us.

Abraham's fear was warranted. God *was* going to go back and claim the law of primogenitor, demanding the death of the firstborn, just not ours.

The Agony of the Heart of God

We have listened in our stories for the heart of our God. In this story, God dramatically invites us all to step into the most horrible experience of his heart.

Through the Isaac event, God compels us all to reflect on what it would be like to sacrifice your only son for someone you loved. How horrific would that act be?

By inviting Abraham (and us) into this heartbreaking choice, God is opening his heart and saying, "Behold the horror of what I called Abraham to endure. Do you feel the nightmare of it: the call to bring about the death of your only son?! That is what *my choice* was like. That is what it was like to walk *my son* up that hill. That is what it was like to kill *my son* because of my love for you. Abraham was right, I did "provide for myself the lamb." The lamb was my beloved one.

Know me. Feel the agony of my sacrifice. This is the horror my son and I faced for you."

This story is horrible because God's story was horrible. And in it we are forced to witness something that we often don't want to face: that our salvation cost our precious God everything!

Lift this passage up in your hearts. Never forget this troubling story. I want to invite you to let it speak to your hidden fears and deepest vulnerabilities about your relationship with God. I want you to live every day seeing that at Calvary, God's love was "tested" like Abraham's. And that, in response, his heart covered those hills with his love – and with the blood of his son.

And now, because of God's sacrifice, we can cast off the fears and doubts we so often feel about God's love for us. Because we can now echo God's words to Abraham *back to God*, saying,

"Father, now I know that you love me.

Because you did not withhold your son, your only son, from me."

Chapter Six

Moses I: The God of Flame and Belonging

Let's review our One Story so far. God created a perfect Way for his people in Eden – a Way that he still wants and is busy redeeming. Adam and Eve left his side, but instead of destroying them, God began his One Story by promising a redeemer to save us all. He committed with Noah that his approach to our sinfulness would no longer be total destruction. And then he began his family. He found Abraham and promised him a son who would be the beginning of a great nation. Remember, God has always wanted his people at his side.

Soon, that family of Abraham indeed becomes a great people, a nation in fact. And this will lead us to the next installment of our One Story, the story of Moses. We're going to look at Moses over the next three chapters because his story is so rich, and because with Moses, the complexity and depth of God's One Story is going to expand to a new level of wonder. We can't miss a drop of it!

From a Family to a Nation

Jacob's gift

After the promises, fulfillment, and protection of his chosen Abraham, God continues his story. Abraham's son, Isaac has Jacob; and Jacob has his own experience in God's covenant plan. He has a dream!

In Genesis 28, Jacob dreams he sees a ladder. It is set on earth with its top reaching into heaven, "And behold, the angels of God were ascending and descending on it." (Gen. 28:12) In this dream, God comes to Abraham's grandson and reaffirms the promises he had made to Abraham himself.

He says to Jacob,

> I am the LORD, the God of your father Abraham and the God of Isaac. I will give you and your descendants the land on which you are lying. Your descendants will be like the dust of the earth, and you will spread out to the west and to the east, to the north and to the south. All peoples on earth will be blessed through you and your offspring. I am with you and will watch over you wherever you go, and I will bring you back to this land. I will not leave you until I have done what I have promised you.
> – Genesis 28:13-16

Hear the themes from the promises to Abraham? The land, the descendants, and the blessing of God's eternal presence *with* him. Two generations after his original promise, God is still on the job, making the same promises he made to Abraham, only now, to Abraham's grandson.

As we have already seen however, with each manifestation of God's promise of salvation, the story gets richer and fuller. Jacob gets a reaffirmation of God's promises to his grandfather, but he also gets more. Jacob not only gets the promises; he also gets the image of "the ladder."

I remember singing a little song as a child growing up in Sunday school. "We are climbing Jacob's ladder, Jacob's ladder, Jacob's ladder, soldiers of the cross!" As we sang, we made little climbing motions with our hands and feet.

Like "Noah and the Ark," "Jacob's ladder" has often been relegated to the Bible schools. But Jacob's vision is not a childish image. As you will see, it is yet another graphic gift from God's arsenal of redemption. In this image, Jacob actually receives a wondrous foreshadowing of the inner workings of God's ultimate promise.

So what's God up to with the ladder? Psychologists love interpreting dreams, but if I were to have taken a crack at understanding this one for Jacob, I would have had to wait a couple of thousand years to get its true meaning. I would have had to wait until the days of John chapter 1, when Jesus encounters Nathaniel.

John tells us that Nathaniel meets Jesus after having had a little siesta under a fig tree. When they are introduced, Jesus tells Nathaniel that he saw him sleeping under that tree. Because of this, Nathaniel immediately believes Jesus and believes in who he is. Jesus is obviously moved by his simple strong faith and says to Nathaniel, "You believe because I told you I saw you under the fig tree? You shall see greater things than this. I tell you the truth, you shall see the heavens open, and the angels of God ascending and descending on the Son of Man." (John 1:50-51)

In this statement Jesus finally interprets Jacob's dream. Essentially, he is saying, "You want to understand the ladder? You want to understand the staircase? You want to understand God's access to us and our access to God; how heaven reaches down to earth? Then understand *me*. The Son of Man is the staircase. I am the ladder. It is only through me that you will reach the Father."

In other words, in his dream, Jacob is shown a picture of the very way of salvation that will be provided by God, the "ladder" that is Christ. How can God bridge the gap between himself and man? How can God come and develop these loving relationships with lost sinful men like Abraham, Jacob, and us? Only if there is a ladder, only if there is a bridge. Jacob gets to see that picture, foretelling the one who will come and bring God to man.

Welcome to Egypt

The next step in our One Story involves Jacob's family. Jacob has twelve sons, one of whom is Joseph. And because of Joseph's unusual dreams and the way he chooses to handle them, (not to mention the notorious "coat of many colors") some very unpleasant family strife develops. As a result of their envy, Joseph's brothers end up selling him into slavery in Egypt. (And you thought you had a dysfunctional family!)

Joseph ultimately becomes sort of a 'grand deputy administrator' under the pharaoh of Egypt, and at about the same time, there's a famine in Joseph's homeland of Canaan. So Jacob and all of Joseph's brothers flee to Egypt to survive the food shortage. Since Egypt had the Nile River, it was less dependent on the weather than other countries. (This was one of the reasons for its world power, and why they worshiped the river as a god. Preview of coming attractions!)

Egypt was the perfect place for the family of God to ride out the famine, so perfect in fact that they decided to stay. And they multiplied.

The book of Exodus picks up their story, describing how well the people of God prospered in Egypt. We are told in Exodus 1:7 that they prospered so well that they began to be seen as "exceedingly mighty" by the leadership in Egypt. God told Abraham at the covenant cutting ceremony that his people would be exiled in another land for 430 years, but that they would become "many." Well, here we go! The covenant with Abraham was God's promise that Abraham would not only have a family but that it would multiply greatly. Now, according to that promise, the *family* has become a *nation*. And we come to the part of our One Story that deals with Moses and God's nation of people.

The Rise of Israel

As we address this story of Moses, we're going to be looking at Egypt, the plagues, and the Ten Commandments. And as we do, I want you to try to get that movie, *The Ten Commandments,* out of your head. Remember Charlton Heston bellowing, "Let my people go!" Remember Yul Brenner constantly declaring, "So let it be written, so let it be done!" I know you do, but let's reformat our brains just a bit.

Firstly, the focus of God's story here is not the Ten Commandments. I don't know why they would name the movie that. The focus of this story is an aggressive, loving God coming to rescue his people. He wants to make them his own. He will only set up the law much later as a structure for their hearts and for his relationship with them. That will only happen *after* he saves them from the most powerful nation in the world in a show of might, wonder, and love.

Secondly, what was Edward G. Robinson doing in that movie? The character he played in the film still talked like one of those smarmy goodfellas Robinson always played in those old gangster movies like *Little Caesar!* "Yeah, Moses, we're goin' to the promised land, see! We're gonna rub 'em out, see."

Anyway, back to our story.

We are told that "the Sons of Israel were fruitful in Egypt and increased greatly and multiplied and became exceedingly mighty. So the land was filled with them." (Ex. 1:7) A little nod there by Moses, who is writing these books, that God was already fulfilling the promises to Abraham. Just as God had promised, the people are becoming as many as the sands in the sea and the stars in the sky.

Then suddenly, we are given a major plot point:

"Now a new king arose over Egypt who did not know Joseph." (Ex. 1:8) This is going to spell trouble. The new pharaoh starts looking at the people of Israel, and says, "Behold the people of the sons of Israel are more and mightier than we." (Ex. 1:9) God's people have prospered so much that they are now greater in number than the people of Egypt, and Pharaoh starts to worry. He says, "We need to deal wisely with them less they multiply, and in the event of a war, join themselves to those who hate us and fight against us and depart from the land." (Ex. 1:10) So he decides to afflict God's people with "hard labor and made their lives bitter."

This is how the whole slavery thing started. Egypt's oppression of God's people was basically a strategy to prevent them from becoming too numerous and therefore potentially allying themselves with one of their enemies! (That's one way to keep them friendly, right?) Regardless, it doesn't work. The more the Egyptians afflict the people of God, the more they multiply and spread out – so that "Egypt was in dread of Israel." (Ex. 1:12)

So, as they say in New Orleans, the Egyptians "kicked it up another notch." The pharaoh told the Hebrew midwives to put to death any male children born to Hebrew families. Incidentally, do you remember any other time in which male infanticide is ordered by a king? The only other time we hear of such a thing is in the book of Matthew, with King Herod's attempt to destroy young King Jesus by killing all of the little Hebrew boys. Matthew is the only one of the Gospel writers who talks about this. The reason he puts his focus here is because Matthew is writing very specifically to Jews, and he wants to highlight the historical identity of Jesus – that Jesus is in essence the "new Moses." This is why he also reminds us that Jesus takes the people out into the wilderness. He also takes them to a mountain where he feeds them and speaks to them about the truest understanding of God's Law. Matthew is saying in essence, "Alright, you Jewish folks who have been following Moses all along, there is a new Moses, a better Moses, and his name is Jesus of Nazareth. He is the one to whom God's great story has always been pointing!"

The One who Draws Out

The Little Egyptian Boy

The first five books of the Bible (which theologians call the Pentateuch) were written by Moses. Well, these books are about to become an autobiography because, thanks to the clever work of the Hebrew midwives, as well as God's loving hand of protection, baby Moses is born. We are told, "A man from the House of Levi (the priesthood), married a daughter of Levi, and bore a son – and she saw he was beautiful, and she hid him for three months. And when she could hide him no longer, she got a wicker basket and covered it in tar and pitch. She put the child in it and placed it among the reeds by the river bank." (Ex. 2:1-3)

The Hebrew word used here to describe Moses's little basket is *tebah*, the same word used for Noah's Ark. You recall God's promise of protection and salvation to his people in the Noah story. How perfectly appropriate it is that God again sends another ark to protect and provide for his people in the person of Moses.

So Moses's mother puts him in a little ark "and sets it among the reeds on the bank of the Nile, and Moses's sister stands at a distance to see what will happen." (Ex. 2:4-5)

The daughter of the pharaoh comes down that day to bathe in the Nile, sees the little basket, and decides to adopt this baby. The child grows and bonds with Pharaoh's daughter and becomes her son. And "she names him Moses, because 'I drew him out of the water.'"

(Gen. 2:10) Moses's name means "one who draws out;" which is perfect, given what Moses will later accomplish in his life.

Now, since Moses, the writer doesn't tell us much about his childhood, I will allow you to fill in the details here from the movies if you want: the little prince of Egypt, Moses, running around with little boy Yul Brynner (who's already bald as a kid for crying out loud). But by Exodus 2:11 Moses has grown up and become a leader in Egypt, trained in all the wisdom and culture of mighty Egypt. (Acts 7:22) He seems to know his Hebrew heritage as well, a heritage that obviously still motivates him. He tells us that one day while venturing around the land, he witnesses an Egyptian beating a Hebrew slave. In his rage, he kills the Egyptian on the spot. This deed gets discovered pretty quickly, and before you know it Moses is a wanted man. He runs from Egypt, and settles in a land called Midian.

The Shepherd of Midian

The Bible is filled with powerful and wonderful "coincidences," and we get another one here in Moses's choice to settle in Midian. Of all the places Moses could have landed, he chooses this one. Midian is "Covenantland." Midian just happens to be the area where all of Abraham's adventures occurred. This is where Lot chose the fertile ground for his flocks. This is where Abraham entertained his shadowy guest, Melchizedek. This is the land where Abraham experienced God walking through the pieces of the covenant in his promise to provide for Abraham and for us. Moses has suddenly arrived in what we in the South would refer to as Abraham's "stompin' ground." This is the land of the people of God.

Now, there is a priest in Midian named Jethro, and Jethro has a nice set-up. He has flocks, he has his own well, and he has seven daughters! This whole arrangement is apparently very appealing to Moses, so he marries one of Jethro's daughters, settles down there and becomes a shepherd. I'm sure that this process itself would have been an interesting one to observe. I imagine that Moses had not had a lot of "shepherd training" growing up in the pharaoh's palace, but despite what I imagine was a steep learning curve, Moses becomes a shepherd in Midian.

Moses is now residing in the land of the covenant. That's the good news. But we have a problem. At this point in history, our One Story isn't progressing very well, and it really hasn't been for over 400 years. We've heard God's promises to Abraham, and we have seen the beginnings of their fulfillment. By the days of Isaac and Jacob, God had a people and now even a nation. But currently, they are a nation in slavery. They are not in the land that God promised to Abraham, Isaac, and Jacob, and they are not receiving the promises that God has made. So God is going to intervene to get his people back! In our next two chapters we will get to watch as he begins their rescue.

The Meeting

In Exodus 2:23, we are told that, "In the course of many days, the king of Egypt died, and the sons of Israel sighed because of their bondage, and they cried out. And their cry for help rose up to God. And God heard their groaning and (check out the verb here) God *remembered* his covenant with Abraham, Isaac, and Jacob."

Remember what "remember" means? We're talking covenant jargon here. It's like if you walked up to a group of guys and one of them is saying, "We just need our offensive line to protect the quarterback better in the pocket." You don't have to say, "Are you boys talking about football?" You already know what they're talking

THE ONE STORY

about because of the lingo, right?

So here, God "remembers" his covenant again! He is coming in faithfulness. He sees the sons of Israel, takes notice of them, and feels his connection to his promises. I love the simple phrase of Exodus 2:25. It simply says, "God saw the people of Israel – *and God knew.*"

God remembers his people. And in response to his remembering, God is going to come and bring them home.

The rescue operation begins on a lonely mountain top.

We are told that "Moses was pasturing the flock of Jethro, his father-in-law, the priest of Midian. And he led the flock to the west side of the wilderness and came to Horeb, the mountain of God." (Ex. 3:1)

Another Bible coincidence alert: Horeb will play heavily in our One Story. You may know this mountain better by its more common name, Sinai. Yes, long before the Ten Commandments, Moses is meeting God at Sinai! Moses and his sheep have wandered into "ground zero" of God's work with his people.

As Moses grazes his flock, we are told that "the angel of the LORD appeared to him in a blazing fire from the midst of a bush; and [Moses] looked, and behold, the bush was burning with fire, yet the bush was not consumed." (Ex. 3:2)

Blazing fire! Remember what appeared to Abraham in the covenant ceremony? This is the same blazing fire that walked the covenant pieces with Abraham. This is the very presence of God himself, picking back up with his covenant plan!

Seeing this, Moses says, "I must turn aside now and see this marvelous sight, why the bush is not burned up." And God calls to him from the midst of the bush and says, "Moses, Moses."

Moses says, "Here I am."

And God says, "Do not come near here. Remove your sandals from your feet, for the place on which you are standing is holy ground. And he said, "I am the God of your father, the God of Abraham, the God of Isaac, and the God of Jacob." And Moses hid his face, for he was afraid to look at God.

Then the Lord said, "I have surely seen the affliction of my people who are in Egypt and have heard their cry because of their taskmasters. I know their sufferings, and I have come down to deliver them out of the hand of the Egyptians and to bring them up out of that land to a good and broad land, a land flowing with milk and honey." (Ex. 3:5-8)

What has just happened here at Horeb is one of the most graphic and powerful events in God's story. We are about to watch God set in motion a series of events that will define the history of Israel for centuries, as well as establish a bold, new chapter in the One Story. But before we rush ahead to witness God's incursion into the enemy territory of Egypt, I want us to slow down and take a careful look at his meeting between Moses and God at Horeb. Aside from Moses probably setting the new world record for "taking one's sandals off," a lot is about to happen on this mountain. As we stand at Moses's side, we are about to be personally reintroduced to the holy God of the universe, the God of the One Story.

Moses Meets the Covenant God

Holiness

The first thing to notice at Horeb is God's *holiness*. To my understanding, God's engagement with Moses here is the first time that God and his presence is referred to as "holy" – right here, right now. The very ground upon which Moses stands is weighty with the holiness of God. We are receiving an introduction here to God in his otherness, his purity, his set-apartness. We have seen God as creator and loving father, seeking his children. We have seen him as the wrathful vindicator of the weak and the pursuer of redemption. We have seen him make and keep his blessed promises.

And he is also holy.

God introduces us here to the awe and reverence that is due the one who loves us tenderly but is also exalted in splendor – worthy of invoking trembling fear and wonder. He is holy, dwelling in majesty and absolute purity. He is beyond all of his creation. His glory spreads above it like the cosmos surrounds us when we gaze up at the stars on a silent, clear night. His presence should evoke awe and submission in all the earth. He is the one who "dwells in inapproachable light!" (1 Tim. 6:16) He is holy.

In fact, in Isaiah 6, a passage in which Isaiah the prophet encounters the glory of God filling the temple, he will hear the seraphim (the burning ones) refer to God as "Holy, holy, holy!" repeating the praise three times.

Within Hebrew literature, repetition was used like exclamation points, pouring intensity into a statement. When God calls Abraham to stop his sacrifice of Isaac, he calls out, "Abraham, Abraham." When God speaks to Moses from the burning bush, he says, "Moses, Moses." When Jesus wants to draw keen attention to his words, he often says, "Verily, verily."

Well, if repeating something twice expressed intensity for the Hebrews, imagine the volume communicated by a repetition of *three times*! And only one attribute of God is ever raised to that level of power: his holiness. The seraphim are proclaiming to the universe, "This is He! He is Lord of all! He sits upon the throne of the universe. He rolls and flames in roaring majesty.

And beyond all else, he is holy!"

Moses is given the privilege (and the fright) of encountering this God of holiness. This is a moment of infinite solemnity and wonder on this mountain. And in response to the brilliance and gravity of this holiness, Moses is told something that we rarely hear God say to his people.

"Do not come near!"

Many times in scripture we see individuals encounter God or his angels and respond in terror, but then they are softly comforted to "fear not" or to "draw near." We so often live under God's assurances of his safety and approachability. But not here. Here we (and Moses) are warned of the glory and might of the covenant God. As the book of Hebrews reminds us, though we have a God of grace and love, he is also a God of "consuming fire." (Heb. 12:29)

As Moses withdraws in reverence from this holy presence, God also instructs Moses to remove his sandals. In Hebrew culture, feet were a symbol of creatureliness. We are told that the seraphim in Isaiah 6 have six wings: with two they fly, with two they cover their faces from the glory of God, and with two they cover their *feet*. (Isa. 6:2) And remember what Christ does in the upper room to symbolize his servanthood, as well as to demonstrate our desperate need of cleansing? He washes the disciples' *feet*. (John 13:4-10)

So this is Moses, the creature, meeting God. Before this Holy One, the smallness of Moses's humanity is exposed. And as a result, Moses hides his face in fear (just like the seraphim).

Continuity and family history

As Moses removes his shoes and falls on his face, the holy God speaks to him. He speaks to him with covenant weight, and he speaks to him of the One Story. He says, "I am the God of your father, the God of Abraham, the God of Isaac, the God of Jacob."

I'm calling this book *The One Story* because I believe that God's redemptive plan isn't just a collection of arbitrary events scattered through the Bible. It is a sequential story, growing ever richer as God comes to each of his patriarchs, building his salvation throughout history. God has come to this mountain to engage Moses in the rescue of Israel from Egypt, but God has also come to engage Moses in the One Story. And he begins by introducing Moses to his place in it. He begins with personal introductions.

Notice that God doesn't say, "Moses, you don't know me, but I'm God, and I want to save my people." He begins by recounting his history with his people, reminding Moses of his One Story thus far. It's as if God is saying, "My dear Moses, let's begin by recalling that I have a huge history with you. I'm your daddy's God. I'm the God of Abraham and Isaac and Jacob. You and I already have a story together; you just haven't met me personally until now. For centuries I have known you and your people because you are all my beloveds. This is all one story, and now you are going to be part of my story to save you all!"

I don't know about other parts of the country, but when you meet someone in the South, you usually have to go through a bit of a ritual in which you figure out who you know and who you are related to. We say things like, "I'm Ryan Williams. I knew your granddaddy, Joe Whit Johnson. My granddaddy was in his law firm in the fifties up in the Delta." (Around here, I think everyone's granddaddy was a lawyer "up in the Delta" at some point.) That's what we do when we meet somebody in the South and it's what God is doing here.

God is saying, "This is not a beginning-from-scratch relationship here, Moses. We have a history, and I'm coming to you on behalf of a lot of work that I've already done." It's like God is reminding Moses of the history of the One Story that we've looked at up to this point!

This history is as important to us as it was for Moses. So much of God's later relationship with his people Israel will be confusing unless we see it in the context of the Eden, Noah, and Abraham promises. This is why God begins by reminding us of his history. He is the God who has pursued his people over and over again. He is the God who sought his children at Eden and dropped his weapons with Noah. He is the God of grace who reckoned Abraham as righteous. He is the God who promises to his own death that he will save us.

Remembering this history will be the key to making sense of so many potentially confusing developments later in the Bible. For example, before too long we're going to encounter a lot of laws and Old Testament rules and regulations. God's apparent switcheroo into the "God of Law" will be confusing if we don't remember that he is still the "God of Abraham."

In other words, the story of God and Moses pre-supposes you've done your homework, remembering Abraham, Noah, and the protoevangelium of Eden. God begins his interactions with Moses by giving us a 'cheat sheet,' a reminder of where we've been. This is the One Story, and you cannot understand where God is going to go with it unless you understand where we have already been.

Possessive Pronouns

Remember what God wanted in the Eden Plan? All of this began with God wanting a *people*. He wants image-bearers who work at his side and walk with him in his garden. This is what God has always wanted and this is the third major theme in this interaction at the burning bush.

God says, "I've seen the affliction of *my people*." This is the first time God actually uses this term to refer to Israel. He is no longer dealing with individuals such as Adam, Noah or Abraham. He is saying, "I've heard the cry of *my people*." Remember the theme song of the covenant we talked about with Abraham? What does he say? "I will be your God, you will be my people, and I will dwell among you."

Now we see it actually starting to happen.

Don't you love that he uses a possessive pronoun when he talks about us! He says, "*my* people!" Think about it, when can we use possessive language in reference to another person; to speak as if they "belonged" to us? In any culture, we can only use possessive pronouns or prepositions when there is a deep mutual giving and safety in the relationship, when our connection is so intimate that we feel a literal possession of that person. We even speak words of possession in our safest places. We say, "I feel like I 'belong' with you." Or we call our dearest ones, "my wife," "my child," or "my mama."

What a treasure it is that God actually calls us his own. He says, "You are *my* people." He says, "I'm the God of Abraham. I am Abraham's God. I am the God of Isaac. I'm Isaac's God."

"I am the God of John Cox. I am John Cox's God."

And just as marvelously, he invites us to use the possessive pronoun with *him*. He is *my* God. He is *my* Savior.

This is the kind of language people use when they love one another. It is the language of family and of covenant. It is the language of the One Story.

As God's history with his people unfolds, it will be beautiful to watch his expression of his heart for his people become even more personal and dear. By Exodus 4, God is calling Israel "My son, my first-born." This is God's first implication of himself as our father, by the way.

By Exodus 19, he's calling his people by the Hebrew term *segula*, which is usually poorly translated in our English Bibles as "my own possession." But *segula* literally means "my special treasure!" This is the position of God's heart when we come to him. "You are my people, you are my son, and you are my special treasure."

This is also the attitude with which God is going to come to Pharaoh. He will in essence say, "Pharaoh, this is my son we are talking about here. This is my firstborn. This is my special treasure. Let them go!" He will be coming with a vengeance to take his people back.

God's presence

I'm sure that Moses was delighted when he heard God announce that he was coming to free his people. I don't think he liked the next part, however. God wants Moses to help.

God proclaims his intention to free his people, but then adds, "Therefore, come now, and I will send *you* to Pharaoh, so that you may bring my people, the sons of Israel, out of Egypt." (Ex. 3:10)

Moses responds with obvious anxiety, "Who am I that I should go to Pharaoh and bring the children of Israel out of Egypt?" (Ex. 3:11) I love God's response here. He could say things to Moses like "Well, actually you're perfect for the job: a Levite Hebrew who was raised in the palace of the pharaoh! Who could be better?!" But that's not what God says. His reply to Moses is essentially this: "It doesn't matter who you are. *I will be with you.*" (Ex. 3:12) God is saying, "There's only one thing you need to know here, Moses. This is not something I'm sending you to do *for* me. This is something I want you to do *with* me! I will be with you."

Remember what "with" means to God? His longing has always

been to be with his people, and his greatest reassurance to us all is that he will be at our side. Even in this gargantuan task (Moses will essentially be initiating the largest slave rebellion in history), God's comfort and his promise to Moses is simply this: "I will be with you."

His Name

Moses then brings up another concern, and it involves *God's name*. Moses says, "Behold, I am going to the sons of Israel, and I shall say to them that the God of your fathers has sent me to you, and if anybody says 'What is his name?' What shall I say to them?" (Ex. 3:13)

You can comb through God's whole story and find dozens of places where God gives good gifts to his people. Throughout the Bible, we will see him provide food for the hungry and healing for the sick. We will see him intervene in battle to protect his people. We will see him perform miracles and wonders. But here God is about to give a gift that is one of the most beautiful, tender, and personal of all. He is going to tell Moses his name.

Remember the significance of names to the Hebrews? Within their culture, if you named someone, you were establishing your authority over them.

Well then, what would it mean if you *gave* someone your name?

It would mean you were doing just the opposite. If you gave somebody your name, you were bending to their level; you were giving them access to your heart. If you gave them your name, you were saying that you wanted them to reach for you and be close to you. So for God to give Moses his name is for God to welcome Moses (and his people, us) into his deepest heart, into a relationship of warm vulnerability and belonging. He is saying, "I don't want you to just speak to me with formal titles. I want you to reach for me more personally than that. You can call me by name."

So as the holy God of Abraham, Isaac, and Jacob flames from within the burning bush, his glory scattering across the mountaintop, we hear him reach out his hand to Moses and give us all this extraordinary gift:

"Yahweh," he replies. (Ex. 3:14) "My name is Yahweh."

"Thus, you shall say to the sons of Israel. Yahweh has sent me to you...Yahweh, the God of your fathers, the God of Abraham, the God of Isaac, the God of Jacob, has sent me to you. This is my name forever. And my memorial name to all generations." (Ex. 3:14)

We get his name!

His meaning

As you can read in your Bibles, God's name, Yahweh, is literally translated, "I am who I am," (and is subsequently portrayed in our English Bibles as "LORD"). Just to receive his name is an incalculable gift, but there's more. God doesn't just want to give us his name, he wants his name to tell us something wonderful about him.

You can see throughout scripture that an individual's name helps tell the story of who that person is. Hebrew names always reflected the character of the bearer. This is another reason that God would change peoples' names. When a person's heart or mission was radically altered, their names were often changed as well. When Jesus changes Simon's name to Peter, or in the original Greek, *Petras,* "the Rock," he is saying something about who Peter will be.

Our modern Western names don't carry much significance to us. Being called "Bill" or "Katherine" doesn't usually mean anything significant about the individual or say anything about our identities. Celebrities, however, still understand the statement that a name can make. Thomas Cruise Mapother IV surely understood that his image would be improved if he changed his name to Tom Cruise. And Paul David Hewson certainly wanted to communicate something by keeping his childhood nickname, Bono Vox, now simply Bono.

Here God is speaking into a Hebrew world in which names are an encyclopedia of information about the individual. God's name is rich with meaning as well, and he wants us to receive that richness.

So what does God's name mean?

In the Hebrew, God's name, Yahweh, is a play on the verb "to be." Literally, it is the first person singular, "I am" (hence the translation, "I am who I am"). Part of its meaning refers to the fact that God *is*. He simply *is*. He is the foundation of all being. He is God eternal, the creator and sustainer of all existence. For him there is no past, present, or future. His existence floods the galaxy with silent, immovable splendor. "I AM!" It speaks of a holiness and existence beyond measure. His being and his nature are to be worshipped for all eternity.

However there is a more intimate meaning to his name as well, a meaning that I believe also captures his heart. It is a translation of his name that carries with it an energy and a force of personal engagement. I believe the name Yahweh is also translated as a "*being* present," a "*being* with" his people. It is an action verb. It's in motion!

In other words, at its heart, Yahweh's name might be most fully translated something like this: "I AM, that I am with you, and am present with you, to abide with you forever. I am always effectively at your side as you call on me to be your God. I AM!"

This way of hearing his name speaks of the heart God has shown us throughout his One Story. His name reminds us of who he has always been. It captures all that he is and longs for with us:

Is he the one who is there to search for his children at Eden, to clothe them and to promise them salvation? "I AM."

Is Yahweh the one who hangs his battle bow in the sky to protect his people from his just wrath? "I AM."

Is he the one who is willing to pledge to his own death that he will fulfill his promise to Abram? "I AM."

And is he the one who will ultimately sacrifice his own son on an altar that we might live and be his forever? "I AM."

And is he the one who reaches out his hand to you and me, inviting us to walk at his side? HE IS.

Love on a first name basis

We have received an extraordinary gift; God has given us his name, a name that speaks not only of his majesty, but also of his abiding presence and love for us. Just as we saw in his use of possessive pronouns, our Yahweh invites us into the most personal intimacy with him by telling us his name. Imagine what this means in the immediacy of our relationship with him. He wants us to call him by name!

I will sometimes be occupied on the other side of the room when my wife is FaceTiming with our grandchildren. Soon I will hear her say, "Well, hello, Shaw!" as our 3-year-old grandson appears. Then, from across the room, I hear a word from the phone that brightens my heart. I hear his little voice say, "Papa!"

He calls my name – and I come running!

What joy there is in hearing your name spoken by the voices of those you love. Unimaginably, this is how God feels when he hears us, his children, speak his name. That is why he gave it to us. He wants that kind of joy with us. This is his heart. He wants to walk with us in the cool of the day. He wants to come running! My seminary professors taught me the joy of referring to God by his name, Yahweh, and I invite you to enjoy that privilege as well in your own personal walk with him. I will use it henceforth in this book.

The "God of the Old Testament" can sometimes be portrayed as a sort of scary deity, handing down laws and swallowing up people in the earth. Instead, what we find when we really listen to him is the God of Abraham, pledging his own life to save his people, and now the God of Moses, condescending to give his personal name to his people, a name that in its very utterance reminds us that he is ours and we are his. Our goal in this book is to hear his heart for us. This is who he is. He will be our God, we will be his people, and he will dwell among us. I AM.

Truly, only David the poet could begin to capture an adequate response:

> O, *Yahweh*, our Lord, how majestic is thy *name* in all the earth! – Ps. 8:9

The assault begins

The One Story has reached a momentous milestone here on Mount Horeb. We have been trembling in fear at Moses's side as we are confronted with the God of all holiness and power. Though he stoops to give us his name, this consuming God *should* evoke this kind of humility and dread from those who behold him.

And now this God says that he is going to bring all of that scalding glory down upon those who have possessed his people. Egypt is the one who should fear!

He says to Moses, "I have surely seen the affliction of my people who are in Egypt and have given heed to their cry because of their taskmasters, for I am aware of their suffering, so I have come down to deliver them from the power of the Egyptians." (Ex. 3:6-9)

As his glory flames upon the mountain, God says that he has seen that his One Story of salvation has been obstructed by Egypt. He remembers his covenant promises. He has heard his peoples' pain. He has not forgotten them. And the holy God of Horeb is going to come after them.

We will rejoin God and Moses on the mountain in the next chapter as we watch God go to war. It will be Yahweh versus the most powerful nation on earth!

Chapter Seven

Moses II: Who is this Yahweh?

When we last saw our heroes, they were talking on a mountain. God had heard the cries of his people in Egypt and had "remembered" his promises. Now he appears as a dazzling fire before his new man, Moses. And this consuming fire has a name. His name is Yahweh! (This is a tender, loving, consuming fire, if you can wrap your mind around that.)

But Yahweh hasn't come to this mountain just to bond with Moses. This is the war room. God wants his people back, and he is going to send Moses out as his tact team.

Let's pick up our story here. After much persuasion and reassurance, Moses obeys God and heads back to Egypt. Given the fact that Moses was essentially part of the Egyptian royal family, he apparently has easy access to the pharaoh, and he demands on behalf of God that Pharaoh release God's people.

Incidentally, Moses never says "Let my people go," like he does in the movies. Instead, he always says something more like, "God says, 'Let my people go, *that they may worship me.*'" (Ex. 10:3) In other words, this is not just a rescue operation. This is God bringing his people to himself that they may be with him and delight in who he is (that's what worship is). There's always a direction to God's salvation of us. He doesn't just save us. He saves us *unto* something wonderful.

Now, Pharaoh doesn't respond very favorably to this demand from Moses and God. He is not interested in Moses's God, nor is he willing to release his slaves. This is bad news for the people of Israel, but it is going to be even worse news for Pharaoh, because in the process of interacting with Moses, Pharaoh asks a really dumb question. It's a question that is going to set in motion a series of very unpleasant events that are going to last for the next five chapters of the book of Exodus.

The unfortunate question is this: Moses demands that Pharaoh release Yahweh's people, and Pharaoh responds by asking, *"Who is this Yahweh that I should obey his voice and let Israel go?"* (Ex. 5:2)

Here's a little cosmic safety tip: don't ever ask this kind of question! "Who is this Yahweh?" Really? It's like stepping off of a building and asking, "Who is this guy called 'gravity' and why should I do what 'he' says?"

One just shouldn't ask questions like that.

Unfortunately for the ruler of Egypt, God hears this question and responds. He responds in essence by saying, "Alright. You want to know who I am? I will show you who Yahweh is. Get ready."

Thus begin the plagues of Egypt.

I want you to get this. The plagues aren't just for show or to develop Hollywood drama in this story. Neither are they repeated, failed attempts at a rescue. All ten have a very specific purpose. They are designed to speak God's heart and true nature to the pharaoh, to God's chosen people, and to us. They will answer Pharaoh's question for everyone. Let's unpack them and explore what God is really up to in unleashing the infamous "plagues of Egypt."

That you may know

There are ten plagues in total. The bloodied Nile, frogs, gnats, insects, the death of all livestock, boils, hail, locusts, darkness, and Passover. As these plagues are delivered, we will see a pattern take place (ten times) in the next five chapters:

Moses will demand on behalf of God that Pharaoh "let the people go, that they may worship him."

Pharaoh will refuse.

Then there will be a plague.

Pharaoh will then temporarily relent because the plague is quite unpleasant.

Then Pharaoh's heart will be hardened, he will double-down on keeping his slaves, thereby refusing God again.

Wash, rinse, repeat! Times ten.

But why ten plagues? Why this pattern over and over? Couldn't God have accomplished just one "colosso-plague" and avoided this whole drawn out process? Sure he could have, but you gotta understand, God has a not-so-secret agenda here. He legitimately wants to answer the pharaoh's question, *'who is this Yahweh?'* But he doesn't just want to answer it for the pharaoh. He wants to answer it for his people, too! In other words, there's a sense in which you could say that the goal of the plagues is evangelistic! What Yahweh really wants is to reintroduce himself to Israel.

Think about it. At this point in our story, there is no Hebrew currently living in Egypt who has ever interacted with Yahweh. In fact, God's people have been living in a grossly polytheistic culture for 430 years. That's about how long we have lived since Shakespeare wrote Macbeth! Though I'm sure the people have passed down their identity as the offspring of Abraham, God needs to reintroduce himself. That's why before each plague he says things like, "That you may know that I am Yahweh." Or, "Then you shall know that Yahweh is your God." The God of Abraham was ancient history, and the people needed a refresher course. God is going to use the plagues as a gigantic technicolor fireworks show to begin demonstrating his identity as their one true God. Yes, he is coming to save them, but he is also coming to teach them who he is.

Here's God's strategy with the plagues: if you look at them, each one is in some way a direct attack by Yahweh on Egyptian national power or their gods. And with each, he demonstrates his dominance over them. For instance, the Nile River is turned to blood. The Nile, remember, was the primary source of Egypt's self-sufficiency. The Nile was the power of this nation, giving Egypt her fertility and stability. By attacking the Nile, Yahweh essentially knocks out the economic aorta of the nation of Egypt. A contemporary parallel would be someone destroying the entire electrical and electronic substrate of 21st century America – all of a sudden there's no power. You can't pump gas; you can't make phone calls; you can't withdraw money from the bank. Our culture would be crushed. Such was the power of the Nile for Egypt. And Yahweh destroys it.

Additionally, God directly assaults the Egyptian gods: frogs (frog goddess, Heqet); darkness (Ra, the god of the sun); livestock (Remember the golden calf in the wilderness? Where do you think the Israelite people learned about that?).

So despite the fact that the plagues are certainly attention grabbers (what in the world did it look like for an entire country to be overrun with frogs?!), it's important that we not get lost in the razzle-dazzle. The plagues had a purpose. With each of them, God is sort of saying to the Egyptian gods, "You versus me, right here right now," and he's going to destroy their dominion for all the nations to see. Yahweh is going to show that he is the one true God!

And it worked!

The people are shown their God

We are told that not only do the people of Israel see and believe God because of the plagues, but many Egyptians do as well. And the demonstration has a lasting impact. Moses's father-in-law, Jethro, will later say that he saw God's deliverance of the people out of Egypt. He says, "Now we know that Yahweh is greater than all the gods." (Ex. 18:11) Jethro learned the lesson the plagues were teaching.

My favorite recipient of God's message in the plagues is Rahab, the harlot from Jericho. She will show up during the book of Joshua and aid the children of Israel as they invade the promised land. Why does she help them? She says that she and her people saw what Yahweh did in Egypt, "and when we saw it, our hearts melted, and no courage remained in us, because Yahweh your God is the only God in Heaven above and earth beneath." (Josh. 2:11)

So the plague plan works! God produces an evangelistic message to the world through these miraculous works, announcing that he alone is Israel's God – and the world hears it, even as far as Jericho.

Pharaoh's hard heart

Remember how we have said that God mocks posers who would try and take his people from him? An interesting side note about God's assault against the Egyptian gods relates to how he deals with the pharaoh personally. Notice what happens with Pharaoh after each of the plagues. Pharaoh initially acquiesces, but then his heart is "hardened." It's another repeated pattern.

Of course, part of that refers to Pharaoh hardening himself against God, but there's also a nasty little pun imbedded here regarding God's ultimate judgment on Pharaoh.

Within Egyptian religious beliefs, when a person of royal lineage died, their body was mummified, and their organs were removed. The Egyptians believed that in the afterlife, a dead king then went on to be judged by the jackal-headed god, Anubis, while Osiris, the god of the underworld, looked on. Anubis judged the king by weighing his heart on a scale against an item known as the "feather of Mott." (I'm not making this up!) And if the pharaoh's heart was *lighter* than the feather of Mott, he was made a god himself and went on to rule in the afterlife.

This was a difficult judgment to successfully pass, of course, because as you can imagine, the feather of Mott was very light. And if the pharaoh's heart was heavier than the feather of Mott, not only did he not become a god, but a monster that was part lion, part crocodile, and part hippopotamus devoured his heart, and he was condemned to a perpetual coma. (Still not making this up!) Now, instead of becoming a god, he basically went to the underworld of Egypt. In other words, "Egypt Hell!"

The inside joke is this: In Hebrew, when the passage says Pharaoh's heart was "hardened," it is literally saying that Pharaoh's heart was made "heavier." So, with a nasty little wink to the Egyptians' own religion, each time Pharaoh rejects God, his heart is made a little "heavier." Thus condemning him more and more, even within the rules his own religion.

And who said ancient theology wasn't fun?!

The Redemption of Israel

While the plagues create a spectacle that broadcasts the veracity and power of Yahweh, they are really just an overture for God's ultimate salvation of his people. God is about to bring the Passover, a landmark event in his dealings with his people. This final aggressive engagement to free them will define his relationship with his people for the rest of time. God will refer back to this event for the rest of Israel's history, saying things like, "I am Yahweh your God who brought you out of the land of Egypt, who delivered you from the house of bondage." (Ex 20:2) God is about to graphically fulfill his promises to Abraham. He is going to take his people back with bloodshed, sacrifice, and salvation.

The mark of blood

In Exodus 11, Yahweh comes and unfolds the plan. So far, Pharaoh has shaken his fist at God and the plagues. Despite wave after wave of assault, the king of Egypt has not relented. So now God is going to come with a final devastating attack against Pharaoh and the land of Egypt. God says that on the night of the Passover, he will move across Egypt at midnight; and on that night, all the firstborn will die; all will be under condemnation; all are owed. (Remember the law of primogenitor?) The firstborn of ordinary people will die; the firstborn of royalty will die; the firstborn of livestock and cattle will die – all will be under the penalty of death.

But God has not forgotten his people. Though death will reign universally on that night, protection will be offered to those who belong to Yahweh.

God calls the congregation of Israel to take an unblemished lamb, one for each household, and kill it at twilight. They are then to take the lamb's blood and put it on the door posts and lintels of their homes. Gathered in safety beneath the blood, they are to eat the flesh of that lamb with unleavened bread and bitter herbs. God goes on to tell them that they are to have this meal, "with your loins girded, your sandals on your feet, and your staff in your hand ... for this is Yahweh's Passover. For I will go through the land of Egypt on that night and strike down all the firstborn of Egypt, man and beast. Against all the gods of Egypt I will exercise judgment. I am Yahweh." (Ex. 12:11-12)

(Notice he is still answering the question of "who is truly God?")

He continues, "The blood shall be a sign for you on the houses where you live, and when I see the blood, I will pass over you, and no plague will befall you to destroy you when I strike the land of Egypt. Now this day will be a memorial to you, and you will celebrate it as a feast to Yahweh. Throughout all your generations you will celebrate it. It is a permanent ordinance." (Ex. 12:13-14)

That night at midnight, Yahweh indeed strikes down all of the firstborn in Egypt "from the firstborn of Pharaoh who sat on the throne, to the firstborn of the captive in the dungeon, to the firstborn of the cattle. And the entire country cried out in mourning because there was no home in Egypt where there was not someone dead." (Ex. 12:29-30)

Pharaoh calls for Moses and Aaron that night, and not only releases God's people from bondage, but practically runs them out of town. And we are told that "it came about that at the end of 430 years to the very day, that all the hosts of Yahweh went out from Egypt." (Ex. 12:41)

Thus, God accomplishes his rescue. God accomplishes his "exodus." He hears the cries of his enslaved people, and he remembers his promises to Abraham. He comes to find his special treasure, his *segula* – bringing death and judgment, but not to them.

For them, there is only preservation and salvation and rescue.

The greatest rescue of all

Gloriously, Passover is not just the means by which God will accomplish Israel's deliverance from Egypt. Passover will also define the nature of God's salvation for his people always, including us! The One Story is not just about God rescuing his people from a tyrannical nation, it is about his rescuing us from death and alienation. At its deepest level, the Passover deliverance is a metaphor for Israel's ultimate deliverance from separation from God, their salvation. After all, he doesn't say, "I want to free the slaves." He says, "I will take you to be my people, and I will be your God." (Ex. 6:7) This isn't just a rescue from Egypt, this is a picture of spiritual redemption, of God pulling his people to his heart. Passover is what God's salvation looks like.

So far in our One Story, God has appeared to his people repeatedly with promises and deliverance. But he has only talked about their need for *spiritual redemption* in the most indirect of ways: an animal had to be slain to provide clothes for Adam and Eve; Noah's sacrifice offered a pleasing aroma to God, leading him to swear protection for the earth; the offering of Isaac is demanded of Abraham, but a ram is provided to spare the life of the promised child.

All of these have spoken to the necessity of some sort of sacrifice in order to heal God's relationship with his people. But here with Passover, we get a very vivid picture, not only of God's love for his people, but also of what eternal salvation will look like. It will involve danger and bloodshed, but also protection, substitution, and sacrifice. God loves his people. His goal has always been to walk with us in his garden. But we broke our relationship with him. And for him to have us back (which is his greatest desire), there has to be a restitution. In order for him to have us again, there must be a sacrifice – a Passover lamb.

The Passover event echos how God *still* saves us. If someone were to ask you for an image or a word picture that illustrated our salvation as modern-day Christians, you might conjure a story such as this: a death sentence is owed. All are under condemnation. Someone's blood will be shed. But God arrives and creates a story in which a blameless lamb is sacrificed instead of his beloved people. Their safety is marked by blood. And within the bloodstained house, God's people gather together as his protected children. We are slaves to death, just as the Israelites were slaves to Egypt. And by the blood of a lamb, we are freed. With Passover, God vividly begins to paint the picture of atonement: the sacrifice of one on behalf of another, the death of a lamb to protect his people.

The True Lamb

Like all of the animal sacrifices in the Old Testament, we know that the Passover lamb itself had no power to defer God's judgment. The Passover lamb just pointed to another Lamb who dies that we all might be "passed over" from death.

This story ties in dramatically with the New Testament when we get to join Jesus, Peter, James, and John as they meet with some visitors on the Mount of Transfiguration. In Luke chapter 9, we are told that Jesus meets with Elijah and *Moses*! Then we are enigmatically told that they are discussing something they call Jesus's *departure,* which he was "about to accomplish in Jerusalem" (v. 31).

I always wondered what that meant, yet assumed it simply referred to his coming death. Unable to stop my curiosity, I looked up the word in the original language. The literal Greek word that is usually translated "departure" here, is the Greek word *exodon,* literally, "exodus!"

Elijah, Moses and Jesus sit engulfed in Christ's glory on the mountain and discuss *his* coming Exodus; *his* leading of his people out of slavery; *his* deliverance of his children from bondage by blood and by miracle.

They are talking with the *Passover Lamb* himself!

Not long after the Mount of Transfiguration, and over a thousand years after the first Passover, we see Jesus and his disciples gather for their own Passover in the upper room. And like all Passover celebrations,

Jesus speaks over the elements. But on this night, Jesus doesn't take the unleavened bread and speak of the haste of leaving captivity. He takes the bread and says, "This is my body." He then takes the wine, and says, "This is my blood of the new covenant, shed for the remission of sins." (Matt. 26:26, 28) Jesus doesn't mention the bitter herbs of captivity because he was the only one who would taste bitterness that night. He doesn't speak of a Passover lamb because the True Lamb has come. He is sitting in the room with his disciples and is about to depart for the hill upon which he will become the true sacrifice. He is about to lead his people in the Greater Exodus!

The lamb at Moses's exodus does not prevent the death of the firstborn; it just delays it until the death of *God's* lamb. Exodus chapter 12 graphically describes the depth of mourning and sorrow that swept across Egypt on the night of the first Passover. Fathers' hearts were crushed at the loss of their firstborn sons. Surely, therefore, we cannot fathom the depth of the sorrow that was wept in heaven as God watched the death of *his* beloved son. On that Passover day that we call Good Friday, Egypt did not weep, heaven did, God's tears instead of ours.

But Yahweh and his true lamb of Passover suffered together in order to gather unto themselves their people, their own possession, their special treasure, the Sons of Abraham – as many as the stars of the sky.

And it is now *we,* all who take refuge under the shed blood of the Lamb, who are the treasured people of God. We are God's "possession." Paul even uses this term when speaks about us New Testament Christians in the book of Ephesians. He says that we are sealed with Christ through the Holy Spirit "with a view to the redemption of God's *own possession,* (us!) to the praise of His glory." (Eph. 1:14)

We are now his *segula,* freed, redeemed, and treasured.

So, Pharaoh, *this* is who Yahweh is!

He is the one who appears to a man shepherding sheep in Midian. He comes in a fiery blaze like the one who walked the promised pieces of the covenant. And he is the God who viciously assaults the evil that imprisons his people.

And through his own death, he sets his children free.

Chapter Eight

Moses III: Love and Law

A preacher once asked his Sunday school class, "What do you do with the commandments in the Bible?" A little old lady raised her hand and answered, "I underline them in blue."

All of history is about God's preparation of the world for his Redeemer. It is all One Story, a single odyssey of hope. He comes after Adam and Eve, calling "Where are you?" He surrounds the world in a rainbow-colored blanket of protection in his interactions with Noah. He swears to his death with Abraham that he will bring forth an offspring and a people who will be his. And now he has redeemed his people from slavery. The story continues, richer, fuller and more beautiful.

The people of God are now free. As we rejoin them, over two million people are crossing the desert outside of Egypt. Super Bowl LIV hosted over 62,000 fans. This wilderness hosts almost thirty-four Super Bowl stadiums worth of freed slaves.

But, the Israelites are in the wilderness.

The idea of "wilderness" is a theme throughout scripture. For some reason, God tends to meet his people and provide for them in these empty places; probably because the wilderness strips us all of our delusions that we are fine apart from God. Wilderness is difficult. Wilderness clues us into reality. Wilderness forces us to see that we are small creatures who need our Father.

It is no accident, therefore, that wilderness is where God will engage his next chapter with his people.

Another Deliverance

The children of Israel left Egypt 430 years to the day after their ancestors arrived. They carry in their caravans tons of Egyptian treasure, the spoils of Yahweh's war. They also bear the bones of Joseph, the son of Jacob, who had established his family's foothold in Egypt in the "good ole days." Joseph believed God's promise to his great-grandfather, Abraham, that his people would leave Egypt one day, and he requested that his bones be taken along when that day finally came. His descendants honored his wishes.

But now, almost immediately after Israel has begun leaving their world of pain and slavery, God has told them to delay their progress. They have obeyed. All of Israel now waits in the desert outside of Egypt, on the shores of the immense Red Sea.

Meanwhile, back in Egypt, Pharaoh has yet again reconsidered his offer to give God's people their freedom. His nation has lost one million slaves, crushing not only his pride but also the infrastructure of daily life in Egypt. Imagine waking up and facing life without the entire workforce of a country. I imagine he is also rageful with grief at the loss of his son, as well as humiliated by Yahweh's domination of his nation. Pharaoh has been dispossessed of his heir and dethroned from his position of being an Egyptian demigod. He is now a grief-stricken father and an impotent leader, and determines to reacquire his slaves or kill them all in the process. Consequently, he unleashes his army to go and bring the Israelites back.

Now, as the people of Israel stand before the vast, uncrossable expanse of the Red Sea, the army of the ancient superpower Egypt begins to roar across the desert toward them. We are told that Pharaoh comes at them with 600 of his best chariots and an innumerable number of cavalry and soldiers. Military scholars tell us that the chariot was the ultimate weapon of war in the ancient Near East. Egyptian chariots were manned by a driver and an archer, one to pilot the chariot and the other to act as artillery. This is like 600 modern-day F-22 Raptor fighter jets, screaming across the desert, laser guidance locked on you and your family. And the people of God are sitting ducks.

The people's response is not encouraging. They don't turn to Moses or Yahweh for help. Instead, they bark at them in sarcastic rage, "Is it because there were no graves in Egypt that you took us out here to die in the wilderness? Didn't we say to you in Egypt, 'Leave us alone, that we may serve the Egyptians'?" (Ex. 14:11)

In the psychology business, this statement is what we call a "distorted reframe," a reinterpretation of reality to suit our own agenda. Their claim is preposterous! We just read this story, remember? This is not what they said at all! But now, they act like they *wanted* to be slaves; that they miss the lash and the whip. As if Moses and Yahweh were thoughtless and cruel, dragging them away from their awesome life of making bricks without straw!

Despite the people's immaturity and lack of faith, Moses stands before them and says, "Do not fear. Stand by and see the salvation that Yahweh will accomplish. The Egyptians you have seen today you will never see again. Yahweh will fight for you while you keep silent." (Ex. 14:13-14) (I have to wonder if Moses added the "while you keep silent" part as a personal editorial comment.)

God tells Moses to lift his staff toward the sea and then sends a wind that blows throughout the night. As a result, the Red Sea is pulled apart for God's people, allowing them to walk across its floor, safe, dry and protected.

As the children of Israel cross the dry seabed however, the Egyptian army follows, hot on their heels. But seeing the parted sea, even the Egyptians recognize that they are out of their league. They correctly observe that, "Yahweh fights for *them* against *us*!" (Ex 14:25) In that moment, God has Moses withdraw the hand that parts the sea, allowing the waters to rush back in upon the Egyptians, destroying their entire army. "Thus," Moses writes, "Yahweh saved Israel that day from the hand of the Egyptians, and Israel saw the Egyptians dead on the seashore." (Ex. 14:30)

The sea is often an image of judgment in scripture (surely the Egyptians experienced this as true). Now, just as God sheltered his people from death in his Passover, he completes his salvation of them by allowing them to pass through the "waters of judgment" completely unscathed. They are preserved again, safe in Yahweh's arms. In this miraculous act, God completes his redemption of his people from Egypt.

There's a great old story I remember from seminary (probably apocryphal). An old-style conservative preacher was talking with a liberal skeptic about the story of the Red Sea. The old preacher says, "Praise the Lord! God parted the Red Sea and the children of Israel walked across on dry land. Then God drowned the whole of the enemy army. Praise the Lord!"

The liberal skeptic, having read the "informed literary criticism" of the Old Testament literature, condescendingly responded, "Well, actually our current archeological research shows us that at the time of year this occurred, that particular area was actually known as the 'Reed Sea,' and it was later miswritten as the 'Red Sea.' During that season, the 'Reed Sea' was only about a foot and a half deep. So the Israelites could have easily crossed through that shallow spot unharmed. There is no need for a miracle to have saved them."

Undaunted, the old preacher retorted, "Well, then praise the Lord! Praise the Lord even more!"

"What do you mean?" the confused skeptic asked.

The old preacher exclaimed, "Your story means that somehow God managed to drown the whole Egyptian army in a foot and a half of water! What a miracle! Praise the Lord!"

Worship is a Gift

The people worship

In back-to-back chapters of Exodus, Yahweh has delivered his people. And again, he is killing two birds with one stone: he's saving his people, and he is demonstrating to them who he is. "That you might know that I am Yahweh."

And again, it works!

We are told in Exodus 14:31 that "When Israel saw the great power which Yahweh had used against the Egyptians, the people feared Yahweh, and they believed in him and in his servant Moses."

As a result, the people worship!

Exodus 15 is a song of Moses and a celebration of the wonderful God they are getting to know. Moses has watched for the last eight chapters as Yahweh has flooded the north of Africa and the Near East with power and wonder. Now, he and all of God's delivered children launch into a song of joy on the eastern shores of the Red Sea; celebrating Yahweh the warrior, Yahweh the bringer of sanctuary. They are all flooded with the wonder that is the God of Israel.

Moses's song is the first real worship that formally occurs in scripture. So far, we've heard people talk about God or talk to him. They've bowed or feared or made sacrifices, but here we begin to see them take joy in him and celebrate who God is. In Moses's song, we start to hear the delight and adoration that comes from God's people as they begin to realize what it means to be Yahweh's "special treasure."

Listen to these excerpts from Moses's song and hear the peoples' relationship with God developing. In this song we actually get to listen to Moses and the people worship. They sing,

> "I will sing to Yahweh, for he is highly exalted; the horse and its rider he has hurled into the sea."
> "Yahweh is my strength and song, and he has become my salvation; this is my God, and I will praise him; my father is God, and I will extol him."
> "Yahweh is a warrior; Yahweh is his name. Pharaoh's chariots and his army he has cast into the sea."
> "Thou wilt bring [thy people] and plant them in the mountain of thine inheritance, the place, O Yahweh, which thou hast made for thy dwelling, the sanctuary, O Lord, which thy hands have established.
> "Yahweh shall reign forever and ever."
>
> – Exodus 15:1-4, 17-18

This is who he is. Moses and God's delivered people see it. As Yahweh's people today, may we likewise worship him.

We get to worship

Worship is a vastly misunderstood concept in our culture. We so often hear God's call to worship him as some sort of demand to grovel and spend our time extolling his virtues (as if he needed narcissistic stroking). We have it backwards. Worship is at its most basic personal level a joyful act for *us!* It's a gift!

You don't know it, but you actually "worship" all the time. You take a bite of food at a restaurant, and you exclaim to your fellow diners, "Oh my gosh! You *have* to taste this! It's amazing!" You witness a solar eclipse (as I did a few years back), and you feel overwhelmed with the grandeur and glory of such a sight. At times like these, we don't need a sign on the lawn saying, "Be Awed! Be silenced. Weep with wonder!" We are just flooded with natural awe, and we delight in this glory! In fact, we seek it out. Why? Because we love the experience of being washed over with wonder.

At the most basic psychological/spiritual level, this is what worship is: the exultation and joy of beholding and experiencing wonder and awe. God simply invites us to pivot that sight around toward him, the fount of all wonder.

A major reason for my writing this book is to point us to who God really is, what his heart is like. I believe that to the degree that we see even a glimpse of him, none of us will need to be told to worship. Our hearts will be irresistibly drawn to him. Our voices will cry out in the joy of witnessing who he is, just as we do when we encounter natural wonder.

Remember that when the seraphim in Isaiah 6 encounter the holiness and glory of God they say *to one another*, "Holy, holy, holy is the Lord of hosts; the whole earth is full of his glory!" (Isa. 6:3) I love that as they are drawn to worship, they are speaking to *each other*. It is as if they cannot contain their wonder. They have to share it amongst themselves, just as we do when we encounter delight and joy. They *worship!*

I believe if we see him, like the seraphim (or Moses), we will be overwhelmed, delighted, and unable to contain our expressions of wonder. We will worship. And we will worship *together*! Let us worship continually by constantly seeing who he really is. Let us be the recipients of that gift of awe. Let us "Glorify God and *enjoy* him forever!"

We are saved too

In the song of Moses, we get to hear the joy of a people who have been saved, and it is the same joy that we can share. Don't forget that our One Story is the tale of the emergence of *our* salvation, too. We can see by the Passover and Red Sea events that Israel's story is no longer just about promises and covenants. God is now at work doing some legit salvation! In fact, if you think about it, their story is starting to sound more like *our* story of salvation; more like the relationship *we* have with God now.

I believe that if you had grabbed one of the children of Israel in the wilderness, pulled him out of the line as the caravans rolled along and asked him about his people and God, he would have said something that might sound familiar to your ears. He might say, "We were in slavery and bondage, but Yahweh came and he delivered us – not by our own death, but by the blood of a lamb. We're free now. We still wander in the wilderness, and we are still immature and learning, but he promises to teach us to be like him. He also promises us a land one day, and in that land, we will be like him and with him forever!"

Doesn't that sound familiar? Isn't that exactly what we still say?

It's the same story, the same God.

The One Story is coming alive!

The Law: A Whole New Level

The people of God have crossed the Red Sea and their enemies are now nothing but the chorus of a song. As they begin their new life, God is going to add the next big installment in the One Story: The Law.

For the last many chapters of the Bible, the developments we've seen in the One Story have essentially just been more fully formed versions of something that has already existed; bigger and better types of what was already there. We had promises of preservation and blessing to Adam, and then an even more serious vow of protection with Noah. With Abraham, we had the addition of a promised son, a family, and ultimately, a nation. With Moses, God started to "put meat on these bones" by actually intervening and rescuing that nation. Now they are his people, and he has shown them (and the watching world) who their God is. He is the Lord of all, and his name is Yahweh.

But with God's giving of his Law in the wilderness, we're going to get something new. The structure of God's relationship with his people will no longer just be about promise and salvation. It's time to begin re-forming the lives and hearts of his image-bearers. God has always wanted his people to bear his image. He is about to begin teaching them what that looks like. This is going to be the "One Story 5.0 upgrade download." Let's teach these saved people what the children of Yahweh can look like!

And contrary to what we often expect, the Law is going to be glorious!

The Goodness of the Law

Maybe it surprises you to hear me say that the coming of the Law could be a good thing. In our modern-day culture, the notion of law often gives people pause. We enjoy learning about the God of grace and love, but then the idea of the Law of God can conjure images of an angry bearded deity sitting atop a mountain throwing down scary commandments.

Our salvation is indeed God's gracious gift in Christ, so what do we do with the fact that we're about to get book after book, chapter after chapter, of laws, rules, and regulations? Not to mention the potential consequences–good or bad–of keeping or breaking them. How do we make sense of that? When we bring the Law into this story of God's love and grace, it's easy for us to feel like, "Bummer! Fun-time's over. Time to go to Sunday school!" Be honest, were you excited when you saw that this chapter was going to be about law? "Yeah, Doc! I need lots more burdensome rules in my life!"

And yet, somehow, centuries later, David will say that he "loves" God's Law (Ps. 119:97); that God's statutes are his "delight" (v. 24); that God's ways are more precious to him than "a thousand pieces of silver and gold" (v. 72); that they are "sweeter than honey and the honeycomb." (Ps. 19:10)

David apparently sees something about God's Way that we have missed. What is it we're not seeing? How do we make sense of all the laws of God and yet not lose the loving God who walks the covenant pieces with his "friend" Abraham?

To answer these questions and to begin our chapter on the Law, I feel it's appropriate for us to begin by gettin' honest. Let's talk first about why none of us like law in the first place.

I hate being told what to do

It's true. I do. My wife says I have unresolved authority issues – probably due to something in my adolescence. I usually respond by saying something like, "Get off my case with all your rules, man!" Thus, proving her point.

However, I'm in good company. It is innate in us humans to not want to do what we're told. If you have kids, you know that when they are born, they essentially hold a household board meeting and elect *themselves* chairmen. We want to be in charge. We don't like being told what to do. We don't like law.

In Romans, Paul tells us that we are all born at "enmity" with the Law. We don't like anyone bossing us around. Something in us naturally turns away from it. Our reaction to the Law is often like Hawkeye's in that episode of the TV show, *MASH,* in which he sneaks in and cuts out all of the "nots" from Father Mulcahey's Ten Commandments. Then, when the chaplain reads the Bible the next day, he says things like, "Thou *shalt*...commit adultery; thou *shalt*... steal."

Something in us does not want what is good and wise. In fact, we are naturally attracted to things that are bad for us. Plus, in order to obey God, we would have to (horror of horrors), disobey *ourselves!*

Something in us is broken

One thing that has intrigued me throughout the years of my practice is the fact that there seems to be something deeply basic in humans that "runs downhill." We find it easier to spend money than to make money. It's easier to gain weight than to lose it. It's more natural to be selfish and unkind than to be wise and loving. It's like gravity. We are always, curiously pulled downward.

Think about it, why is it easier to lie when you are caught than to tell the truth? Why is it natural to be unkind to your spouse and hard to be humble? Or for the passive types, why is it easier to live as the oppressed victim than to be powerful and assertive? Why do we naturally incline toward that which is bad for us and other people? The reason is that our hearts got crippled when we turned from God at Eden. Now, they "play off key." Our hearts are now naturally imbedded with selfishness, fear, shame, and entitlement as a default. It's one of the nastiest results of our fall in Eden, and unfortunately, it is a fundamental condition for humans. I know this – it's my job.

I remember listening to two psychoanalysts debate a therapy case at UCLA when I was in grad school. One of them spoke at length about the ways in which a destructive, pathological patient had been wounded and deprived in his childhood (and indeed he had). The analyst went on to discuss his (unsuccessful) strategy of helping the patient by using nurturing reparative therapy: "This patient needed more love."

The other analyst, a distinguished Englishman, then stood up and reminded us of one thing had not been considered in this patient's analysis: the fact that this individual *enjoyed* being harmful, that his desire to live in grandiose control of others was a fundamental driving force in his life. This natural inclination toward destruction was as much a part of his psychopathology as were his injuries. The analyst maintained that from infancy, humans are oriented toward selfishness and anger, and for this patient to heal, his therapy would have to take into account the fact that even when good *was* given to him, the patient would often thoughtlessly and instinctively destroy it. He would rather be in control than be loved. For this patient to heal, his innate destructiveness would have to be addressed.

The UCLA crowd nodded in silent agreement. We all knew he was right. He was describing every one of us at some level.

I don't think this analyst was a Christian (this was UCLA!). He was just a brilliant expert on the true nature of the human heart. And he had the wisdom to know that human hearts frequently enjoy darkness more than light.

If you want to understand sin, understand this. Sin is not the "bad things" we do. Sin is that odd background inclination inside of all of us that finds it so much easier and more automatic to believe that we are right and that others are wrong, that we deserve better, and others deserve less. It's the part of us that *likes* not forgiving. And unless confronted with an outside force (like God's Way) those hearts will go on taking and taking and taking until all of the darkness is satisfied (which is never). Come to my office sometime and tell me I'm wrong!

Fortunately, most of us do *wish* that we were more loving and truthful than we are, and I believe that wish is a gift from God. Remember he promised that he would "put enmity" between us and the Serpent? I wonder sometimes what it will be like to be fully redeemed in God's image, and for our natural reflexive inclination to finally be what is life-giving and loving.

I believe that when it happens, we will all be intensely relieved.

This is why we resist God's Law: our human hearts are "out of alignment" with that which is lifegiving and good. So how could it be that David experienced God's Law as such a gift? How could law be something we *treasure*? Let's talk about that for a bit. Look with me at the beautiful context of the Law and then seven ways in which it is one of God's greatest blessings to us.

Remember the Giver and his history

If you want to read the Ten Commandments, go read Exodus chapter 20. But if you want to *understand* the Ten Commandments, you have to begin by reading Exodus 19.

This is key. The giving of the Law does not begin with God announcing a list of rules. The giving of the Law begins in the same way that God began his relationship with Moses at the burning bush: with personal introductions. God doesn't just start thundering rules from Sinai. As he steps up to bring the Law, he leads with tenderness.

Listen to the affection with which Yahweh begins his introduction to the Law. He says, "You yourself have seen what I did to the Egyptians and how I bore you on eagle's wings, and how I brought you to myself. Now, then, if you will indeed obey my voice and keep my commandments, you shall be my special treasure (my *segula*) among all the peoples, for the earth is mine. And you shall be to me a kingdom of priests and a holy nation." (Ex. 19:4-6)

Let's not miss this: God begins giving the Law by saying, "Remember who we are, my dear ones. We are Savior and *segula*; we are Yahweh and his special treasure. You were captives and I brought you on eagle's wings out of the land of Egypt, out of slavery, misery, and imprisonment. I love you!"

"*Now* – you shall have no other gods before me. Only now, after you remember that everything I'm about to tell you comes from the one who loves you and saved you. This law is just another facet in the love affair that we already have!"

We have to hear God's heart in the giving of the Law. If we miss this relational context and this loving God, we will never understand his commandments. The giving of the Law at Sinai is just another step in the same relationship God has had with his people since he came bursting into the Garden seeking Adam. It's the same One Story. With Moses and the Law, the relationship doesn't change, it just deepens. Nothing is taken away; something new is revealed.

The Law-giving chapters in Exodus even line up like a sandwich. Chapter 19 is a renewal and reminder of God's passion for his people. Chapter 20 is the Ten Commandments. Chapters 21, 22, 23 are sort of sundry laws ("Eye for an eye, tooth for a tooth" kind of stuff.) And then in Exodus 24, we're going to see loving promises and relationship again.

It's a covenant sandwich! Two pieces of relational, loving "bread" at either end, with slices of law in the middle. God begins and ends all of this with his love for his people.

Besides, remember what the people are actually *beholding* as they receive the Law in the wilderness: They see before them the very presence of God in a pillar of cloud and fire. They are witnessing the same image that appeared to Abraham in Genesis 15, the smoking fire that walked the covenant pieces. As the Law is given, the people are beholding the God who pledged his life to redeem them.

MOSES III: LOVE AND LAW

The Gift of God's Law

Remember Satan's lie to Adam and Eve in the Garden of Eden? His point was that God's Way was not designed to bring them joy. He wanted them to believe that God's desire was to deprive them, and that if they were to follow God's Way, they would go without.

This is patently untrue. The fact is that God's Law is unfathomably good, and I'm gonna tell you why. Let's talk about *seven ways* in which God's Law is actually an enormous gift!

1. God is taking care of his wandering children.

Before we get too theological, there is a very practical role that the Law performs here in the wilderness. Think about where we are here: we have more than two million freshly freed slaves, exiled to the desert. They have no understanding of ruling themselves, solving their problems, or surviving as an independent group. Heck, they've been slaves in Egypt for four centuries! This is a disaster waiting to happen. Unless some order and structure is given to these people, they will self-destruct. Basic principle of psychology: out-of-control, chaotic people need limits and structure. It is the most loving thing for them. This is Psychology 101, gang! They need to be told what to do and what not to do (like kids). God's people need structure for their own survival as a nation, and with the Law, God is going to give it to them.

The giving of the Law actually begins in Exodus 18 with a discussion between Moses and his father-in-law, Jethro. Moses is spending all day every day mediating the disputes of the chaotic people. Jethro sees this and says to his overburdened son-in-law, "What is this you're doing? You sit alone and judge from morning till evening and deal with all of these people's problems? You'll surely wear out. This task is too heavy to you" (v. 14-18) (The world's first burnout counseling, by the way!)

So Jethro introduces a major plot point in verse 20. He says to Moses, "*Teach them* the statues and the laws. *Make known to them* the way in which they are to walk and work. And seek out able men to help you do [it]."

Then we get the Law!

In other words, the giving of the Law, isn't just God showing up to announce that the party's over. The Law is introduced through Jethro's idea, based on Moses's need, to solve the problem of the people's chaos! Boom! What a gift!

2. When all else fails, read the instructions.

There's been a joke in our family for decades: My wife, Norma, would present me with the kids' "biggest gift" on Christmas Eve, just in time for me to discover that it required hours of assembly. Inevitably, I would dump the box out as hundreds of pieces scattered on the ground; accompanied by a little plastic bag full of screws and an Allen wrench. Folded inside would also be an incredibly complex set of instructions written in a tiny font (the French and Chinese versions of which were on the back).

Since I hate reading instructions, I would often finish my cursing and just try to put the darn thing together using only my wits. Of course, my attempt to construct the Barbie Dream House without instructions inevitably failed, which led to many nights of blissful Christmas Eve togetherness with my spouse.

There is a way that things should be put together and a way that they should not. God is a designer and maker; he is a manufacturer. And there are ways in which his creations work, and there are ways in which they do not work. Once we understand this, we can see that his Law is not a list of rigid rules, it's part of the "instruction package" for human beings, the best owner's manual for our hearts. The Law is about how we operate properly.

Years back I was asked to preach at my favorite church in Atlanta. I eagerly accepted, always glad to have any excuse to be with those dear people. The only catch was that I had to preach within their current sermon series. Currently, they had been preaching through the Beatitudes, and my visit involved my preaching on "Blessed are those who hunger and thirst after righteousness." (Matt. 5: 6)

Frankly, this topic stumped me at first. I mean, I knew that I hungered and thirsted after God's *love*. And I often hungered and thirsted for his *mercy and grace*. But hungering and thirsting after righteousness? Had I ever really done that? Do I really long to be more righteous?

Then I researched the original Greek word that Jesus uses for "righteousness" in the passage (*dikaios*). To my surprise I found that it didn't just refer to virtuous behavior. It also meant that which is "correct or fitting." In a very real sense, it referred to living "accurately," the way things should properly be.

Then the lights came on! To hunger for God's kind of righteousness isn't about staying off the naughty list. It is about living the way humans were created to live. That's when I realized that "righteousness" is not so much about *morality* as it was *reality*. Righteousness is about living a life that works and satisfies! Why? Because God created us to function a certain way, and when we live according to that way, we thrive!

Don't we long to function "accurately?" People fill my office and pay good money to learn how to overcome depression or heal their marriage or help their children. In other words, they are seeking (hungering) for the guidance of a professional, someone who might finally be able to help them live "accurately," in a way that would make life work for them. They hunger and thirst for it!

I've always enjoyed cooking, and I can cook many things well, but for decades, one thing that eluded me was how to make the perfect Southern biscuit. I'd tried innumerable recipes to get that exact texture and flavor that I was looking for. None of them were quite right. I searched recipes and talked to chefs. I watched YouTube videos and read old cookbooks. I "hungered and thirsted" after how to make biscuits "accurately." I wanted to make a "righteous" biscuit!

I actually was given the accurate way to make biscuits after I preached that sermon in Atlanta. As I explained in the sermon what I had learned about righteousness, I used my hunger for "righteous biscuits" as an illustration. The result? I was met in the back of the church after the service by a half-dozen Atlanta grandmothers who were all too happy to share their recipes for making biscuits. One of them held the secret I had been looking for, and I use her recipe to this day. (See Appendix 8.a. for your own personal copy of the recipe for "Righteous Biscuits!")

There is a way that biscuits work and a thousand ways that they don't work. And there is a way that humans work as well. It was an intriguing realization to me (once I had been practicing psychology for a couple of decades and finally knew what I was doing), to see that the ways of living and relating that were the most psychologically sound (the ones that were bringing my clients the richest and the fullest lives) all "accidentally" paralleled what God had been telling us for millennia. It was the day I learned that his Law is a precious gift.

I learned things like this:

Living in a deceitful way makes us alone. And not only is loneliness deeply painful, the hidden, alone parts of us are also the breeding ground for our deepest problems: depression, anxiety, addictions... pick a card, any card.

Covetousness and entitlement guarantee that we never feel loved. That is because our best-case scenario is that, even if we get what we demand, we don't feel happy. We just feel like we've finally gotten what we've deserved all along (*It's about time!*). Ergo: we never feel grateful or loved, just self-righteously smug.

Lust objectifies us as much as it objectifies the object of our lust. It also exercises the part of our brain that "imagines," which is the same part that generates anxiety and shame. The more we lust, the more we cultivate our fear.

Controlling other people will get you just that: control. It will never get you another person's love or trust. (Ergo: you'll be alone again.)

Being untrustworthy makes us paranoid, because how are we to know that others aren't as dishonest as we? Like the saying goes, "He who hides behind the door, looks there."

Being judgmental creates a world of shame inside of us. That critical eye you have toward other people is turned on you every moment. The sword cuts both ways.

I could go on.

What I just recited is psychology, folks, not religion. I do it every day at the office. It just happens to reflect the truth of God's Law. It's accurate.

God's Way is not a set of moralistic rules for learning how to be a squeaky-clean ice cream boy. They are an instruction manual for the human heart. The Law is not so much saying, "Eating soap is wrong." It's more saying, "Eating soap will make you sick; maybe even kill you. Don't be an idiot!"

God himself explains his intent for the Law in Jeremiah. He says, "I will give them one heart and one way, that they may fear me always, *for their own good, and for the good of their children after them."* (Jer. 32:39)

What could be more valuable to us than for the Maker himself to teach us how we best operate!

3. See me and you've seen the Father.

One of the primary reasons that I am writing this book is to reflect with you about what God is like, what he is *really* like! As we have said, God wants to be known, and he has done a lot of things to try to help us see his true character. In the background (and sometimes the foreground) of the One Story, he has poured out his heart so that we can see who he is.

Another wonderful value of the Law is that it gives the people (and us) an even more vivid picture of the heart of God. Again, the Law is not just a list of rules. In many ways, it is a personal resume of God himself, like a social media profile. "If you want to get to know me, these are the things that I like and don't like! This is what brings me joy. This is what I love and value. Get to know me!"

As New Testament Christians, we have a living, breathing, technicolor portrayal of what God is like. Think about it, who says, "Look at me and you see the Father?" Christ is our picture of the nature of God. (John 14:9) The book of Hebrews says, "God, after he spoke long ago to the fathers in the prophets in many portions and in many ways, in these last days *has spoken to us in his Son*." (Heb. 1:1) We are blessed beyond measure that we can read the words and actions of our Lord on earth and get an "incarnated" picture of Yahweh.

But if you were an Old Testament believer, where would you look to understand who God was? After 430 years in Egypt, God's people probably knew a great deal about the Egyptian gods. Like the gods of Olympus, the Egyptian gods were abstractions of natural phenomena (like sun or rain), or anthropomorphized humans, full of pettiness and jealousy, demanding constant obeisance from their puny subjects.

As we currently stand with God's people at the foot of the mountain, they are free and belong to Yahweh, but their relationship with him is brand new. God has a lot of work to do to teach them who he is. The Law will be his teaching assistant. In other words, if Jesus says, "Know the Father by looking at me," the God of the Old Testament says, "If you want to see my heart – *then look at the Law.*"

The Law talks about restoration for people who are wronged, provision for the widow, care for the alien, love for your neighbor. The Law calls for purity and kindness and living in a way that is safe, just, and trustworthy to the people who are close to us.

Look deeper at the Law and you will hear his heart of promise:

When God says to "remember the Sabbath" in the fourth commandment, he is declaring that he is the God who gives us rest. "I will not enslave you to work every day of your life, demanding that you perform and work to earn my love. I invite your hearts to finally settle; to be at peace."

His Law says to "honor your father and mother." In other words, he is the God of family, of belonging, of thriving relationships. "I am a father and mother to you. I am the safest home. You are mine and you need ever be alone again."

When he says, "You shall not commit adultery," he declares his own faithfulness: "I will never cheat on you, grow bored with you, or dishonor you. I am the faithful God. We are wed forever, and I will remain faithfully yours."

You shall not steal – "I will give you everything you need because I own everything. All is mine and you are my children. You don't need to live trying to take. All that you could ever desire will come from my hand."

You shall not lie – "I bring you the safety of knowing that there aren't any secrets or deceit between us. And I want to protect you from the terrible isolation that your lies will weave. When you lie, you are alone. I don't want you to be alone. With me, you are safe to tell the truth."

See him here! Hear him here! This is his true heart spoken in the Law if we only look. He is loyal and tender. He longs to protect us when we are weak. He loves truth. He wants purity and honesty. He is a God of dangerous holiness, but he protects us from that danger by his boundless grace. This is Yahweh. You want to know what he looks like? The Law is a word picture of the heart of God.

4. The remodeling project.

Do you ever wonder why, if we are saved by God's grace (apart from works), that the Bible still insists that we live righteously? Why is obedience still such a big deal to God if he saves us by his mercy and favor? Here's why: we are still called to obey God not because obedience earns us some sort of merit in his sight, nor because we would lose our relationship with him if we didn't, but because *living and looking like him is the very point of our salvation.* The whole reason that God creates and saves us is to have a people in his image. Remember the Eden Plan!?

One of the most unfortunate mistakes that people make when thinking about their faith is to believe that God's plan is *only* a "plan of salvation." In other words, we look at God's story and think that his only goal is to make sure that we "get saved and go to heaven." But here's the secret: of course, he wants to save us, but that salvation is not an end in itself. It is a *means to an end!*

What God has wanted since Eden is to restore his Way, to bring his people back to himself, and to re-form us into his image. Jesus will later call this renewed world God wants to create, the Kingdom of God.

In other words, to be saved and to not be becoming more like him defeats the very purpose of being saved in the first place. Next to his longing to live in a close, loving relationship with us, our being like him is the reason he saved us. He is restoring the Eden Plan! (See how understanding the One Story helps us make sense of puzzling questions like this?)

I have a friend who bought a beat-up 1964 Austin Healey 3000. It was a classic "barn find" automobile. David had saved it from a slow rusty death, purchased it, and brought it home on a trailer; covered in hay and dirt. David loved that little car even when it was a rusty pile of junk (I have to admit to breaking the 10th commandment about it a couple of times myself). But he bought it and saved it and made it his own.

But guess what–David was not satisfied with the condition of his salvaged car. He loved the wreck he had bought, but he had bought the wreck for a purpose: to restore it.

And restore it he did. For months he worked on it, sometimes allowing me to help. He was constantly grabbing me in the halls at church and announcing that he had rebuilt the carburetor or the transmission. One weekend we even pulled the engine out, redid the clutch and shoehorned that baby back in! He painted it classic "Healy Blue" and now it is a shining, beefy little car with a throaty rumbling exhaust when the engine roars–restored to its pre-Beatles glory – and a blast to drive.

But what if this story had played out differently? What if David had purchased this little heap of junk, brought it home on a trailer, and saved it from the pit, only to have the car say to him, "I just am so happy that you wanted to buy me and save me. I just want to live here with you forever, but I don't want to be restored. I kind of like this trailer, and the garage is really nice. I'm not really interested in becoming shiny and rebuilt, but I celebrate the fact that you love me just the way I am."

That would make no sense!

The *reason* David bought the car was to restore it. And that's what the Law is for in our lives as Christians. To buy the little wrecked sports car without restoring it is nonsensical. God saved us *so that* we might be like him. "We are his workmanship, created in Christ Jesus *unto good works*, that we should walk in them." (Eph. 2:10)

So is obedience relevant to whether we are loved by God? No! We are saved and loved by grace alone. So why do we need to obey? Because the goal here is not just your salvation. The goal is for you to look like God again and to be glorious with him one day in his kingdom. It's what he created you for. He wants this very badly. In fact, he wants it so badly that "He made him who knew no sin to *be sin*," (Why, so you could just go to heaven? No!) …so that "we might become the <u>righteousness</u> *of God in Him*." (2 Cor. 5:21)

This is the reason he saves us, and this is the reason he calls us to follow his Law. And every day that you spend submitting your heart to his "restoration" brings you closer to being like him. It's what you were made for! It's what will bring you joy.

5. The happiest hopelessness.

There's another role that the Law plays, and it's one of my favorites. One of the most powerful goals of the Law is *to show us that we can't do it.*

Let me ask you: You hear about God's Law all the time, right? You go to church and probably know a lot about what God wants by now.

So, how's it going?

Has knowing all about the Law helped you be more obedient, more like God? Maybe a little, but if you're like me, you probably aren't totally satisfied with your daily godliness. (I'm pretty certain that your spouse is not satisfied with your daily godliness.)

Think about it, how well have you done this week managing your selfishness or petty irritations? How have you done with lust or envy or unforgiveness or gossip? Let me see those hands! The truth is that we are all walking disasters!

I basically make my living on the premise that everyone is really screwed up. And the fact that we know how to do better doesn't really seem to help us change very much. In fact, when Paul laments his own frustration with obeying God in Romans 7, he implies that the Law actually supercharges sin! Being burdened or obsessed with the Law actually makes us *less* capable of keeping it. (By implication therefore, and psychologically speaking, to the degree that *we* function as "the Law" in anyone else's life, living in a position of judging them, criticizing them, or demanding that they change, we virtually guarantee that they will *never* change. Food for thought.)

The truth is that though the Law is pretty good at telling us how we *should* live, it is incredibly bad at *helping* us actually be more obedient! The Law really isn't that good at solving our sin problem. And though that sounds like a lousy set up, it's actually one of the most beautiful roles that God's Law plays in our lives.

One reason God gives us his Law is to show us that we can't do it ourselves.

The Law holds up a standard to "be perfect as your Father in Heaven is perfect" (Matt. 5:48) and hopes that you'll hear that call and despair. Then you may realize the most important truth in the universe: how badly you need a savior! (We will see Jesus play this card masterfully during his ministry on earth.)

Paul calls the Law a *didaskolos*, a "schoolmaster," to teach us that we don't stand a chance without Christ. The Law works hard to show us we can't do it. As Paul later says in Galatians 3:22, the Law "shuts all men up under sin."

So try to obey and then talk to me.

You will probably "shut up!"

Paradoxically (as all true things are), thanks to the Law, we can be made hopeless that we could ever fulfill it, and then we can at last run to the arms of our Savior, washing ourselves in his righteousness, death, and glorious resurrection. "He is the beginning, the firstborn from the dead." (Col. 1:18) And we are reborn too. Because after his wonderful cleansing and tender renewal, we will often see obedience begin to flow naturally from us. Once we are free, we tend to become more like him. That's the Gospel, my friends!

6. How to be friends with God: The Gift of Substitution.

In that wonderful paradoxical way that Yahweh often works, after humbling us with the realization of our inability to obey, the Law is going to warmly invite us to come *closer* to God. Woven throughout the background of God's dealings with his people, there is some sort of notion that, though we are alienated from God, there is a way to make things right again. For the first time in the One Story, the Law will begin to spell out how this process will work. The Law will tell the people how the impure can be made pure. It will teach them how death and sacrifice are required to pay for evil; and paradoxically, how the stain of blood is the only thing that can make us clean. The Law will spell out specific forms for sacrifices, cleanliness, holidays, debts, and forgiveness. It's going to begin teaching the people how to be friends with a holy God. And one of the most powerful ways it will do this is by introducing a theme that will define God's salvation from here on out:

Something I call the *principle of substitution*.

Bible quiz time: What's the deal with all the animal sacrifices we've been hearing about since we began our story? God slays an animal to cover Adam and Eve; Abel brings a pleasing animal sacrifice to God in Genesis 4; Noah's burnt offering; Abraham's ram in the bushes; even the Passover lamb, all show us God meeting his people in the context of the shedding of blood. The reason for this has not been explicitly spelled out thus far in the Bible. The Law is about to do so.

The situation is this: When Adam and Eve turned from God in the garden, they incurred upon themselves (and us) a death penalty for rebelling against the King. "The wages of sin is death." (Rom. 6:23) (See appendix 8.b. if you want to explore more about why treason against God requires a death sentence.)

This death sentence is obviously a problem for us, but fortunately it's a problem for God as well. Remember the story of Noah? God doesn't want to destroy his children; he doesn't want us to die. But if he turns a blind eye to the destructiveness of our sin, doing so will violate everything holy about him.

In other words, how is he going to be "just and the justifier?"

His solution?

Somehow God creates a plan in which *you* sin, *you* owe a death penalty, *but someone else dies!* Substitution! God's justice is satisfied, yet his people are also preserved.

This is where the sacrifices come in.

There has been a tender, hopeful voice whispering in the background of the One Story all along. It has said, "You are condemned to die, but a sacrifice can be made on your behalf. You owe a death penalty, but someone else can pay it." The Law announces this miracle outright! It tells us that (in some way I don't fully understand) a penalty we owe can be paid by another. A sacrifice can be made as a substitution for our own death.

This is a fundamental lynchpin of our salvation, and the Law begins to spell it out – graphically!

In the old days of Israel, it will work something like this: you bring an animal to the tabernacle. As you stand there and confess the ways in which you have harmed God and others, you watch that animal die on your behalf. You see the gravity of how destructive your heart can be. You see the horrifying cost, and you see that somehow you are not the one to pay it. The Law spells out the severity and price of our turning from God. But, it also announces the wonderous news that a substitute can die in your stead. This concept has lain in the background of the One Story. With the coming of the Law, it now moves to the foreground. Substitution will now be the way that Yahweh will save his people. A sacrificial lamb will die so you might live!

I wonder what it would do to our often-casual repentance ("Dear Lord, please forgive me for all my sins – again.") to experience this kind of sacrificial substitution firsthand. What would it be like to confess our own hurtfulness and then watch the throat of an animal being slit on our behalf? We hear its pain; we watch it die; we see the lifeblood run from its throat. Scholars say that during the Day of Atonement, the Temple in Israel was literally flooded with the blood of thousands of sacrifices. "Here was a royal fellowship of death." [3]

What would it be like to hear someone else's screams and see someone else die instead of us? God gives this opportunity to his people as he sets up the sacrificial system in the Law. He announces this mysterious, wonderful solution to our sin: somehow our relationship with God can be healed if someone dies for us.

It is only through the Law's model of sacrifice and substitution that God's people will be able to one day make sense of the *real Substitute* that God will bring. These rituals of killing animals and shedding blood to pay for sin are only just a symbol, a "play" to demonstrate what God's justice really demands. The blood of bulls and goats can never really atone for sin. (Heb. 10:4)

Real payment for sin can only be accomplished by the death of the guilty, or by the death of the *"not guilty,"* who sacrifices his life for many. (Matt. 20:28)

And on those days in which God gave the Law to Moses, I believe that our True Substitute, Christ, stood next to the Father and spoke at his side as they told their children the way of salvation. A lamb must be slain to pay for their sins. In that moment, our True Lamb watched and waited, knowing that one day he would be that substitute for us all. He would be the one to die. And somehow the knowledge of that horror brought him joy. Because he loves us so much.

7. Our obedience brings him joy!

How could it be that he so deeply wants us? This God has been seeking us since day one. He has worked to protect us and make us his own. If we really touch his love for us, it is our dream come true, our greatest joy!

So here's a lovely question: how would you like to be able to bring joy to *his* heart?

Of course, he needs nothing from us and nothing we can do could ever make him love us more or less, but he tells us over and over that our obedience to his Way makes him *happy;* it *pleases* him. (1 Sam. 15:22, Hosea 6:6, Heb. 11:6) Imagine this: you can actually bring delight to the heart of Yahweh of Hosts, the one who has laid down his life because he loves you!

His Law shows us how.

You know that feeling when you walk into a store and spot something that you know someone you love would just delight in? You know that excited anticipation of the moment when you will see their eyes grow wide with disbelief as they open the gift: "Where did you *find* this!?" When we live in the ways that God treasures, we get the incalculable privilege of bringing the holy Giver of Gifts one of the gifts he loves the most: our hearts following his. When we turn from an opportunity to indulge in the "passing pleasures of sin," when we curb that desire to strike back at someone with cruelty or harshness; when we push back on our own desires (like Christ did) and honor the will of our Father, we give him something he treasures. We bring him joy. One of the richest gifts of the Law is that it teaches us how we can respond in love to the one who has given us everything. We get the gift of learning how to delight the Sovereign of the Universe!

We are his adopted children, and through the Law, we get to discover how to better bring joy to our Father! (Perhaps this should have been reason number one!)

The Happiest Ending

While we've been talking about the goodness of the Law, a lot's been going on with God's people waiting at the mountain. As we said, God began the process of delivering his Law with a renewal of his covenant promise to his people, just like the one with Abraham. Only then does he give them his Law. And he's going to end this whole experience by coming back to his favorite place – his covenant home with his children.

Here's what it looked like on that day: we are told that, after receiving the Law, Moses wrote down all of the words of Yahweh. He sacrificed burnt offerings and young bulls as peace offerings to God. He then sprinkled some of the blood on the altar and read all that God had said to the people. (Ex. 24:3-8)

The Israelites all promised to be obedient to God's Way. "All the words that Yahweh has spoken; we will do" (v. 3) This is a promise we know they cannot keep any better than we could. Fortunately, God's relationship with us does not hinge on our ability to obey.

Instead, the next thing that happens is that Moses takes some of the blood from the sacrifice and literally sprinkles it on the people, saying to them, "Behold, the *blood of the Covenant* which Yahweh has made with you in accordance with all these words." (Ex. 24:8)

In other words, God's next act immediately after giving the Law is to make yet *another covenant promise* with his people.

But what is the promise? How is God going to bless the people in the midst of all these laws which he knows they will break?

We will see it in the next thing that happens.

In Exodus 24:9-11 something astonishing occurs. As Moses sprinkles the people with the covenant blood from the altar, all the priests and Moses see *God himself*. They look, and beneath God's feet there appears "a pavement of sapphire as clear as the sky itself." And despite the fact that God has just spent three chapters laying down laws and penalties against transgressors, we are told that as they encounter God "he did not reach out his hand against the nobles of the sons of Israel, and they *beheld God* and they *ate and drank*."

What is happening here?

What is happening is called a *peace offering*.

Of all the offerings and sacrifices that are prescribed in the Old Testament, my favorite is the peace offering. In this lovely form of Old Testament sacrifice, I go to the temple and confess my sins to the priest. I bring a lamb along, and as I stand there the priest takes the lamb and slits its throat in front of me, and I watch it die instead of me.

But at that point I don't go home mopey and guilt-ridden.

Instead, I call all of my friends and family and we have a big feast with this lamb. We have a celebration that John is forgiven! John's death was owed; he was supposed to die; but this lamb died in his place! I am set free from my sin, and my relationship with God is restored!

A peace offering is what is happening here at Sinai.

Here on the mountain of the Law is God, who is pure and holy, upon whom the children of Israel cannot even look. He is a God of blisteringly righteous law. Yet a burnt offering and a peace offering are made and blood is sprinkled upon the people, and not only are they not killed in retribution for their violations of the Law, they are at *peace* with God.

So much at peace that they get to sit and eat and drink a feast of celebration with Yahweh. What we're seeing here is the intimacy of a sit-down meal with God himself — not because the people were obedient to the Law, but because the blood of a substitute was sprinkled.

This is how the story of the Law at Sinai ends!

Remember what God has always wanted: his people together with him. Here, we see upon the sapphire floor, a God who has finally achieved what we have seen him working toward for countless chapters. We see a God who wanted his people, but they ran from him. A God who sought out a man and started a family. The family that became a nation, but was imprisoned. And a God who rescued them all and brought them to himself.

Of course, he throws a party!

Yahweh has achieved a deep richness in the progress of his One Story, and he wants a meal with his children to celebrate.

This is who he is!

But this banquet at Sinai is only an appetizer. It is glorious, but it is only a dim foreshadowing of an ultimate banquet that is to come:

the marriage supper of the Lamb, where God's bride (us!) will finally be made complete, "clothed in fine linen, bright and clean." There she will meet her bridegroom and see heaven open "and behold, a white horse, and he who sits upon it is called Faithful and True, and in righteousness he judges and wages war." (Rev. 19:11) And because of *his* perfect obedience to God's Law (not ours), we will get to shine at his side.

Get to know this "thundering God of Sinai." He is also the one who provides himself as the sacrifice that the Law demands so that he can have his people at his side to sup with him forever.

Now, after seeing his heart, wouldn't you like to be more like him? His Law shows you how.

Chapter Nine

David and The King of Israel

Thus far in our One Story, God has been re-creating a world that reflected his deepest desire. He has always wanted a dear people who loved him as he loved them. Once they turned from him, his story became an odyssey of restoration and redemption. How could God ever get his people back? The One Story is the tale of how he has fought for and rescued us.

We watched as he began by seeking Adam and Eve, and then laid down his weapons with Noah. He brought forth a new family though Abraham, and, as that family became a nation, he rescued them from bondage with Moses at his side. He later gave them his Way again at the mountain, expressed in the Law.

During the ensuing 40 years in the wilderness, God grew his people into a more mature nation. They needed that time, a generation, to shake off four centuries of Egyptian rubbish in order to learn to be the People of God. During those years, Moses shifted from being the peoples' liberator and lawgiver, to becoming the *first advocate* between God and man. Forevermore, we too will have an Advocate before the Father. (1 John 2:1) (Appendix 9.a. has more about Moses's role as our first advocate before God.)

As we pick up our story, the people of God, the nation he promised to Abraham, have at last arrived at the Promised Land. Now we will witness the establishment of God's nation in the land that God promised Abraham. And we will see the next beautiful step in God's restoration plan:

God's people will have a king!

Joshua fights the battle of Jericho

The book of Joshua covers the checkered history of Israel's attempt to inhabit the land that God has promised. Surely in an homage to Moses's deliverance of his people across the Red Sea (as well as lovely bookends to the wilderness adventure of Israel), God parts the Jordan river and allows the people to cross on dry land. God tells Joshua to have the priests carry the Ark of the Covenant into the river. As they set foot in the water, the river stops. (Joshua 3:8-17) The people then cross on dry land into their new home, flowing around the Ark like water around a stone.

After the people cross the Jordan, Joshua has each of the twelve tribes choose a stone and stack them on the bank of the river as a reminder of God's miracle. (Joshua 4:1-7) The ancient Hebrews called such markers *ebenezers* (literally, "stone of help"). An ebenezer was a tangible memorial of God's faithfulness for the people. God knows his people, and recognizes (as he does with his covenant signs) that we sometimes need visual and tactile reminders of his protection and provision. Joshua leaves the people a marker that says, "Here, Yahweh brought you into the land that he promised to Abraham centuries ago. Do not forget his love!"

As they set foot in the Promised Land, God calls the people to take the land from the Canaanites, a command that they will only partly obey. When the people do act in faith against the Canaanites, however, God intervenes on their behalf.

In Joshua 5, Joshua encounters a mysterious figure who claims to be the "commander of the army of Yahweh." This person says something to Joshua that should sound familiar to those of us who have heard the Moses story. He tells Joshua to take off his sandals because he is standing on holy ground. (Joshua 5:15) Then, he lays out a battle plan.

The people are to conquer the city of Jericho simply by marching around its impenetrable walls while carrying the Ark of the Covenant, the symbol of God's presence. After seven days, and at the sound of the Israelite trumpets and war cry, the walls will crumble down before them.

Forty years prior, ten of the twelve Hebrew spies sent to check out the Promised Land had doubted God's faithfulness to be a warrior for his people. They became overcome with fear at the enemies they saw, and determined that Canaan would be impossible to conquer. The only two who believed were Caleb and (you guessed it) Joshua! Surely, this story of the miraculous fall of Jericho demonstrates the power that God was holding in reserve, ready to bring forth on behalf of his people if they had but trusted him forty years earlier.

One of the reasons that I love looking at the big picture of the Bible is that we get to pull together these two stories that are separated by more than fifty chapters and more than forty years of history. When God told the people that they could take the land, way back in Numbers 13, he was the dead serious. Now, we get to be with Joshua and Caleb as they witness this promise becoming a reality.

During the Jericho campaign, the people encounter a friend in Rahab. I love Rahab's inclusion in the Jericho story. She's often referred to as "Rahab the harlot." It seems unfortunate that for all history she is identified by her sinful choices. God makes it very clear that she is a prostitute. Why do you think he would do that? I think the answer is found in Matthew 1, where Rahab is identified as being in the very lineage of our Jesus. God wants to make it very clear that in his kingdom, even in the lineage of his Messiah, there is room for people who are called even the worst of sinners.

As the book of Joshua continues, the people continue to take the land, again with the miraculous assistance of the warrior God. On one occasion, God rains down large hailstones on the enemy, enabling his people to win the battle. We are told that "there were more who died because of the hailstones than the sons of Israel killed with the sword." (Joshua 10:11)

On another occasion, he drives out the opposing army with swarms of hornets. We are also told about how, in a very unusual event, Joshua "himself" bade the sun to stand still in the sky so that his army might complete their victory before nightfall – and it did! Even the passage recognizes this bizarre circumstance, saying "there has been no day like it before or since, when Yahweh heeded the voice of a man, for Yahweh fought for Israel." (Joshua 10:14)

The people are taking the land that God had promised so long ago to Abraham. However, despite God's ready intervention to help his people take Canaan, they do not fully obey him. They leave many Canaanites roaming free among them, a choice that will cost them enormously in the years to come.

A call to follow

In Joshua 24, Joshua ends his book by telling the One Story back to his people. Like we are doing, he reminds the people that this is all the *same story*. He speaks for God and reminds them of how their heavenly Father had pursued Abraham, even though he worshiped other gods. He tells them of how God gave Abraham a son, and from that son he made a nation. He reminds them of how they were captives in Egypt, but that God had rescued them. He reminds them of how God had provided for and protected them in the wilderness. And finally, he tells them again how God has given them this land.

One of the reasons that it is so important for us to know and remember this One Story is because it has always been important to *God* that his people remember his story. Yahweh is a God of memory and of history. Over and over in scripture, he reminds his people who he is and who they are. Part of my desire in writing this book is to remind you of the same. We can become so focused on small parts of scripture that we lose the scope of God's massive story with us and for us. We've talked about how one of the most powerful things that God does in his relationship with his people is that he "remembers" his covenant promises to us. He calls us to do the same. He calls us to remember.

Joshua ends his book with his famous charge to the people and to us. The people are surrounded with countless options, countless "gods" to whom to they can pledge their hearts. He says to them "choose this day whom you will serve … but as for me and my house, we will serve Yahweh." (Joshua 24:15)

This directive will hang with great weight around the future of Israel. Whom will they serve?

Chaos and Order

The wackiest book in the Bible

As we said, the next step in our One Story is going to bring the advent of a king for Israel. But I don't think we can fully apprehend the importance of the coming of this king unless we understand the context in which he arrives.

That context is the book of Judges.

Think about what you remember about this unusual book – I'm sure you recall some of the stories.

Remember Adoni-bezek who captures seventy kings and cuts off their thumbs and big toes, forcing them to scrape for food from under his table?

How about Ehud, the left-handed judge, who killed Eglon, the king who was so fat that when Ehud stabbed him, the fat flowed out over the hilt of his sword?

There's also Jael who kills the Canaanite general, Sisera, by driving a tent peg through his head. And the guy who kills the concubine, cuts her into pieces and mails the parts all over the country! There's lowly Gideon and the fleece, and let's not forget Sampson, his hair, and all of his strange adventures. This is bizarre stuff. Basically, if you're wondering what to teach to a sixth-grade boys' Sunday School class, this is your go-to book. The strangeness, disorder and almost comic book violence of Judges is sure to bring in your big numbers!

In other words, Judges shows us a world of chaos and upheaval in Israel's new homeland.

And I think it does so intentionally.

The nature of futility

As a nation, the people of Israel are partially unified, but they're still quite tribal. The land has been moderately taken, but there are still many Canaanite enemies running around creating all sorts of trouble. This, combined with all the strange stories in the book of Judges, give us an opportunity to notice something: there is a futile, cyclical nature to the story of Judges. As we have seen in several places in our One Story so far, there is a pattern.

It goes something like this: the people turn from Yahweh and begin to serve other gods. God brings enemies against them, making their lives miserable. In their misery, they cry out to God. He hears their groaning, has compassion on them, and to protect them, he raises up another judge to lead them out of chaos. The judge then brings order, and the people prosper. That is, until the judge dies, and the people then turn from God again to serve other deities.

That's the story of Judges, the story of the Israelites (and dare I say the story of us), over and over again.

It's like the old joke my Uncle Allan used to tell us when we were kids, the story of Pete and Repeat:

"Pete and Repeat are walking down the road; Pete falls in a hole, who is left?

"Repeat."

"Ok! Pete and Repeat are walking down the road and Pete falls in a hole. Who's left?

"Repeat."

"Well, if you insist!"

You get the idea. Judges is sort of like that. For an entire book.

So far in our One Story, each installment has created a progression, a development, an evolution of God's rescue plan of redemption. With each telling, the story has become richer and fuller. Then, suddenly, we sort of get caught in this feedback loop of Judges where nothing is really happening at all. In fact, the book of Ruth is the only story that takes place during this historical period in which anything redemptive happens. And Ruth is a *Canaanite* for crying out loud!

But among God's people, nothing is happening.

A better idea

So if you read Judges and it feels futile, pointless and chaotic — you are correct! In fact, the commentators I've read on this book have said the reaction of futility we experience reading Judges actually shows that the writer of Judges knew exactly what he was doing. He is wanting us to see (and learn from) this pointless cycle.

Here's the secret. The book of Judges is not just a history book. It is an *argument*. There is a polemical goal to the book of Judges. It is supposed to be persuasive in nature; it's supposed to lead the reader to a conclusion.

Do you remember those old movies they used to show us in driver's ed class? Movies with titles like *Blood on the Asphalt!* "Billy and Tommy thought they could make it in front of the oncoming train. THEY WERE *WRONG!* It started out as a joy ride, but it would be their last!"

Sound familiar?

Anyway, they showed us those movies because we were supposed to watch them and think, "Wow! I sure don't want to be like Billy and Tommy. I think I've learned a real lesson here today!"

Well, welcome to the book of Judges. One of the goals of the book is for you to read it and conclude something. Hopefully, you (and those in Israel who heard these stories) would see all of this chaos and pointless repetition and say, "Gee, the way things currently are really isn't working. Something else is needed for Israel."

And if you said that you would be correct. Because there are two refrains that repeat themselves throughout the book, two statements that echo over and over that describe the real problem: *"Everyone did what was right in his own eyes,"* and, *"There was no king in Israel."*

The time has come for Yahweh to take the next step in his One Story.

God Hears

God's next step in his One Story begins with a man named Samuel. Samuel's parents are Elkanah and Hannah, and for years Hannah has been unable to have children. Elkanah has another wife who mocks and torments Hannah for being infertile. Hannah is heartbroken at her inability to bear children and by the other wife's cruelty.

One day, Hannah is praying at the temple for God to give her a son, and even pledges to give him back to God if God would only answer her prayer and open her womb. She is praying so vehemently that Eli the priest thinks she is drunk. In response to her prayers, and using language that we are now familiar with, the story tells us that God "remembered" Hannah and blessed her with a son. Hannah names him Samuel which means "God hears." (1 Sam. 1:1-20)

Certainly, God heard Hannah.

Hannah responds with a song. (1 Sam. 2:1-10) She sings, "My heart exults in Yahweh," the very words later echoed by Mary as the angel announces the coming of Christ.

Technically, Samuel is one of the judges, and the last in the line of Israelite judges. Further, he is a Nazarite, which was a very special Old Testament office, reflecting a life of deep dedication to God. In Numbers 6:1-8, God spells out how his people could take a solemn vow and live in special, sacred consecration to Yahweh. In the case of Samuel, his mother had already committed her son to God as a Nazarite in her prayer for a child. (1 Sam. 1:11) There are only three Nazarites mentioned in scripture, Sampson, Samuel, and John the Baptist. A Nazarite could not have contact with the dead, drink wine, or use a razor. They were hairy, wild-looking characters. This is why John the Baptist ate only locusts and honey, lived in the desert, and wore only camel skin as clothing.

Nazarites lived unique, dedicated lives in service of God. And here's the key – they tended to be transitional figures. Their presence in the Bible meant that big change was about to happen.

Obviously, with John the Baptist, we see an extraordinary "advent" occur, a transition to the new era of Christ. And, with Samuel, we will likewise see a new era ushered in, an era that will never end, an era under which we still live.

God's people will be ruled by a king.

The coming of a king

Bad king

Remember how God called Israel to exterminate all of the Canaanites? Despite Yahweh's command, they had not done so. The Philistines (offshoots of the Canaanites) will cause Israel constant trouble, even to the point of stealing the Ark of the Covenant at one point. (Though they end up sending it back after God brings plagues on them for having it)

When Samuel was an old man, the elders of Israel were fed up with the Philistine assaults and came to him, demanding that instead of appointing his corrupt and unreliable sons as new judges over Israel, he should give Israel a *king*. Samuel consults with God about this question, and after presenting warnings to the people about how difficult life under a king might be, God directs Samuel to go ahead and appoint a sovereign for the people.

Now, for those of you who have been regular Sunday school attenders in your life, you are undoubtedly a bit confused at this point. I have been talking excitedly in this chapter about the advent of a king for Israel. Yet, if you're like me, you were probably taught this "king story" quite differently.

I had always heard it something like this: Samuel comes to God, broaching the subject of the peoples' desire for a king. God responds to this angrily, as if the people are rejecting him in their request. After all, were told in Samuel 8 that God says, "it's not you they have rejected, it's *me* they've rejected." Yet God reluctantly capitulates to their request.

That's how I was always taught this story, but that is not what is happening. The problem here is not that the people want a king. God is not saying that they are rejecting him by simply wanting an earthly sovereign. In fact, God had always intended for them to have a king. He promised Abraham and Sarah that "kings shall come forth from them." (Gen. 17:6) In Deuteronomy 17, God tells the people that one day they would ask for a king, and he is very specific about the qualities he would like that king to possess.

God is rejected in the people's request, not because they want a king. He is rejected because they say they want a king "like other nations." In wanting such a king, God knows they are turning from him. *That* is the rejection.

But God gives them what they ask for, a king "like other nations." He gives them a king who is exactly what they want. Their new king will be handsome, tall, and warrior-like – but also power-hungry, cowardly, and disobedient to God. Indeed, he gives them a king like other nations. He gives them Saul.

God's king

As Saul is in the midst of his 40-year-reign, God begins working to crown his own king. God makes it immediately clear with David, that he is choosing his man by different standards than the peoples'. God is not looking for might or prowess; he is choosing his king based on the quality of his heart. "For Yahweh sees not as man sees. Man looks on the outward appearance, but Yahweh looks on the heart." (1 Sam. 16:7)

To call his own king, God sends Samuel to the household of a man named Jesse, where he meets all of Jesse's big, strapping sons. (1 Sam. 16:1-10) As he meets each one, however, God essentially says to

Samuel, "not him, not him, not him," one after the other. Samuel ultimately runs out of brothers, and since God told him this is where he would find the new king, he is a bit stumped.

Confused, he asks Jesse, "Are all your sons here?"

Jesse responds, "Well, there is the youngest, but he is out tending the flocks." In the Hebrew, the literal word that Jesse uses when speaking about his youngest son is the "runt." (v. 11) "The 'runt' is out in the fields." Thanks, Dad!

David is immediately brought to Samuel and is anointed as God's king on the spot. We're told that in that moment "the Spirit of Yahweh rushed upon David, from that day forward." (1 Sam. 16:13)

Indeed it did.

Our One Story has been the gradual unfolding of God's restoration project. With David, God's story is going to take a massive leap forward. God has always wanted man to rule his garden on his behalf, like Adam did at Eden. Now that God has his people and the people have the land, the fulfillment of the Eden restoration takes another step: the people will have a *ruler* who is a "man after God's own heart." (1 Sam. 13:14)

Let's spend the rest of our chapter looking at some ways in which David actually starts to embody the One Story restoration that God has been working toward. So much of what God has always wanted is going to come together in the reign of his new king.

The man who rules for Yahweh

The people possess the land

We have to go way back in our One Story to remember the first time that God talked about "the land." As you remember, Abram was minding his own business in Ur of the Chaldeans, and God interrupted his day with a promise saying, "Go from your country and your kindred and your father's house to the *land* that I will show you. And I will make of you a great nation." (Gen. 12:1-2)

Notice God didn't just say, "Follow me and I will be your God, and we will abide together." Nor did Abram say, "Sure, Lord, I'll be glad to go, but where am I supposed to live?" In his very first call to Abram, God *leads* with the promise of a "land."

God has always wanted this – his people in his land. Initially it was a garden; currently in our story it is the land of Canaan. (One day it will be the New Heavens and the New Earth!)

Though the people of God have made significant movement into the land during the years of the judges, it is still not fully theirs. Philistine Canaanites continue to assault them. The peace and rest that God wanted for his people has still not been accomplished.

Then along comes David. The new king is going to cement the possession of the land, bringing peace, unity, and organization to God's people. David begins by obeying God and finally, completely obliterating the Canaanites. Throughout 2 Samuel we are inundated with stories of David slaughtering Philistines. As God says in 2 Samuel 3:18, "By the hand of my servant David, I will save my people from the hands of the Philistines, from the hands of their enemies."

In these chapters, David is sort of Alexander the Great, The Terminator, and Conan the Barbarian all rolled in to one. In one story, he kills so many Philistines that the grip of his hand is locked on his sword so tightly that he can't let go of it. You wouldn't let your kids watch this stuff on TV! But finally, after 800 years, God's promise to Abraham is finally fulfilled. The people of God, the children of Abraham, fully possess the land.

There's a sense in which we could say that God is attempting to 'kill two birds with one stone' in his deliverance of the land to his people. He wants his people to have the land, and he also wants to eliminate the incredibly destructive culture of the Canaanites.

There are hints throughout the Pentateuch that God is deeply troubled by the culture of these brutal people. (Lev. 18:21-25, Lev. 20:22-23, Deut. 9:5, Deut. 12:29-31) Indeed, history confirms the Canaanites as being a very cruel race, even to the point of sacrificing their infant children in the furnaces of their fire god, Molech. Despite God's promise to Noah to never again destroy the whole world, he continues to intervene with judgments upon particular nations (and individuals) who embrace destructive ways of living. He has told his people to take the land and destroy all of the Canaanites. David finally obeys.

And there <u>was</u> a king in Israel

Remember the repeating refrain from the book of Judges: "And there was no king in Israel." With David, God's man finally reigns! Once David conquers the enemies of God's people, he centralizes government in Jerusalem and unites the tribes of Israel. They have a country now and even a capital city, and David sits on the throne. As he did with Adam before the Fall, God finally has a man in authority over his creation.

Think about it: what was the first commandment in the Bible? It was God's call to Adam that he be ruler of the earth. He told Adam to subdue the earth and to name the animals. We have said numerous times that within Hebrew culture, being given the power to name anyone or anything signified complete authority. God has always wanted his people to rule over the world that he created.

Our king, Adam, fell, and with him fell mankind's godly dominion over God's creation. So, for millennia, there was no man who ruled on earth under God. But at last, we have David. He conquers the land;

he unifies the tribes of Israel; he is a warrior, a poet, and musician. He creates a standing army for Israel and even extends Israel's boundaries. He creates a government with wise elders and counselors to assist him, beginning a dynasty that will last over 400 years. Just as God has always wanted, his man is bringing order and grandeur to God's creation.

An even greater King

So David reigns over Israel. But don't leave just yet.

David is about to take things one step further. Not only is he going to centralize government and rule as king, he is also going to do something else, something extraordinary.

He is going to bring the *Ark of the Covenant* to Jerusalem.

In 2 Samuel 6, David assembles 30,000 chosen men and journeys to Kiriath Jearim to the house of a man named Abinadab. (The Ark had been hidden there for about 20 years, ever since the Philistines sent it back, after having learned a nasty lesson about messing with Yahweh.)

David repossesses the Ark and brings it back to Jerusalem, and he does so with extravagant celebration. This event apparently means something incredibly powerful to David. As he brings the Ark into the capital city, he dances before it, wearing the clothing of a priest, and every six paces, he sacrifices an ox and a fatling to glorify God. Everyone is celebrating with "songs and lyres and harps and tambourines and castanets and cymbals." (2 Sam. 6:5)

What's happening here? Why is King David throwing his regal dignity to the wind and dancing with all his might? And why might we, as followers of the One Story, want to pull out our own lyres and castanets and join this party?

Well, remember what the Ark represents? It's not a secret Hebrew weapon like in the movies. The Ark represents the *presence* of God himself. The Ark is God's *throne on earth*.

As David brings the throne of God into Jerusalem, the city which houses the throne of David, he is joyfully declaring to the world that, "Yes, I am God's man, and I am ruler over his people, but there is someone whose throne is greater than mine, someone whose lordship is Lord over me. Yes, I rule, but I rule only under someone else. Yahweh of Hosts is his name!"

All have bent their knee to King David, but here David bends his knee to God. In this moment, we have a slice of the Eden being restored! Man is ruling creation, yet dancing in joy that Yahweh is the true King of all!

Reflecting the Heart of God

God's Image

Remember that other refrain we kept hearing in the book of Judges, "And everyone did what was right in his own eyes?" Well, as 1 Kings 15 develops the history of David's reign, it takes a clever jab at the people from the book of Judges. While they lived doing what was right in their *own eyes*, it tells us that David "did what was right in the *eyes of Yahweh*." (v. 8)

Of all biblical characters (excepting Christ), somehow it is David who most truly reflects what a "man after God's own heart" would look like. David deeply submits his life and his character to God's Way. But he doesn't do it out of some sort of pious religiosity. He is not an "uptight" Christian. David is a man of aggression and powerful passion (sometimes to his demise). He seeks after God because he "gets it." He gets that *most true* of things: that engaging God and knowing him is the wildest, most exciting adventure anyone can embrace. Someone who lives killing lions and giants would not want a tame, pious religion anyway. He would want to be absolutely in love with a wild and passionate God. And he is!

This is what David's "religion" looks like, the joyful dance of a shepherd boy who finds the most wonderful person in the universe and fills an entire book of the Bible with poetry about him. David is a warrior and a singer and a sinner and a king. He is brave and wise and noble and frail. He kills countless foes in battle and yet spares his greatest enemy.

In other words, he *bears God's Image*.

If it surprises you that I would call someone this wild a glorious image-bearer; if your idea of a "man of God" is just soft and pious; then you do not yet understand what the image of God looks like. This is what God has been working toward since Eden: not gilded, pasty saints, looking like they just stepped out of a painting by Fra Angelico, but free, powerful beings with whom he can live and create and delight forever! Again, David reaches back to the Eden Design and reminds us of what God originally wanted. He wanted a people who would echo back some of the bright life and rich wonder of what God is really like.

But David is not just God's man because of how he reflects God's power and goodness. He also poignantly lives as a man of God by showing us his own deep need for a savior. David was indeed flawed. David galactically sinned. He knew this better than we do. He talked about it and grieved over it. The Bible is not a book of heroes. We are shown David not just because he is good. We are shown David because he is *God's*. Sometimes David does it best, and then he is beautifully broken when he fails, guiding us as to what real repentance and restoration before God looks like. He is a man after God's own heart.

Pointing us to God in his Psalms

David knows this God. He abides with Yahweh throughout his life. As he says in Psalm 139:14, "Wonderful are your works; my soul knows it very well." He says that God is "always with me; he is right beside me." (Ps. 16:8) Have you ever wondered what it would be like to experience God through the eyes of David? Staggeringly, we are actually given that gift! In the Psalms, we are given the chance to see God as David's heart saw him. Let's look at Yahweh through David's eyes as we listen to him sing about his beloved God in his Psalms. Let's let him show us the God he so deeply knows.

Are we even worthy to look at God as we stand at David's side? David comforts us reminding us that his God "knows our frame; he remembers that we are dust." (Ps. 103:14) And David knows what "remember" means to God. David tells us that we are safe in the hands of someone who is not surprised that we are so broken.

Those sins that plague your life – David tells us that they are as far removed from God's heart as the "east is from the west." (Ps. 103:12) I love that he does not say "the north from the south." Given the right instruments, one could actually measure the distance from pole to pole. But the distance between the east and the west is impossible to measure. It is infinite!

David knows about pain. He tells us that though there may be weeping at night, a shout of joy will come in the morning (Ps. 30:5). He reminds us that we may "cast [our] burdens on Yahweh, and he will sustain [us]; he will never permit his righteous ones to be moved." (Ps. 55:22) Surely David learned these comforts firsthand as he walked at God's side through the sorrows, failures, and dangers that he endured.

In the 23rd Psalm, David tells us something wonderful about God's pursuit. He says, "Surely goodness and mercy shall follow me all the days of my life, and I shall dwell in the house of Yahweh forever." Just as it reads, this is a beautiful image. But if we dig just a little deeper, we find that the Hebrew word for "follow" here is the word *radaph,* and it means more than just to "follow." It refers to a stalking pursuit, even like a predator stalks his prey. David, the slayer of wild beasts, tells us that God's goodness and mercy seeks us relentlessly, like a hungry lion whose longing is to bless us deeply. Do we recognize this in our lives? Truly, our God seeks us with a hunger that will not be satisfied until we are consumed by his blessing!

David lives delighting in who God is and what he has done. He calls us to enjoy our God: "Oh, taste and see that Yahweh is good! Blessed is the man who takes refuge in him!" (Ps. 34:8) In Psalm 103:1-5, he says, "Bless Yahweh, O my soul, and do not forget his benefits, [he] forgives all your iniquity, [he] heals all your diseases, [he] redeems your life from the pit, [he] crowns you with steadfast love and mercy, [he] satisfies you with good so that your youth is renewed like the eagle's."

The Hebrew word "bless" that David so often uses in the Psalms (*barak*) refers to a personal heart reaction. It means that when David reflects on who Yahweh is, his heart is moved to kneel and rejoice in adoration at the same time. Though his knees bend low, his soul is lifted high in exultation. In fact, God's love is so delightful to him that he can say in Psalm 63 that Yahweh's "unfailing love is *better than life!*" (Ps. 63:3)

What stunning wonder! My prayer is that we can all grow to the place that we can join David there, knowing and experiencing a love from God that is so encompassing that we would gladly trade our lives for it.

This is what God's chosen king does. He reaches down to his people, lifting us up and making us "blessed" too, as he shows us the majesty of our True King and his love that is better than life itself!

The Ultimate Image Bearer

In David, God finally has a man who begins to reflect what God has always wanted man to look like. And as we will soon see, from David, God will ultimately bring us a man who is *wholly* like God. As we read the stories of David, we get glimpses of this greater King who will come from his line, Christ himself. One of my favorite David stories that points us to our Savior, is the tale of David's hand-to-hand battle with the giant, Goliath. (1 Sam. 17)

You remember the story: the people of Israel are still at war with those Philistine Canaanites they failed to eliminate when God first told them to. The nature of the warfare has now been reduced to chants and threats, but the Philistines have a champion. We're told that their warrior, Goliath, stood "six cubits and a span" in height. (Curiously, Goliath is the only individual in the whole Bible about whom we are told his exact height.) This would've made Goliath stand about 7 feet tall. His armor weighed about 120 pounds, and his spear was approximately 12 ½ feet long and 2 ½ inches thick. Quite a formidable opponent.

Goliath makes a habit of daily mocking the cowardly Israelites who listen, quaking from the hillside. Not one among them is powerful or courageous enough to engage this monster.

Until David shows up.

A teenage David is coming to the battlefield to bring bread and cheese to his big brothers in the army, and he is incensed at how this Philistine insults God. He immediately volunteers to take the giant's challenge and defeat this beast himself. (The therapist in me is tempted here to add, "typical teenage impulse control behavior," but I'll resist.)

Declaring Saul's offered armor too heavy and bulky for him,

David decides to play his own game, that of a crafty, deadly shepherd – one who defends himself and his sheep with staff and slingshot.

The slingshot of that day was not a toy. It was a leather pouch with two long cords attached. A smooth rock was placed inside. Actual experiments have shown that the ballistic impact of such a weapon was roughly equivalent to that of a .45 caliber handgun! In your Sunday school lessons, David is portrayed as the underdog. He was not. Though he *was* severely underestimated.

David responds to the taunting threats of the Philistine by rushing Goliath, slinging a stone that strikes the giant between the eyes, sinking into his forehead and dropping him to the ground. I'm reminded of that scene in *Raiders of the Lost Ark* in which Indiana Jones simply pulls out his pistol and shoots the guy waving his big, curved sword. And I love what David says to Goliath before 'pulling the trigger,' "You come to me with a sword and with a spear and with a javelin, but I come to you in the name of Yahweh of hosts, the God of the armies of Israel, whom you have defied." (2 Sam. 17:45)

But here is our focus: The Sunday school takeaway from this story is that we should all learn an important lesson from David's faith: "Oh, that we would so trust in God that we could face our foes with the bravery of David."

But what if there's a different story happening here?

What if David is not the character in this story who is meant to represent us? Be honest, as you look at your Christian life, which of the characters in the story most remind you of *you*? (Hopefully it's not Goliath.)

If you're anything like me, you don't often live filled with the confidence and faithfulness of a David, rushing headlong at the enemy, overflowing with the power of God. Frankly, when I look at my own life and the lives of the clients in my office, the truth is that we more often feel like the overwhelmed army of Israel. We face enemies, internal and external, that shake their weapons at us, and we wonder how we can possibly overcome them.

I hear so many sermons in which folks beseech us to be more faithful and obedient. We are told that we should move out of our complacent faith and become more committed to God. But the problem I see most Christians struggle with is not a lack of commitment or a lack of desire to serve God. The place I see most Christians struggling is that they are *defeated*. They feel deeply committed to wanting to serve God, but they are exhausted and demoralized from trying and failing. They even fear, given their chronic failure, that God may not even want them anymore. The enemy is too strong. The challenge feels too great. So, like the Army of Israel, we live our Christian lives cowering on the hill, being mocked by our adversary.

But here's the key: in this story, we are not David. We *need* a David! We are the frightened, helpless army of Israel, defeated and battered, hopeless and needful! And God knows this. The takeaway from this story is not that we should be as faithful and powerful as David. The moral from this story is that *we need a champion*. We need someone who can live with power and victory on our behalf. Someone who will win that victory for us.

In this story David is 'Christ,' God's man sent to save his people. David points us to Jesus, our true champion, the one who will finally step onto the battlefield, and though bruised, will crush the Serpent and free his defeated children forever.

A King Forever

In the Goliath story, David lives out his role as a powerful precursor to Christ, but God has one more gift in store for David and us. He is about to make David's connection to our Jesus very real and very official, because in the story of David, we are going to get one last Old Testament covenant. Through David, God is not just going to give us a king; he's going to give us a *King Eternal*.

All through the One Story, God has built his restoration plan on a series of promises or covenants. He made a covenant with Noah to no longer destroy but to save. He walked the covenant pieces with Abraham, promising redemption through faith. He renewed his covenant with Moses and the people at Sinai, making them his special treasure. With each covenant promise, God has made his story richer and fuller. Now, with David, the story will not just be about the redemption of a people, it will be about the establishment of the Kingdom of God.

Because from David, the True King will come.

The story goes like this: after David has established his rule, creating government and prosperity for the nation of Israel, he has a realization that I find to be quite dear and loving. He is obviously thinking about his own prosperity and how God has cared for him. Then he seems to begin reflecting on how he can give back to God. He muses to Nathan the prophet, saying that it feels oddly inappropriate that he dwells in a house of cedar while the God of Israel continues to live in a tent. At this point in history, the tabernacle of God was still the same tent arrangement that God had established with Moses in the wilderness. In 2 Samuel 7:1-2, David tells Nathan that he wants to build God a house – a temple.

God's reaction to this gesture is priceless, and expands the One Story exponentially. God essentially responds to David saying, "You believe that you are someone who should build a house for *me*? I've not dwelt in a house since I brought the sons of Israel up from Egypt. All along, I've been moving around in a tent. And never during that time did I ever speak a word to any of the tribes of Israel, asking them to build me a house of cedar. Now to you David, I say this. As you recall, I took you from the pasture, from following your sheep, and I made you the ruler of my people. I've been with you wherever you have gone; I've cut off your enemies; and, like Abraham, I have made your name great and given you the land I promised him. And now you say you want to build a house for me? Well, Yahweh declares to you that Yahweh will build a house for *you*! When your days are complete and you lie down with your fathers, I will raise up your *descendent* (or "seed," same word from the protoevangelium, *zera*) who will come forth from you and I will establish his kingdom. And I will be a father to him, and he will be a son to me… and your house and your kingdom shall endure before me forever and your throne shall be established forever." (2 Sam. 7:4-16)

Again, I love God's ironic, poetic humor. His reaction reminds me of his words in Psalm 50. There, God is essentially mocking again, saying, "You can't give me anything! Your sacrifices? I don't need them. If I were hungry, I would not tell you, for the world and its fullness is mine."

God doesn't need anything from us or David. David wants to build God a literal house. And God's response is, "Oh yeah? You want to build me a house? I declare that I will build *your* 'house!'" By which God means David's lineage, his heritage, his "seed." He will bring forth from David a "house" that will exist always, an offspring, a "descendent," who will be king forever – Christ the true King.

That "seed" that we heard foretold in Genesis 3, the one who became a promised son to Abraham, the one who became a sacrificial lamb at Passover, will now also be a King reigning at God's side forever. And from now on, nobody in the Bible ever stops talking about it.

Isaiah will tell us that "his name will be called Wonderful, Counselor, mighty God, eternal Father, Prince of Peace ... on the throne of *David* and over his kingdom, to establish it and to uphold it with justice and righteousness." (Isa. 9:6-7)

The prophet will later tell us that "a throne will be established in lovingkindness, and a judge will sit on it in faithfulness in the tent of *David*; moreover, he will seek justice and be prompt in righteousness." (Isa. 16:5)

And one day, centuries later, an angel named Gabriel will appear to a young woman named Mary and say to her, "Don't be afraid Mary, for you've found favor with God. (Like Noah did.) And behold you will conceive in your womb and bear a son and you shall name him Jesus and he will be great. And he will be called son of the Most High. And the Lord God will give him the throne of his father *David*. And he will reign over the House of Jacob forever and his kingdom will have no end." (Luke 1:26-33)

Apparently, Gabriel had not only read 2 Samuel 7, but had also studied God's earlier covenants, recalling his promises to Abraham and Jacob that began our whole story.

The book of Hebrews drives this point home with blistering clarity. In chapter 1, the writer speaks of the excellence and uniqueness of Christ, and in so doing, quotes this very passage from 2 Samuel, saying, "For to which of the angels did God ever say, 'You are my Son, today I have begotten you'? Or again, *'I will be to him a father, and he shall be to me a son to me'?* Hebrews is quoting this very covenant promise to David. (Heb. 1:5)

Ultimately, one of the last things we will ever hear before the curtain closes on the One Story are the words of the Seed himself as quoted in Revelation 22. Jesus speaks, identifying himself before everyone. And what does he call himself? He says, "I am the *root and the descendant of David*, the bright and morning star." (Rev. 22:16)

With David we have the last new development in the One Story before Christ himself comes. Surely, the promised Seed will arrive, and he will be a king over God's people, and he will live and die and rise again. Then he will sit on that throne. He is sitting on it right now, at the right hand of Yahweh – he has been for 2,000 years. But one day he will stand again and come to fully take his rightful kingdom, gathering all of his beloved children to himself.

David responds to God's covenant with a prayer. (What else could you do?) It's a prayer by David, a king's prayer about himself. But it is also a king's prayer about his people, Israel. In other words, it's David prayer for God's people, *even for us!*

Think about it. God has essentially just told David that his people, Israel (who spiritually speaking are now us), will belong to David forever. So, we get to hear our king pray for his children – and all of his future children! As you read excerpts of this prayer and hear David invoke God's blessing on Israel, remember that he is talking to God about you as well.

> "Who am I, O Yahweh, and what is my house, that you have brought me thus far? And yet this was a small thing in your eyes…for there is none like you, and there is no God besides you, according to all that we have heard with our ears. And who is like your people Israel (*us!*), the one nation on earth whom God went to redeem to be his people. And you, O Yahweh, became their God.
>
> And now, O Yahweh, confirm forever the word that you have spoken concerning your servant and concerning his house, and do as you have spoken. And your name will be magnified forever, saying, 'Yahweh of hosts is God over Israel,' and the house of your servant David will be established before you…

Now therefore may it please you to bless the house of your servant, so that it may continue forever before you. For you, O Yahweh, have spoken, and with your blessing shall the house of your servant be blessed forever."

– 2 Samuel 7:18-29

It is a great and mighty king indeed to intercede like this on behalf of his people. We have that priestly king both in David and in his descendent, Jesus, who continue to intercede for us before the Father. The king prays for you. If you love and seek God today, surely it is because his prayer is continually being answered.

Chapter Ten

The Prophets I: The Heart of God

The Son of David

We have just watched as God promised David that he would build David's "house." In our last chapter, we focused on how this was ultimately a promise to provide for us all a king who would reign forever, a promise of Christ. But God's promise to David is also a promise for a *contemporary* blessing in David's time. A *literal* offspring of David will occupy the throne. And soon, David's son Solomon, is crowned the next king of Israel.

There's a sense in which you could say that, during the reign of David and Solomon, God's promise of restoration and blessing to his people reaches its highest fulfillment, at least as it regards temporal history. God's promises to Abraham are profoundly fulfilled, perhaps more than they will ever be until Christ himself fully reigns. Under the reign of Solomon, the people are as many as the sands of the sea and they are indeed a great nation, just as God promised Abraham. There is peace and plenty in the land; Israel is a blessing to other nations; God's presence is with them in the temple. And as God promised, an offspring of David sits on the throne.

Solomon seems to understand this richness. Solomon fulfills his father's desire to "build God a house" by constructing the grand temple of Jerusalem (see 1 Kings 7 for details of its splendor). After completing this majestic place of worship, Solomon offers a great prayer of consecration. (1 Kings 8:56-57) In it, he speaks of how Yahweh has fulfilled his One Story promises to Moses and the patriarchs. He says, "Blessed be Yahweh who has given rest to his people Israel, *according to all that he promised*; not one word has failed which he promised through Moses." (I Kings 8:56) Solomon understood the One Story. He knew that what he was experiencing was the fulfillment of commitments that God had made for generations. In gratitude to God, he sacrifices 22,000 oxen and 120,000 sheep.

A Visit from Yahweh and a Snapshot of the Future

In the context of all this great fulfillment, God is going to pay Solomon a visit. *And as he speaks to Solomon, God is in some ways going to spell out a dynamic that will exist between him and his people for the next several hundred years, a pattern that will bring pain to both parties.* As we begin our chapters on the prophets, it is important that we understand this dynamic.

Yahweh says to Solomon (in my paraphrase), "I've heard your prayer, and I've consecrated this house, and I will put my name here forever, and my eyes and my heart will be here perpetually. And as for you (and by implication, future kings), if you walk before me as your father David walked, with integrity and uprightness, I will establish the throne of your kingdom over Israel forever, just like I promised your father David. But, (and here's where it gets sticky) if you or your sons turn away from following me, and go and serve other gods, then I will cut off Israel from the land which I've given them, and I will cast them out of my sight. And Israel will become a proverb and a by-word among the people, a heap of ruins. And people who pass by will be astonished and hiss and say, 'Why has Yahweh done this to this land and this house?' And they will say 'Because they forsook Yahweh, their God, who brought their fathers out of the land of Egypt, and they adopted other gods and worshiped them and served them. Therefore,

Yahweh has brought all this adversity on them.'" (1 Kings 9:1-9)

This statement to Solomon from Yahweh is vital because it is like a preview of the rest of the history of the kings of Israel. As we read the books of Kings and Chronicles, we will see played out over and over the exact dynamic that God describes to Solomon. Kings will come and go. Some will honor Yahweh, but many will turn from him. And, just as God promises, he will engage his kings and his nation to bring them back to him, sometimes with the most devastating discipline.

But God does not deliver this judgment in isolation. He will send messengers, emissaries, who will plead with the people to return to him.

As he engages his people to return to his side, he will send the prophets. In our common language we think of a "prophet" as someone who can foretell the future. But technically, a biblical prophet is someone who serves as a mouthpiece of God, a man who speaks God's message to his people. Sometimes it is about the future, but as we will see, it is mostly about God's heart for us.

Over the next two chapters, let's listen to three themes the prophets will proclaim to God's people:

— *The prophets will richly and overtly speak the heart of God for his people. God's people have left him (again), and the prophets will show us his heart and work to get them back.*

— *The prophets will begin unfolding the future of God's promises and the ultimate fulfillment of the One Story: the Kingdom of God.*

And in our next chapter:
— *They will give us the deepest picture yet of the nature of the coming Messiah.*

Unveiling the Heart of God

God speaks his heart

Let's remember what the situation is here: God is the king and creator of everything, but from day one, he relates to his people as more than just a sovereign ruler. From the beginning, he repeatedly lays aside his mantle of cosmic authority in order to have what he desires the most, closeness with us.

But like all relationships, this belonging requires the participation of both parties. And in God's life with us, he repeatedly encounters us violating our side of the bargain. At Eden we saw him long to walk with Adam and Eve, but he tells them that in order to have such belonging, they must live according to his Way. The result? They immediately turn from him. When he comes to Moses in the burning bush and declares his intention to deliver "his people," he is almost using the language of betrothal. We will see in his judgments through the prophets that one of his favorite analogies to describe his people's faithlessness is that of a wife who betrays her husband.

God's people continually forsake him.

One of the most common fears that I hear with clients in my office is a fear of rejection. Almost universally, we humans fear that horrible feeling of scorn that comes when people we love exclude us. Maybe all of your friends get together but don't include you. Maybe your wife is angry, and you feel that chill in the house as she silently sends her message of rejection. A boyfriend breaks up with you; you are ignored by your parents – all of us fear that feeling of being not wanted.

One of the things that becomes painfully obvious if you read the Bible with any sort of awareness, is that to be God is to experience rejection. I find it quite heartbreaking when I try it on. Most of us are reluctant to tell anyone when our hearts are broken. God doesn't seem to mind admitting it. From the first pages of the Bible, we see God reaching for the people he loves, and then watching as they turn from him. Yet as we saw in Eden, his response is to consistently work to bring them back to himself. In fact, as we've said, the theme of the One Story is God's centuries-long work to create a "happy ending" to the story of his painful relationship with us.

Here is the key if you want to really engage the richness of the prophets: so far, we've watched this dance of invitation, rejection and pursuit take place from the *outside*. We've heard his stories and *surmised* his heart from what we have seen. Our focus will be the same in the prophets, but instead of listening for an objective story or narrative, we're going to hear God's <u>subjective experience</u>. *We are going to hear his heart from the inside rather than the outside.* In the prophets, God is going to actually tell us about himself as he engages his people.

These two chapters are a brief departure from the plotline of our story. Instead, I want us to receive the gift of hearing *God's own words* in the prophets, speaking his accusations, restoration, and love for his people. I will let *him* eloquently tell you this part of his story.

I invite you to read these passages carefully. Listen to them. Hear his song. Hear his poetry. Yahweh is going to pour out his hurt, anger, and, ultimately, forgiveness and joy, as he speaks to us in the breathtaking poetry of the prophets.

The accusations of God

The bad news first

God is not okay with rejection from his people. Through the decades, as kings come and go, God's people repeatedly turn to the worship of other gods, often involving demeaning fertility rites or even the sacrifice of their own children. They have also become a society of lawlessness and cruelty: the weak are oppressed, judges are bribed, and commerce is deceitful and corrupt. But mostly, the people simply no longer care for Yahweh, and when they do, their "worship" is lame and meaningless. This is what he means when he says, "These people come near to me with their mouths and honor me with their lips, but their hearts are far from me." (Isa. 29:13) When he speaks like this, he's not just condemning their empty religion, he's mournful at how their *connection* to him is empty. They don't really want his heart. But he wants theirs.

As a result, God comes at the people with strong charges against them. They have turned from him and the ancient covenant he has made with them, both by worshiping other gods and by living in destructive ways with one another. God is going to work to regain their hearts, but for a time, things are gonna get ugly. Thus, he begins his assault in the prophets.

> In Jeremiah, God recalls the love he has lost. He says,
>
> I remember the devotion of your youth,
>   your love as a bride,
> how you followed me in the wilderness,
>   in a land not sown.
> Israel was holy to the Lord,
>   the first fruits of his harvest.
> ...What wrong did your fathers find in me
>   that they went far from me,
> and went after worthlessness, and became worthless?"
>   – Jeremiah 2:2-5

Listen to his hurt here! We often turn sin into some sort of naughty choice that displeases a heavenly judge. But God is turning himself inside out in this passage. He is telling us what it means to him when we reject him. He is saying in essence, "I cared for you and gave to you. Remember when we were close? You were like a bride to me. What fault did you find in me that you would leave me?"

In Isaiah, God speaks to us of his hurt and anger in some of the most beautiful literature ever written. Isaiah 5 speaks in the voice of a woman who loves a vineyard owner. She tells of how her beloved planted his vineyard and protected it, but it yielded only pain for him.

> Let me sing for my beloved
>   my love song concerning his vineyard:
> My beloved had a vineyard
>   on a very fertile hill.
> He dug it and cleared it of stones,
>   and planted it with choice vines;
> he built a watchtower in the midst of it,
>   and hewed out a wine vat in it;
> and he looked for it to yield grapes,
>   but it yielded only wild grapes.
>
> – Isaiah 5:1-2

The woman speaks on behalf of God, reminding the vineyard how Yahweh nurtured and cultivated it. But it yielded only bitter fruit. God then hammers home the metaphor to his own people, saying,

> For the vineyard of Yahweh of hosts
> is the *house of Israel*,
> and the men of Judah
> are his pleasant planting;
> and he looked for justice,
> but behold, bloodshed;
> (he looked) for righteousness,
> but behold, an outcry!
>
> – Isaiah 5:7

In other words, Isaiah says, "*You, Israel,* are that worthless vineyard, and God will dig you up and press you like grapes if that's what it takes to bring you back to his arms."

At the heart of our One Story is the God who spoke the words of Genesis 3:9, "Where are you?" In the prophets, he does not just speak these words to his people, he laments them, sometimes with the cry of an abandoned lover, sometimes with that of a brokenhearted father. Hear him grieve his loss of us, his children:

> Hear, O heavens, and give ear, O Earth;
> for Yahweh has spoken:
> "Children have I reared and brought up
> …they have rebelled against me.
> The ox knows its owner,
> and the donkey its master's crib,
> but Israel does not know,
> my people do not understand."
> – Isaiah 1:2-3

Despite the fact that he has loved and nurtured his children, this Father has been rejected by them. Again, his comparisons are so rich and poignant: "Even an ox or a donkey are more faithful than you are." (And I can't help but wonder if this image of the donkey at its master's crib isn't a tender, hopeful reference to the nativity.)

In the meantime, God's people have completely lost their bearings. In leaving Yahweh, they are practically delusional in their understanding of reality. Isaiah 29 continues:

> Ah, you who hide deep from Yahweh your counsel,
> whose deeds are in the dark,

> and who say, "Who sees us? Who knows us?"
> You turn things upside down!
> Shall the potter be regarded as the clay,
> that the thing made should say of its maker,
> "He did not make me;"
> or the thing formed say of him who formed it,
> "He has no understanding"?
> — Isaiah 29:15-16

How can the creature look at his creator and say, "He doesn't know what's going on, but I do!" You have it all backwards, Yahweh says. "You are the creature, and I am your God. And your way has neither truth nor wisdom. Your thinking is bent and twisted."

The best therapeutic interventionist could not have said it better!

As we listen to God's heart in the prophets, let's not forget his sense of humor (he invented humor, remember). In Isaiah 44 he speaks incredulously to those who worship idols. He's mocking again; even sarcastic. Let's listen in.

> He [the idol worshipper] cuts down cedars, or he chooses a cypress tree or an oak and lets it grow strong among the trees of the forest.... then it becomes fuel for a man. He takes a part of it and warms himself; he kindles a fire and bakes bread. Also, he makes a god and worships it; he makes it an idol and falls down before it. Half of it he burns in the fire. Over that half he eats meat; he roasts it and is satisfied...and the rest of it he makes into a god, his idol, and falls down to it and worships it. He prays to it and says, "Deliver me, for you are my god!
> — Isaiah 44:14-17

It's as if God is saying, "Let me get this straight. You're going to grow a tree, cut it down, use some of it for firewood – and then use the rest of it to make a *god to worship*!?" You can feel the personality of God in these remarks. He is not just condemning sin here; he's dumbfounded by the stupidity of it. And he will have nothing of it. In Isaiah 42:8, he says,

> I am Yahweh; that is my name; my glory I give to no other,
> nor my praise to carved idols.

In the prophets, God so often comes home to his metaphor of marriage. Their (our) betrayal of him is not just a rejection. He experiences it as an adultery – and he is graphic about it. Be careful reading Jeremiah chapter 2:20-24 – "parental guidance" is suggested!

> For long ago I broke your yoke
> and burst your bonds;
> but you said, 'I will not serve.'
> Yes, on every high hill
> and under every green tree
> you bowed down like a whore.
> ….Look at your way in the valley;
> know what you have done–
> (you are like) a restless young camel running
> here and there,
> a wild donkey used to the wilderness,
> in her heat sniffing the wind!
> Who can restrain her lust?
> None who seek her need weary themselves;
> in her month they will find her.

This passage should both offend us and rip our hearts. Listen to him! He says, "I set you free; I broke your bonds. I am the liberator, the one who brings joy, and yet instead of turning and walking with me you have acted like a prostitute, a wild animal controlled by her primitive sexual instinct." And he almost mocks her: "Your suitors would not even become weary searching for you. You are all too easy to find!"

Someone once said that listening to God in the prophets is like hearing a lover's quarrel through the wall of the next-door apartment. There's injury and hurt; there's an "I did this for you," and a "Look at what you did to me," kind of tone. In fact, the entire first part of the book of the prophet Hosea revolves around a living metaphor of betrayal, a real-life parable in which God has Hosea literally marry a prostitute. Yet, despite the fact that she is unfaithful to him, taking lover after lover to her bed in order to enjoy the gifts and delights she receives, God calls Hosea to take her back to his heart (just as God does with all of us, routinely). If the prophets are doing their job (and we are paying attention), we should be heartbroken.

He invites our appropriate response to this kind of sinful destructive betrayal in Jeremiah 2:12-13, where he says,

> Be appalled, O heavens, at this;
> be shocked, be utterly desolate, declares Yahweh,
> for my people have committed two evils:
> they have forsaken me,
> the fountain of living waters,
> and hewed out cisterns for themselves,
> broken cisterns that can hold no water.

Not only have they left God's endless overflow of abundance, they have traded it for empty, dry wells. They have forsaken his tender wonder and richness in exchange for worthless desolation.

Should this sadden us? He asks. Should we be surprised?

No, we should be *appalled*, shocked, utterly desolate!

Indeed, we should.

Welcome to the prophets. The One Story is about God's work to get his people back, but through these poetic messengers, God is devastatingly eloquent about how wounded and offended he is by their rebellion and flight from him. And he will do anything to bring them home.

The consequences of leaving God

By the time of the prophets, God has been dealing with the destructiveness and rebellion of his people for almost 900 years. (Define "patience!") During that time, he has used divine intervention, disease, famine, and even death, to bring his people to their senses. None of these has turned their hearts back to him with any consistency.

The coming of the prophets is essentially a last call to repentance before God plays his final card, the complete ruin of Israel. By 722 B.C., most of Israel will be obliterated by the Assyrians. By 586 B.C., the remaining tribe of Judah will be taken in captivity to Babylon. As Dr. Knox Chamblin, one of my seminary professors, once said, "Yahweh is 'long-suffering,' but he is not 'forever-suffering.'" Or as one of my psychology professors at Rosemead once said, "God never 'enables' sin. The last thing he is, is a 'codependent'." Hosea concurs, as he channels God, saying, "For they sow the wind, and they shall reap the whirlwind." (Hosea 8:7)

God further lays out their options in Isaiah chapter one:

> If you are willing and obedient,
> you shall eat the good of the land;
> but if you refuse and rebel,
> you shall be eaten by the sword;
> for the mouth of Yahweh has spoken. – Isaiah 1:19-20

Yahweh is very clear: if his people remain positioned against him, he will do the only thing that will ever change their hearts (or the hearts of any destructive human), he will allow the calamity they are sowing to ravage their lives.

In Isaiah 5:24-25, he begins to describe their fate.

> Therefore, as the tongue of fire devours the stubble,
> and as dry grass sinks down in the flame,
> so their root will be as rottenness,
> and their blossom go up like dust;
> for they have rejected the law of Yahweh of hosts,
> and have despised the word of the Holy One of Israel.
> Therefore, the anger of Yahweh was kindled against his people,
> and he stretched out his hand against them and struck them,
> and the mountains quaked;
> and their corpses were as refuse
> in the midst of the streets.
> For all this, his anger has not turned away,
> and his hand is stretched out still.

God will respond to their rebellion against him by burning down the blossom that was once Israel. His anger will shake the mountains! The tender Yahweh, who has lived with his hand extended, absolutely refuses to tolerate his people turning their backs on him.

Ever eloquent and graphic, Isaiah describes how God will literally *summon* the nations that will bring this kind of ruthless judgment upon his people. He calls them into hostile action personally here:

> He will raise a signal for nations far away,
> and whistle for them from the ends of the earth;
> and behold, quickly, speedily they come!
> None is weary, none stumbles,
> none slumbers or sleeps,

> not a waistband is loose,
> not a sandal strap broken;
> their arrows are sharp,
> all their bows bent,
> their horses' hoofs seem like flint,
> and their wheels like the whirlwind.
> Their roaring is like a lion,
> like young lions they roar;
> they growl and seize their prey;
> they carry it off, and none can rescue.
>
> – Isaiah 5:26-29

He will "whistle for them" and "none is weary!" Wow! I find God's judgment frightening, but I am also dazzled by the beauty and wonder of how he communicates his heart, even his heart of anger. Be awed, even at his wrath. It comes swiftly to those who love to destroy. (And, paradoxically, it is their only hope for having real Life again.)

In Ezekiel, you can hear the exhausted rage in God's voice as he finally says enough is enough.

> Thus says Yahweh: Disaster after disaster! Behold, it comes...now I will soon pour out my wrath upon you, and spend my anger against you, and judge you according to your ways, and I will punish you for all your abominations. And my eye will not spare, nor will I have pity. I will punish you according to your ways, while your abominations are in your midst. Then you will know that I am Yahweh, who strikes.
>
> – Ezekiel 7:5-9

I love that even in this diatribe, God gives a little hint at his ultimate goal, the reason he is bringing such disaster. It is not just to destroy. It's not because he's some kind of angry deity, relishing in his vengeance. It is so that one day, "then," the people will finally know that "He is Yahweh."

This has been his goal all along. Remember the plagues of Egypt? They were not just attacks on the pharaoh, they were attacks on the Egyptian gods, "That you may know that Yahweh is God." God's goal is and has always been for his people to know him and live at his side. His goal is to give them this ultimate joy. The people of Israel, like us, were made for it, for him.

The tragedy of humanity is that we typically resist the very thing that will give us life. I see this in my office every day. People who long for love will often destroy it at every turn. People who seek revenge live lives of obsessive bitterness. And those who want forgiveness will often run from it when it is offered. Being a therapist is a strange graphic exposure to the futility of how humans live. And it often takes the most radical of interventions for people to let themselves be open to what they need the most. But it is beautiful to witness the moment when we finally let down our guards and let love in. This is what God is doing to Israel. He is battering down the forces in their hearts that run from the warmth of truly belonging to him.

God's judgments on his people happen just as he said. In the destruction of Jerusalem and the people's deportation to Babylon, God finally takes away everything that Israel and Judah were. In other words, their insistence on living apart from God results in the very loss of themselves. Their national identity was wrapped up in who they were as the "children of Abraham" (Rom. 9:7), and in their possession of the land. Being deported to Assyria and Babylon strips what was once the great nation of Israel of everything. During that season, God was deeply severe in his discipline of them. It was the only thing that would bring them home. God took away everything they were, until they could realize that he was everything they could ever want.

Making sense of God's judgment

Despite the fact that we can point to a redemptive goal to God's judgment, it is natural for us to find his assault on his own people disturbing. Try as I might, I am unable to sanitize it into something simple and palatable. How do we make sense of the violent nature of God's judgment on his own children?

In several parts of our One Story, we see radical examples of God's vengeance and wrath: the Noah flood, the 40 years in the wilderness, the Book of Judges, and now the prophets. In each of these, we are confronted with a God who brings great pain and even death upon his people. How are we to make sense of that?

Like we said regarding the Noah story, I don't want to shy away from these kinds of questions or gloss over them with pat answers. Judgment is as much a part of who God is as mercy and love. I want us to remain curious, even about his scary parts. There seems to be a trend in our current pop-religion culture toward reframing everything God does so as to portray him as only meek and gracious. His love is truly unbounded, but that's not all he is. We cannot defang God's just wrath or try to subdue his wildness. If we do, we will never really know him. And we will also make the vengeance we see at the cross meaningless.

If you have trouble making sense of how our God's heart seems to be full of astonishing love and gentleness, and yet also radical judgment, you are not alone. We even saw God himself wrestle with this very question in the Noah story. For my entire life as a thinking Christian and a psychologist, I have sought to understand this question: how do we integrate these parts of his personality – his grace versus his wrath?

Bottom line: I'm still not sure I understand it. I see God make choices that I do not understand. I see the pain he brings to his people, both in the prophets and in my everyday life; and I so often do not know how to make sense of him. (Is it okay for the author of a book to say that he's not sure? Don't you sometimes feel the same way?) But let me ask you this question: does this uncertainty leave us in such bad company?

What we do know

Think about it – we extol the noble faith of men like Abraham or Job. And since we have the gift of perspective, we can look back into their lives and see what God was doing. We can do that, but they could not. They didn't have the perspectives that you and I have.

Like us, they often did not understand.

When God allowed calamity in Job's life, the heavenly Father was looking toward countless centuries of people who would read of his faithfulness to Job, even in the context of the pain that he brought into his life. But Job had to live not knowing.

What did Abraham think when God called him to sacrifice the very son that he had promised? He was not sure what God was doing. He heard promises, yet he saw wrath; and I imagine that he was unsure. Again, we have the gift of perspective that looks back and knows that God will provide a ram. But Abraham did not know.

Are we now not in the same position as they?

We read of God's actions in the prophets or witness his actions in our daily lives, be it with the death of a loved one or financial disaster, and we do not understand him. Ironically, what many of us do at that point is stand in *judgment* against God's *judgment*. We say things like "I just can't worship a God of such vengeance." My question is, why not? Do we so understand God's heart that we can know what he is doing and judge it?

Somehow, I think that a rich and powerful place for us to stand is in a place of *not knowing* and *not being able to make sense* of all that he chooses; and perhaps just hold on to the things that we *do know*. In a sense, isn't that the definition of faith (and also of emotional health)? It was certainly the answer for Job and Abraham. Perhaps it is our answer as well.

So, what do we know?

- I know that what God wants the most is for our lives to be rich and flooded with overwhelming joy. And, I know that his destructive judgment somehow serves that end. He allows pain, but he desires our joy. I know this even though I don't fully understand how it works.

- I know that God's desire is to show his people that following our bent desires will lead us into deep harm, both to ourselves and to others. As we said, deep inside of us all is a "downward" pull that will ultimately destroy us, others, and our relationship with God. He will do almost anything to prevent that, at least with those who love him. With people who wholly turn their backs on him, he often does nothing. He "gives them over" to their choices, the worst judgment ever. (Rom. 1:24) As C.S. Lewis says, "There are only two kinds of people in the end: those who say to God, 'Thy will be done,' and those to whom God finally says, in the end, 'Thy will be done.'" [4]

- I know that in the background of God's judgment is his constant appeal for justice on behalf of the weak and the oppressed. We hear his harsh condemnations of those he judges, but we forget that behind the scenes of these stories are the oppressed who are being harmed. These are people crying out for an advocate to stop the destruction that is being inflicted on them. Don't you long sometimes for God to intervene and stop the assault of destructive people in your life or our culture? I know that God is that advocate. He comes in the whirlwind, not just to be destructive to the wicked; he comes on behalf of the weak and the vulnerable.

• I know (from reading the Bible and, overwhelmingly, from my clinical work) that unrepentant evil will never stop on its own. If it is not stopped by an outside force, it will continue to swallow everything in its path. Cruelty, bitterness, and entitlement will continue relentlessly until they ruin lives and destroy everything. I know that something external must stop evil because it will never stop itself.

I was working once with a guy in my office whose wife was chronically destructive and hurtful, both to him and to their children. It soon became clear to me that this was not merely a case of marital strife. Instead, his wife was an individual who thrived on control, cruelty, and criticism. (I'm coming across more and more of these in my practice for some reason). Such people never grow by receiving more "love," and they rarely come to therapy. Her husband was beginning to realize this, having spent the last 20 years trying to "turn the other cheek" or explain to her how her behavior was hurtful, hoping that she would finally "get it." "Honey, don't you see?" That never worked.

People like this woman only grow by being forced to run headlong into the destruction they create. I told her husband that the only possible way for her to ever have a chance to change was for him to become very skilled at powerfully confronting her, even bringing consequences and pain into her life in response to how she treated her family.

Kindness and "turning the other cheek" are a great way to relate to repentant, humble individuals, but with unrepentant, destructive people, growth can only happen if they encounter the *tangible pain* that their lifestyle creates. I didn't make that up, it is simply a basic principle of human growth. And it is sometimes the only way to save an individual or a family. God already knows this principle (he wrote the instruction manual, remember?), and it is a major reason he brings his judgment in the prophets. After 900 years of unrepentant evil, his discipline needed to graphically get their attention.

- I know that God waits for us with open arms when we choose to come back to him. His ultimate desire is not to destroy. His judgment on his people is always designed to bring them back to himself. We've seen it since the beginning of our One Story in the Garden of Eden. Come back to God and he will wrap you in his deepest embrace. Come back to life and you will live.

- And finally, I most deeply know that by the end of the One Story, we will see God turn the worst of his judgment upon *himself* in order to guarantee that none of us ever have to experience such a thing again. The judgment that God inflicts on his people in the stories of the prophets is nothing compared to the obliterating wrath that he blisters down on his precious only son centuries later on our behalf. Judgment is part of God's story, but he is committed to it never being the end of his story for those who are his own.

Many things we know. Many things we do not understand. In the meantime, can we live with *the mystery that is God*? Can we live trusting that, somehow, he knows what he is doing, even though we do not?

He likes us this way

Living this way is called "trust," and "faith," and they are things that God values enormously. I am not sure why, but he seems to *like* us in places where we are uncertain but trusting him. He wants us there. He seems to prefer it to our living in control and certainty. Apparently (and often unpleasantly) it is one of his favorite ways to relate to us.

Having to live trusting him makes us terribly frightened, of course. He becomes our only security, and he is invisible, often *unfeelable*. Yet he chronically puts us in situations in which we are hanging out over the precipice, supported only by his hand.

Though we don't like this, he seems to.

Strangely, however, I have found that when I release my fear and fall into the (seemingly dangerous) arms of faith, I am flooded with something that feels "right." God likes us having to rely on him because it is our natural state, like a bird who is finally in the air, or a fish in the water. We were *created* to be so deeply vulnerable and dependent on him. Something about living in hopeful trust in him is our truest home. We often don't know the outcome, but never forget that we do know this Yahweh.

So how do we make sense of God's judgment in the prophets (or his countless other confusing choices)? By remembering what we *do* know, and by returning to the place he created us to live: not knowing, but walking at his side.

But don't close in prayer just yet. Because there is one other thing that I *do know*. For Yahweh's people, judgment is never the end of his story!

The Restoration of God

His face shines again

We've seen God build a devastating case against his people in chapter after chapter of the prophets. We've heard his heart as he has been wounded, angry, and planned interventions against them. History tells us that the hammer indeed did fall as the idols were destroyed and even the holy city of God was flattened. Yet one of the most beautiful things about the God of the prophets is that, somehow, in the midst of all of this calamity, *God's heart is constantly weaving a foreshadowing of hope.*

When it comes to God's relationship with his people, his judgment is never simply an act of anger or retaliation. It is always a means to an end. It is always a tool to achieve something he has wanted since the beginning of the One Story, the restoration of a beautiful relationship with his people; for us to live out the purpose for which we were created, full satisfaction in him.

The prophets are full of Yahweh's joyful anticipation of that reunion.

One of the most graphic and intense pictures of God's dream of restoration is given to Ezekiel in chapter 37. The prophet is brought by God to the middle of a desolate valley. Looking across it, Ezekiel sees that it is strewn with death, covered with dried bones. God looks at him and thunders, "Son of man, can these bones live?" (Surely, we have all been asking this same question as we have watched God annihilate his own people throughout this chapter. Ezekiel seems uncertain as to how to answer as well.)

God answers for him by instructing Ezekiel to speak to the bones, and say to them, "O dry bones, hear the word of Yahweh... Behold, I will cause breath to enter you, and you shall live. And I will lay sinews upon you, and will cause flesh to come upon you, and cover you with skin, and put breath in you, and you shall live, and you shall know that I am Yahweh." (Ezekiel 37:1-6) (I love the echoes of Eden creation in these verses, by the way.)

Ezekiel obeys God and suddenly hears the dry rattling of bones coming together, "bone to its bone." Then sinews and flesh and skin begin to knit over the staggering skeletons. God tells the prophet, "Speak and say, 'Thus says Yahweh: Come from the four winds, O breath, and breathe on these slain, that they may live.'" (Ezekiel 37:7-9)

And out of the absolute hopelessness of death, God reaches down and breathes again the breath of life into his people. In Ezekiel's desolate field, God's discipline of his people has a "breathtaking" (pun intended) resolution. The shattered bones of his desolate people will live again!

God predicted as much back in the book of Deuteronomy, where he says, "When you are in tribulation, and all these things come upon you in the latter days, you will return to Yahweh your God and obey his voice. For Yahweh your God is a merciful God. He will not leave you or destroy you or forget the covenant with your fathers that he swore to them." (Deut. 4:30–31) God promises even before his people betrayed him that he will restore them to his arms. His covenant, he will "not forget."

Remember Hosea's wife, the harlot? We have to come back to her! He says this, speaking of his precious prostitute:

> Therefore, behold, I will allure her,
> and bring her into the wilderness,
> and speak tenderly to her.
> And there I will give her vineyards
> and make the Valley of Achor a door of hope.
> And there she shall answer as in the days of her youth,
> as at the time when she came out of the land of Egypt.
> And in that day, declares Yahweh, you will call me *Ishi* (My Husband), and no longer will you call me *Baali* (My Master).
> For I will remove the names of the Baals from (your) mouth,
> and they shall be remembered by name no more. …
> And I will betroth you to me forever. I will betroth you to me in righteousness and in justice, in steadfast love and in mercy. I will betroth you to me in faithfulness.
> And you shall know Yahweh.
> – Hosea 2:14-20

This is God's goal all along: to reunite the lovers at the end of story, to bring us to that place where we will at last "know" Yahweh (in that deepest Hebrew intimacy) once again.

Whatever our befuddlement about his wrath and justice, we can never forget that this is his goal: to have us! After all, God had told Jeremiah to buy land in the region of Judah before the people were dragged into captivity (Jer. 32:8-15). God was saying, "Whatever happens, I am going to bring you home!"

With Hosea his restoration continues as he describes his own heart changing and softening. He says,

> My heart is changed within me;
> my compassion grows warm and tender.
> I will not execute my burning anger;
> I will not again destroy Ephraim;
> for I am God and not a man,
> the Holy One in your midst,
> and I will not come in wrath.
> – Hosea 11:8-9

I love how his rationale for his compassion is that he is not like men. Ironically, as we said, we often judge God for his judgment, yet he reminds us that he is compassionate, unlike we could ever be. He is not like a man, he is Yahweh. This too is the heart of God. He holds compassion and judgement, love and wrath, all in perfect, never-ending balance. And he does so in a way I'm not sure we will ever understand until we meet him.

A new life together

In the prophets, we have seen God's accusation, threat, and follow-through of judgment. And we have heard him promise to bring his people home. But the prophets bring us even deeper promises as well, promises of an even richer hope. In the prophets, God also tells us about his joyful *future* with his people. It is almost as if, alongside God's meditations on the betrayal of his people, he scatters throughout the prophets anticipations of the wonderful future that he is working to build. Let's conclude our first chapter on the prophets by being washed in Yahweh's dreams of his *Forever* with us.

In Jeremiah, you can almost hear his happiness as he anticipates it.

> Hear the word of Yahweh, O nations,
> ..."He who scattered Israel will gather him,
> and will keep him as a shepherd keeps his flock."
> For Yahweh has ransomed Jacob
> and has redeemed him from hands too strong for him.
> They shall come and sing aloud on the height of Zion,
> and they shall be radiant over the goodness of Yahweh,
> ... and their life shall be like a watered garden,
> and they shall languish no more.
> Then shall the young women rejoice in the dance,
> and the young men and the old shall be merry.
> I will turn their mourning into joy;
> I will comfort them and give them gladness for sorrow.
> ...and my people shall be satisfied with my goodness,
> declares Yahweh.
> — Jeremiah 31:10-14

Please let your heart soar as you read those words and hear his voice, desiring to bring you only goodness. This is what he longs for with you: merriment and joy; dancing instead of sorrow.

In the book of Revelation, God promises us that on the last day, he will sit with us at the marriage feast of the Lamb, and as he finally pulls us to himself, he will wipe away every tear. But John's words in Revelation are not the first time that we hear this promise. Isaiah was way ahead of him. Listen to God foreshadow his Revelation promise in Isaiah 25.

> On this mountain Yahweh Almighty will prepare
> a feast of rich food for all peoples,
> a banquet of aged wine –
> the best of meats and the finest of wines.
> On this mountain he will destroy
> the shroud that enfolds all peoples,
> the sheet that covers all nations;
> he will swallow up death forever.
> The Sovereign Yahweh will wipe away the tears
> from all faces;
> he will remove his people's disgrace
> from all the earth.
> Yahweh has spoken.
> In that day they will say,
> "Surely this is our God;
> we trusted in him, and he saved us.
> This is Yahweh, we trusted in him;
>   let us rejoice and be glad in his salvation.
>   – Isaiah 25:6-9

Centuries before the Book of Revelation, God was promising his people that, not only would their pain one day end, but that he would personally comfort them. The Old Testament has always alluded to a "veil" that shrouded God's people from seeing his full wonder. That veil will finally be torn away (remind you of another veil that was torn from top to bottom?!) and we will see him fully. And like the children of Israel at the covenant celebration in Exodus 24, we will sit at a table of celebration with him and feast.

He goes on to tell us about his future with us, as he describes his desire to satisfy the deepest longings of our hearts. In Isaiah 55, he says,

> Every one that thirsts, come to the waters,
>   And he that has no money;
> Come, buy, and eat;
>   Yea, come, buy wine and milk without money and without cost.
> Why do you spend your money for that which is not bread,
>   and your labor for that which does not satisfy?
> Listen diligently to me, and eat what is good,
>   and delight yourselves in rich food.
> Incline your ear, and come to me;
>   hear, that your soul may live;
> and I will make with you an everlasting covenant,
>   like my steadfast, sure love for David.
>
> – Isaiah 55:1-3

This passage overwhelms me, and in some ways captures the ending of the first part of our journey through the prophets. Certainly, the prophets are full of God's admonitions and calls to obedience, but here God simply invites us to finally be saved from a life of hunger and thirst!

One thing that I know from my work as a psychologist is that, regardless of how bizarre, destructive, or dark a person's choices, that person is always driven by deep hunger. I see people rip their lives to pieces trying to satisfy a longing that cannot be satisfied. There's a lot of talk in contemporary Christianity about "idols." The implication is that if anything in your life has more power to control you than God, it must be an idol. This is not what I see in my office. Though I certainly encounter my share of unrepentant destructive people, what I hear mostly in my clinical work is not people who *desire* to turn their hearts away from God. What I find is people who are so hungry and full of longing, that they become obsessed with finding anything to fill them up in order to *survive*. This is not idolatry; it is a life of starvation. They would try anything to no longer be controlled by their pain and their deprivation. But they hunger and thirst.

So, our God announces like a crier in the town square, "Ho there!! Everybody! Come get what you long for! And it's all free! I've got wine and milk and rich food! There's no need to be hungry anymore!" His desire is not just to restore us, his longing is to make us whole to overflowing. In Hosea 4, he tells us his desire is to "heal" us. Listen to the richness that he wants us to have:

> I will heal their apostasy;
> I will love them freely,
> for my anger has turned from them.
> I will be like the dew to Israel;
> he shall blossom like the lily;
> he shall take root like the trees of Lebanon;
> his shoots shall spread out;
> his beauty shall be like the olive,
> and his fragrance like Lebanon.
> They shall return and dwell beneath my shadow;
> they shall flourish like the grain;
> they shall blossom like the vine;
> their fame shall be like the wine of Lebanon.
> – Hosea 14:4-7

How humbling to hear about his ultimate goal. One might think that after all of his lamentations about his people's sinfulness, that God's goal at the end of the story would be that "my people will all be obedient and righteous." But what he is singing about at the end of the story is not a bunch of good religious people, it is a people who are beautiful and fragrant, flourishing and joyful, "famous" because of how they have been enriched by the "dew" that is Yahweh!

I remain silenced that he has given us the gift of getting to see inside of his heart through the prophets, his heart to bless us and make us his own.

He has plans:

> For I know the plans I have for you, declares Yahweh, plans for welfare and not for evil, to give you a future and a hope. Then you will call upon me and come and pray to me, and I will hear you. You will seek me and find me, when you seek me with all your heart.
> — Jeremiah 29:11-13

This is the promise of God's restoration in the prophets. We have seen him ruthlessly intervene. We've listened as he has brought pain into the lives of his wayward people. And we have seen him use that pain to bring them home. He does not just want things to get back to the status quo. He wants us full and satisfied and richly nourished at his side.

In response to his adventurous, relentless love, and in conclusion of our first chapter on the prophets, what can we do but borrow the simple words of his prophet, (Micah. 7:18)

"Who is a God like you?"

Chapter Eleven

The Prophets II: The Hope of the Redeemer

God asked a lot of the prophets. They brought loads of hideous news to God's people, and sometimes the people literally *did* kill the messenger. They were often alone, hated, even hunted. God tells Isaiah before he begins that, though he will speak a message to the people, they will not listen to him. That's like playing in a ball game after your coach has already told you that you are going to lose! Jeremiah admits at times to deep, even suicidal, misery. (Jer. 20:14-18) Elijah ran away and asked to die. (1 Kings 19:4-5)

These guys were the infantry grunts, coal miners, and garbage men of the Kingdom of God – all the while trying to speak the redemptive poetry of Yahweh. Yet in the context of this thankless, lonely job of being Old Testament prophets, God gives them one of the greatest gifts that he gives anyone in our story: the prophets are given the privilege of unveiling the redeemer of the world.

If you've read this far into the One Story, you know that God has been promising something, someone, for centuries. He began almost immediately in Genesis 3:15, promising a "seed" who would crush the Serpent. He promises Abraham that he would have an "offspring," a son who would be the foundation of God's people. The rest of the One Story has been filled with allusions to some very special person whom God would send. He would be something like the Passover lamb, but he would also be like David, the king. God has been talking about this special One all along, but so far, these promises have remained veiled and symbolic. Now, the prophets are going to turn the lights on. They're going to begin describing this "offspring" of God, and for the first time, we're going to start getting to know him. Who will he be? What will he be like?

He will be a **King**, a **Servant**, a **Sufferer**, and he will bring his **Kingdom** home to us. Let's return to the prophets with an ear to hearing their glorious tale of the coming Messiah (the chosen one). And as we do, remove your sandals again, for the ground upon which we walk is joyfully holy.

The King is Coming

The wonder of the King

Who better to introduce us to the royalty of the redeemer than Isaiah. In chapter 9 of his book, we hear a passage with which all of us are familiar. Listen to it now with the ears we have developed by following our One Story from the beginning. We've been hearing promises of this person throughout centuries of scripture. Now, through Isaiah, God tells us that he will be born, and he will be majestic!

> The people that walked in darkness
> have seen a great light:
> They that dwell in the land of the shadow of death,
> upon them hath the light shined.
> …For unto us a child is born,
> unto us a son is given:
> And the government shall be upon his shoulder:
> And his name shall be called

> Wonderful, Counsellor, The mighty God,
> The everlasting Father, The Prince of Peace.
> Of the increase of his government and peace
> there shall be no end,
> Upon the throne of David, and upon his kingdom,
> To order it, and to establish it
> with judgment and with justice
> From henceforth even forever.
> The zeal of Yahweh of hosts will perform this.
> – Isaiah 9: 2-7

God announces through Isaiah that the One we have awaited, the Seed, will be born and will be a mighty king! He's no longer a shadowy figure; he is the fulfillment of promises we have been given for generations. And he will rule his kingdom with justice and righteousness, forever.

When we began our discussion of the prophets we heard God's declaration to Solomon, calling the kings of Israel to follow him in faithfulness, justice, and righteousness. The reason the prophets arrive on the scene is because so many of those kings failed in honoring God's call. The people have indeed "dwelt in darkness." In the Isaiah 9 passage, God announces that at last a king will come who will reflect the true nature of Yahweh. At last a king will reign with "justice and righteousness." He will even be God himself! He will be called by glorious names: the everlasting Father, the Prince of Peace, and mighty God. One of his names will simply be "Wonderful!" Remember the significance of names to the Hebrews. In Isaiah, God overflows with wonderous names for his coming king. You can almost hear a note of relief and joy in God's voice as he announces this good news, "A son is given! A king is coming! And once he arrives, his reign will just keep growing more and more wonderful!"

THE ONE STORY

And why will this happen? How will it be accomplished? Will it be God's half-hearted concession of grace? A shrugging, reluctant, benediction of kindness? No, it will be accomplished by his *zeal*, his passion, his thrill! "The zeal of Yahweh will accomplish this." (v 7) This is his longing. His deepest desire is to have such a king, and to give this king to us. The zealous passion of Yahweh will accomplish the coming of the Redeemer/King!

In Zechariah 9, the prophet describes the arrival of this monarch.

> Rejoice greatly, O daughter of Zion!
> Shout aloud, O daughter of Jerusalem!
> Behold, your king is coming to you;
> righteous and having salvation is he,
> lowly and mounted on a donkey,
> on a colt, the foal of a donkey.
> I will cut off the chariot from Ephraim
> and the war horse from Jerusalem;
> and the battle bow shall be cut off,
> and he shall speak peace to the nations;
> his rule shall be from sea to sea,
> and from the River to the ends of the earth.
>   – Zechariah 9:9-10

Zecharaiah describes our coming king as one who will bring peace everlasting. In fact, the king announces that he will take away the chariots and the war horses, and proclaim peace to all of the nations. And, I wonder if it is in a beautiful nod to the Noah promise that he declares that even the battle bow (*qeset*, the same Hebrew word from the Noah story) will be broken.

Christ himself obviously has this prophecy in mind when he rides into Jerusalem for the last time. He knows that his most powerful act as our redeemer is upon him, so he enters the city as a king, riding on a donkey.

People often reference his use of a donkey simply as a symbol of his humility, but according to Jewish custom, this was also the traditional means by which a king would be presented. For instance, we are told in 1 Kings 1:33 that as Solomon is crowned king by his father David, he arrives into Jerusalem to the fanfare of trumpets and cries of "Long live King Solomon!" As he is being presented, he is given the noble honor of arriving on David's own donkey. Other passages in the Old Testament (Judges 5:10, 2 Samuel 16:2) also reference donkeys as a symbol of power and royalty. Jesus knew this well, and so did the people. Jesus is coming as a king. And remember what the people proclaim as he arrives. "Hosanna to the son of David: Blessed is he that cometh in the name of the Lord!" (Matt. 21:9) Hosanna means, "Please save us!" And what do they call him? The son of David. They remember God's promise to David and are proclaiming the arrival of the Davidic king. He is king indeed, and if the people had been silent about it, the very stones would have cried out in celebration! (Luke 19:40)

God tells us in Isaiah 11 about how this Redeemer/King will rule (as well as tying him again to his father, David).

> There shall come forth a shoot from the stump of Jesse,
>   and a branch from his roots shall bear fruit.
>   And the Spirit of Yahweh shall rest upon him,
>   the Spirit of wisdom and understanding,
>   the Spirit of counsel and might,
>   the Spirit of knowledge and the fear of Yahweh.
>   And his delight shall be in the fear of Yahweh.
>   He shall not judge by what his eyes see,
>   or decide disputes by what his ears hear,
>   but with righteousness he shall judge the poor,

> and decide with equity for the meek of the earth;
> and he shall strike the earth with the rod of his mouth,
> and with the breath of his lips, he shall kill the wicked.
> Righteousness shall be the belt of his waist,
> and faithfulness the belt of his loins.
> – Isaiah 11:1-5

This king will rule and judge with wisdom and truth. The "fear of Yahweh" will not be something he just possesses; it will *delight* him. Under his hand, even the poor and the powerless will find justice and protection.

We long for a king

You may not know it but you want a king – a *just* king – a *protector* king. Though there is something inside of all of us that instinctively resists the idea of having a sovereign (because we don't like being told what to do), we all long for a world in which justice and goodness reign. Think about what you feel when you read the news. Regardless of your political orientation, you read about the unfairness, injustice and violence of our world, and you feel a disturbance, even an anger at how "wrong" things are. "Someone should make this right!" When you experience this, you are longing for the "rightness" that you were made to recognize. We long for a just king.

In our culture we don't have such a king, so we try to create one. Why do you think legends and epics of great heros are woven throughout our literature and culture, stories of wise and powerful kings who finally bring peace to the land? Why are we consumed with disappointment and criticism of our current leaders? Why are we obsessed with super hero movies?

Psychologically speaking, humans will serve some sovereign. We are creatures oriented toward bending our lives to something bigger than us. God created us to live in service to our holy king, but we are all drawn to lesser kings, lesser gods. Sometimes we live controlled by what others think of us. Sometimes it is a compulsive drive that causes us to bend to knee: money, work, porn, gossip, success, even family. (I think my personal favorite is to simply serve *myself!*) But humans are formed to submit to someone/something bigger than ourselves. And if that thing is something other than our God and King, we will very quickly find ourselves slaves.

I broke my iPhone at about 7 pm one evening. Desperate, I immediately booked a "genius" appointment with the iPhone store, threw on clothes and bolted out of the house. As I careened toward my "salvation," I wondered if there was anything else that might drive me to so urgently put aside everything I was doing and leave the house in the middle of a restful evening. Would the need of a friend evoke such devotion? The cause of caring for orphans and widows? I grimaced at what a slave I was to this "thing." Humans will serve someone, something. But the things we serve will always take from us. *They* will own *us*. God is the only sovereign who will respond to our submission by lifting us up and setting us free. He will always give back to us more than we give to him.

What our hearts really long for is the power and wisdom of our just and loving God and king. Yahweh knows this. He created you to need such wisdom and protection in your life. I believe that even now, as we finally drop our grandiose attempts to be our own "king" and submit to our true Lord, we will be surprised at what a relief it will be. God's people were formed to live under his lordship, and when we do so, we are living in our truest home, under our King as we were created to live at Eden.

In the prophets, Yahweh promises that his King will one day sit on the throne and finally reign. Oppression will finally be stopped. Your servanthood will cease to be slavery and become a warm position of belonging to your Lord. And as he reigns, we are told that the weak will at last be protected. A way will be cleared through the wilderness. The valleys of your life shall be lifted up, and the rough places will be made smooth. (Isa. 40:4) He will delight in making your once-painful life rich and whole.

He is the Prince of Peace.

The Servant

Since the beginning, God has sought a people who would humble themselves and follow him. And since the beginning, his people have consistently refused to do so. But God promises us in the prophets that a *servant* is coming who will fully submit to Yahweh and delight him fully. Again, he tells us about him in Isaiah:

> Behold my servant, whom I uphold,
> my chosen one, in whom my soul delights;
> I have put my Spirit upon him;
> he will bring forth justice to the nations.
> He will not cry aloud or lift up his voice,
> or make it heard in the street;
> a bruised reed he will not break,
> and a faintly burning wick he will not quench;
> he will faithfully bring forth justice.
> He will not grow faint or be discouraged
> till he has established justice in the earth;
> and the coastlands wait for his law.
> – Isaiah 42:1-4

This servant will bear God's Spirit and tirelessly serve him. But the passage also tells us that Yahweh's servant won't just honor God; he will also be a gift to *us*. We are told that this tender one will step down from his royal throne and cradle us in our brokenheartedness. He knows that we sometimes feel as if we cannot go on, like a candle that is barely flickering, battered and bruised. God promises us that the Servant/King will never grow faint or weary in his care for us. In other words, the promised one will be more than a king who finally brings peace, order, and righteousness. He will also have the kind of heart that will look upon the "bruised reeds" among us, and tenderly reach down to care for us.

Throughout the prophets, I love how God refers to this individual as "my servant." This is a little bit of a jab at the people of Israel. If you flip through the prophets, you will hear God routinely calling Israel "his servant" or "my servant, Israel." That phrase is often unpleasantly followed by statements like, "my servant who has turned from me," or "my servant has forsaken their first love."

This servant, however, he invites us to behold. This servant will delight Yahweh's soul and will bring forth justice. He will never grow faint nor be discouraged. God's desire for the Servant who will follow him perfectly will finally be realized. He will delight in his Promised One!

The gift of the Servant

Can you imagine what that must have been like for Christ, the righteous servant of God, to experience the Father's delight in him. We are given one of the most beautiful moments in the New Testament as we witness Jesus being baptized by John the Baptist, and the voice of the Father himself proclaims to the world his joy in his son. "This is my son, whom I love; in him I am well pleased." (Matt. 3:17) Can you imagine the joy that Jesus felt hearing that? If you can, keep imagining, because you can feel God's delight as well!

Remember the principle of substitution? Well, it doesn't just apply to Christ's sacrifice and payment for our sin. It all so applies to the substitution of *righteousness*. One of the deepest gifts that the Servant will give his people is that he will let us partake in the delight that Yahweh has in *him*! His Father is deeply pleased in his servant's perfect obedience, "In him my soul delights!" (v. 1) And when he arrives, the Servant of Yahweh will come and cover *us* in the mantle of that perfect faithfulness to God. When we belong to Christ, we get to appear before the Father as a pure and righteous servant – just like him! Now we can delight Yahweh as well! Because of God's beautifully obedient servant, the Father can now look upon us, his often-failing servants, and only see the glory of this gentle, tireless, delightful Servant. *Somehow God will look at us and see him!* Then God will say about even us, "Behold my servant, whom I uphold, my chosen one, in whom my soul delights."

Imagine with me again. Imagine what it will feel like to look into the Father's eyes and not see the disappointment or anger that we often expect. What will it be like to see him look at you and delight in you, to finally see that you bring him joy!? *"You delight my soul!"* On that day we will be wearing the mantle of the Perfect One. He will present us pure before his Father. (Jude 1:24)

The bringer of good news

The tenderness and the humility of the promised servant was apparently deeply meaningful to Jesus, and quoting the prophets was actually one of Jesus's favorite ways to describe himself.

One of my favorite examples of this occurs in Luke 4:16-21, when Jesus is visiting his hometown church in Nazareth. He is given the opportunity to read the scripture for the day, and he chooses one about *himself!* The passage is from Isaiah 61.

THE PROPHETS II: THE HOPE OF THE REDEEMER

Imagine the scene. Jesus takes the scroll, stands up (as was the custom of his day). He opens his mouth, begins to speak, and this is what he says:

> The Spirit of Yahweh is upon me,
> because Yahweh has anointed me
> to bring good news to the poor;
> he has sent me to bind up the brokenhearted,
> to proclaim liberty to the captives,
> and the opening of the prison to those who are bound;
> to proclaim the year of Yahweh's favor,
> and the day of vengeance of our God;
> to comfort all who mourn;
> to grant to those who mourn in Zion –
> to give them a beautiful headdress instead of ashes,
> the oil of gladness instead of mourning,
> the garment of praise instead of a faint spirit;
> that they may be called oaks of righteousness,
> the planting of Yahweh, that he may be glorified.
> – Isaiah 61:1-3

Then Jesus rolls up the scroll, hands it back to the attendant, and says these words: "Today, this scripture has been fulfilled in your hearing." In response, those in attendance try to throw him off a cliff for blasphemy. It was apparent to them what Jesus was claiming: "I am the chosen Servant/King of Yahweh. I am the one who comes to bring the healing that has been promised for centuries."

I love that of all the passages in the scriptures, Jesus chose to read this one. I mean, he could have picked anything! I wonder if he thought, "How do I best capture for my people who I really am? What is it that I want them most to know about me? Should I read Isaiah 9 about how I will rule forever? How about Psalm 118 and its declaration that I will be the chief cornerstone of my Father's new kingdom? No – I want them to know my heart. I want them to know that as I walk among them, my deepest longing is to set them free from heartbreak and bondage; that I desire to reach into every one of their hurting hearts and bring them joy. They are imprisoned by sin they can't resist. They mourn because this world hurts so much. And I want these broken people to know that I have come specifically for them. I am their liberator. I come to give them flowers and garlands and sweet oil. I have come that they might have life abundant. And I do these things not just to bring them relief. I come because, if they receive these things from me, they will not just be happy; they will not just be obedient; they will become 'oaks of righteousness,' grand powerful images of Yahweh himself, just like he has wanted from the beginning."

Behold the Servant/Redeemer of Israel!

The Sufferer

The one who suffers for us

The Horror

The prophets reveal for us that the Chosen One will be wondrous in his power to rule, heal, and to bring life to his people. This announcement came as no surprise to God's people. Especially after the covenant with David, they looked toward a future that would be ruled by a holy king. "Of course," they thought, "he will be wonderful, a Prince of Peace, like unto God himself."

But then the prophets throw us a curveball. They begin to tell us about his *suffering*. This promised one will also be called the *Ebed Yahweh*, the "Suffering Servant of God." And the Hebrew people hardly knew what to do with this fact.

Zechariah begins to describe him.

> And I will pour out on the house of David and the inhabitants of Jerusalem a spirit of grace and pleas for mercy, so that, when they look on me, on him whom they have pierced, they shall mourn for him, as one mourns for an only child, and weep bitterly over him, as one weeps over a firstborn. – Zechariah 12:10

Hear the Father's voice here. He says he will enable the people to see the horror they have committed against the Sacrificed One. They will mourn as they see his death, like watching the death of one's own child. Again, Yahweh welcomes us into his own heart, for we know that the Father himself certainly wept bitterly over the death of his firstborn.

I believe that some of the most gloriously heartbreaking images of the Suffering Servant are given to us in Isaiah 53.

> Who has believed what he has heard from us?
> And to whom has the arm of Yahweh been revealed?
> For he grew up before him like a tender shoot,
> like a root out of dry ground;
> he had no form or majesty that we should look at him,
> and no beauty that we should desire him.
> He was despised and rejected by men,
> a man of sorrows and acquainted with grief;
> and as one from whom men hide their faces
> he was despised, and we esteemed him not.
> – Isaiah 53:1-3

What is the first thing that comes to your mind when you try to describe someone? What stands out to you? Somehow, the first thing that Isaiah reaches for is that this precious one would live a life in which he is despised; that grief and rejection would be his constant companions; that he would be so brutalized that you and I would want to look away. "Like one from whom men hide their faces." (v. 3)

This is your savior. And Isaiah invites us to not shield our eyes, but to look upon him and witness the horror:

> Surely he has borne our griefs
> and carried our sorrows;
> yet we esteemed him stricken,
> smitten by God, and afflicted.
> But he was pierced for our transgressions;
> he was crushed for our iniquities;
> upon him was the chastisement that brought us peace,
> and with his wounds we are healed.
> All we like sheep have gone astray;
> we have turned – every one – to his own way;
> and Yahweh has laid the iniquity of us all
> on him.
> – Isaiah 53:4-6

The message of the Messiah's suffering, borne for us, is obvious and disturbing in this passage, and to push the point even deeper, Isaiah lays it out in a poetic style that reminds us repeatedly that Christ is our advocate, our substitute. Notice how the poem is laid out in couplets, in pairs. The principle of substitution is again graphically portrayed: *He* is here for *us*.

- *He* was pierced for *our* transgressions.
- *He* was crushed for *our* iniquities.
- By *his* wounds, *we* are healed.
- Like sheep, *we* have gone astray.
- But God lays the iniquity of *us* all on *him*.

Back and forth. Back and forth. Us and Christ. Christ and us. God is driving home that this sacrificial savior has come for *you and me*.

In the midst of this imagery of the Suffering One's sacrifice, there is a feature of verse 6 that has always made my heart feel full and courageous. In our English Bible, verse 6 reads, "and Yahweh has laid the iniquity of us all on him." Another translation reads, "and Yahweh has made the iniquity of us all *to fall on* him." The Hebrew word used here for "fall" is the word *paga*, and it can also be translated as "to meet" or "to encounter."

In other words, this passage could be translated thusly: "And Yahweh has caused the iniquity of us all to *encounter him*." I love this twist on the passage, and believe it is full of hope for us all. If you are like me, you often feel defeated by your sin. How can we ever be a match for its power? Well, I love to remember Isaiah 53:6, and speak back to the forces that can so easily defeat me, saying, "You think you can beat me? You probably can. But now it's time for you to *encounter him*! Encounter the warrior of Israel. He is the Lord of all life and glory! You don't just deal with me anymore. You must encounter him, my savior. Then you will encounter the end of your story, crushed beneath his feet!"

In the midst of this graphic description of the suffering of the Christ, we are reminded what it all was for. In his deepest humiliation and death, he destroys our greatest foe.

Our sin encounters the very Son of God!

Somehow, horror and wonder at the same time

As the Isaiah passage continues, telling us about the warrior who is our sacrificial lamb, we will hear an announcement that stuns me completely. The prophet says,

> He was oppressed, and he was afflicted,
> yet he opened not his mouth;
> Like a lamb that is led to the slaughter,
> and like a sheep that before its shearers is silent,
> So he opened not his mouth…
> *But Yahweh was pleased to crush him;*
> *putting him to grief.*
> – Isaiah 53:7-10

We are told that the Lamb of God, Yahweh's Suffering Servant, is silent. The Lamb submits to his slaughter. And then we are given verse 10, words I can barely comprehend. Isaiah literally says that "Yahweh was *pleased* to crush him." I've been studying this passage for years and I am silenced by it every time I read it. What could it possibly mean?

To understand the gravity of this phrase, we have to get theologically technical for a moment (I apologize, but trust me here).

During my seminary days, my professor R.C. Sproul seemed to delight in ambushing us with impossible theology questions. One day, he mounted his lectern in class and practically assaulted us with the following inquiry:

"Gentlemen," he said. "Who killed Jesus Christ?"

One eager student's hand shot up (we knew he was toast).

"It was 'wicked men,' sir. Like Peter says in Acts 2."

"True, but not completely. Try again," Dr. Sproul intoned, looking for another hapless volunteer.

"It was his own people! The Jews who rejected their Messiah," tried another student.

"In a sense, yes," Sproul remarked with disappointment. "But that's not the ultimate answer. Come on, gentlemen! Read your Old Testament!"

Silence was the only other answer he received from us that day as we cowered under his impatient gaze.

He finally uttered just one phrase:

"God the Father."

Stunned, our silence grew even more weighty.

"Let me ask you the question in a different way," he continued. "To whom was the eternal debt of death owed? Who lived for centuries demanding a capital sentence and a sacrifice for the sins that had been committed against him? Who was the one whose holiness could only be satisfied by the death of one who was pure and righteous? *God the Father* is the one whose justice stood waiting to be satisfied since Eden. And ultimately, *God* is the one whose justice demanded the life of Jesus. *God* was the one who called in the debt that had hung over the lives of his people for centuries. And, so, gentlemen, it was *God himself* who ultimately took the life of his only son so that he would never have to take ours."

He then simply left the classroom silently. There was nothing more important that he could ever say. No one said a word.

Here is what Robert Charles Sproul wanted us to never forget that day. Remember the vicious wrath of Yahweh that we have read about from Noah through the prophets? We've cringed as we've wondered how he could bring such destruction on his own people. Sproul wanted every one of *us* to cringe that day about the fact that the same God ultimately brought the full weight of that same wrath down upon his own son – so that you and I would *never ever* experience it.

And here is the part I want you to let into your deepest soul as you hear God speak in Isaiah 53:10: God loves us so much that somehow, this sacrifice is what he *wanted*. "He was *pleased* to crush him."

The Hebrew word that is used here for "pleased" is the word *chaphets*. Here are some of the other instances of it in the Old Testament:

When Saul favors David, he sends a messenger saying, "The king *delights* in you." (1 Sam. 18:22)

The queen of Sheba visits Solomon and says, "Blessed be Yahweh, your God, who has *delighted* in you and set you on the throne of Israel!" (1 Kings 10:9)

Earlier in his book, Isaiah tells us that "Yahweh was *pleased*, for his righteousness' sake, to magnify his law and make it glorious." (Isa. 42:21)

Shockingly, these passages speak of *chaphets* as a desire and a favoring of something, a wish. Somehow, though I imagine Yahweh's agony at the death of his son rippled the foundations of the galaxy, his love for us is so great that if "crushing" his beloved son was what was required to bring us into his arms, inconcievably, it "pleased" him to do so.

I have no adequate response to this except to fall to my knees.

Perhaps Job's response to God is the only appropriate option.

He simply says,

> Behold, I am insignificant; what can I reply to you? I lay my hand on my mouth. Once I have spoken, and now I will say no more. – Job 40:4

The wonder and the reward

Somehow, it was the Father's desire to sacrifice his son for us. And if there could possibly be even more amazing news – Jesus *felt the same way!* His death for us was his longing as well.

Let me ask you another theology question: why did Jesus die on the cross for us? Why would he be willing to do such a thing? What motivated his heart? Isaiah 53 goes on to tell us.

> When his soul makes an offering for guilt,
> he shall *see his offspring*;
> he shall prolong his days;
> the will of Yahweh shall prosper in his hand.
> Out of the anguish of his soul *he shall see and be satisfied.*
> – Isaiah 53:10-11

Isaiah tells us that Christ's motivation for sacrificing himself was that doing so would allow him to "see his *offspring.*" And that when he sees them, "he will be *satisfied!*"

What is God telling us here through Isaiah? What does this mean?

God is declaring that the reason that Jesus was willing to lay down his life was because he longed for his "offspring," the people whose lives he purchased through his death.

Christ died because he wanted *us!*

We are Christ's reward for his sacrifice. We are his inheritance. Christ dies that he might finally be made "the firstborn among many brethren." (Rom. 8:29) He is willing to be pierced and forsaken so that he can be surrounded by his beloved ones. His reward is that, in the end, he gets to gather *us all* to himself!

Paul points at this in Ephesians 1:18, when he says, "I pray that your hearts will be flooded with light so that you can understand the confident hope he has given to those he called – his holy people *who are his rich and glorious inheritance.*"

Paul is reaching back to Isaiah 53 and praying that we would see this. He wants us to know that *we* are that gift that Christ receives for his sacrifice. Somehow, incomprehensibly, we are his inheritance; we are his reward.

The shepherd may go out to seek one lost sheep, but at the cross the Messiah seeks *all* of his sheep! Jesus tells us in Luke that when that shepherd finds his one lost sheep, he puts it over his shoulders, goes home and tells all of his friends, and they all rejoice! (Luke 15: 4-7)

If the shepherd rejoices like that at the gathering of just one of his sheep, what must have been the joy of Christ on Easter morning? And what will be his tears of joy on the day when he gathers all of us into his arms? Our precious shepherd will one day gather all of his offspring, and indeed we will all rejoice.

The one who suffers with us

The sufferings of the promised Seed are the fountainhead of our redemption. His death pours forth the fruit of life to all who belong to him. But his deep acquaintance with suffering offers another layer of blessing to us.

He suffers not just as our redeemer; he also suffers daily as our friend. He is *with* us in our pain!

"Where was God when this injustice was done to me?" "Why is God letting this happen?" These kinds of questions are asked of me by countless clients in my office. They are questions I too have asked, especially after the unexpected death of my brother at a young age. Where was God? If he is sovereign, couldn't he have stopped this horror? Does he not care? Is he not strong enough to protect his children? We have not shied away from hard questions in this book, and this is one of the hardest. Where is God in our suffering?

Gratefully, like many of the problems that we have regarding God and his place in our lives, I believe that Yahweh has "struggled" with this issue, too. He gave his children the freedom to choose death, and we did so. His response? He immediately began working to solve the problem of the pain that we all endure.

It is a very difficult problem.

So difficult, in fact, that the best solution that God could create to solve it involved the *death of his own son!* That's how big a problem this broken, painful world is. It required a solution that brutal and that horrifying.

The sufferings of our Lord Jesus that we just witnessed in Isaiah were to purchase a redemption for us from the deep pain of our lives. However, it will take centuries for that brilliant, brutal solution to fully heal our sorrows. One day it will. On that day, at the dawn of our new lives, Christ will stand victorious, and death will at last be destroyed. Love will win. Death will die. Pain will be destroyed. (Rev. 21)

In the meantime, we all suffer.

And here is the incalculable gift – so does our Lord.

In the Suffering Christ, we have a Servant who pays for our redemption, but we also have a brother who knows the pain of our lives. He never leaves our side. He grievously knows death and rejection and loss and hopelessness. He knows every bit of it. He feels it. And he is *with you.*

Where is God in our suffering? Though he is deeply powerful and sovereign, he is also somehow our *fellow sufferer*. I believe he is at your side even now, and feels your pain as intensely as you do, perhaps even more so. Even as he is at work to bring you life everlasting, he stoops down to hold you in the darkest sorrow and endure your pain at your side.

That means that he knew what it was like when you were abused. He felt it. He knows the loneliness and rejection you experience since your spouse left you. He feels it with you – today! He touches the fears you have in the middle of the night about money or illness. And of course, our heavenly Father personally knows the heartbreak of losing a child.

God is not some detached deity dispassionately observing the sufferings of mankind from a lofty heavenly throne. For some reason we will never fathom, until his full redemption is accomplished, he chooses to suffer *with* us. I believe that God loves us so much that, though he is sovereign, he voluntarily choses to daily expose himself to all of our pain.

So, where is God in your suffering? *He is hurting with you!*

There is a startling scene in C.S. Lewis's book *The Magician's Nephew* that paints a picture of God's abiding presence with us in our sorrows. In it, the young boy Digory chooses to obey Aslan's command to bring him an apple that can restore life to Narnia. Digory also knows, however, that if he steals a second apple, it could heal his dying mother. In a heartbreaking moment, Digory obeys Aslan, and presents just the one apple to the Lion, knowing that doing so dooms his mother to death.

Then Digory starts to cry. But as he does, he dares to look up into the Lion's powerful face and is shocked to see that "great shining tears stood in the Lion's eyes. They were such big, bright tears compared with Digory's own that for a moment he felt as if the Lion must really be sorrier about his mother than he was himself."

"My son, my son," the Lion replies. "I know. Grief is great. Only you and I in this land know that yet. Let us be good to one another."[5]

This is where our King/Servant/Suffering Redeemer lives – in the *midst* of our pain *with us*. "For we do not have a high priest who is unable to empathize with our weaknesses." (Heb. 4:15) He knows our sorrow and he calls us "my son, my son" as he hurts alongside us. He is our fellow sufferer, living the agony of our current broken lives, day by day, moment by moment – at our sides. And because he suffers, we will never suffer alone. As David says to the Redeemer who cradles him in his anguish,

> You keep track of all my sorrows. You have collected all my tears in your bottle. You have recorded each one in your book.
> – Psalm 56:8

And beyond all of this, don't forget that this is the One Story. The Seed was promised; the Seed has come. The Serpent has been crushed. And because our Redeemer suffered at Calvary, he will one day crush all suffering under his feet.

In other words, we must *also* remember that suffering is not the end of our story!

Thy kingdom come

The prophets have taken us inside the heart of God; we have heard *his* words. Through the prophets, God has opened himself to us, be it about his wrath, his restoration, or his promised one. But there is one last treasure that he will unveil to us through his powerful, poetic messengers. God is going to give us a glimpse into the *treasured Kingdom that his Messiah has purchased for us.* Let's look again at the future God promises through the prophets, but this time with a view toward the future of our *hearts* with his!

When we told the story of Abraham, we heard one of God's favorite songs, a refrain he sings again and again throughout his relationship with his people. He tells Abraham, "I will establish my covenant between me and you and your offspring after you, throughout the generations for an everlasting covenant (and here it is) ... *to be a God to you and to your offspring after you.*" (Gen. 17:7)

Remember when God introduces himself to Moses on Mount Horeb? What does he say? He says, "I will take *you to be my people, and I will be your God.*" (Ex. 6:7) This is God's great Song of the Covenant, and he sings it with growing intensity throughout scripture. And in the prophets, he is going to add deeper harmony to its refrain.

Through the prophet Ezekiel, he promises to restore his people, and the tone of his song gets even richer. He begins to speak to all of us, his people down through the ages, and he promises to transform our very hearts, so that we might be more deeply his and he might be more deeply ours.

> And I will give you a new heart, and a new spirit I will put within you. And I will remove the heart of stone from your flesh and give you a heart of flesh. And I will put my Spirit within you and cause you to walk in my statutes and be careful to obey my way. You shall dwell in the land that I gave to your fathers, *and you shall be my people, and I will be your God.*
>
> – Ezekiel 36:26-28

If you really listen to him here, you will realize that this is your wildest dream come true! Think about it: where do Christians struggle most in their spiritual lives? When I speak with God's people, they struggle with a longing to feel closer to God, and they ache with a constant sense of failure at conquering sin and brokenness in their lives. Where is that warmth and belonging they have searched for with God? Why are they locked in lonely hurtful choices? They long and are unsatisfied. They are exhausted.

I grow tired of the ubiquity of messages that just entreat Christians to work harder to serve God and devote themselves to better obedience to him. If you really talk to Christians, you find that the problem is not that they don't want to be close to God, nor that they wish to disobey him. The problem isn't that they don't care. *The problem is that they feel so utterly defeated by trying and failing.* They are tired of longing for the warmth and joy that could come from walking at God's side and yet instead feeling empty. They are tired of finding themselves standing back in the middle of the cesspool of their own sinfulness, regardless of how hard they have tried to get out. Most of the Christians I know are not purposing to be disobedient, they are weary and frightened.

So God speaks to us frustrated, battered Christians in Ezekiel 36. He says, "Guess what! One day, because of my promised Redeemer, I will remove that exhausting stubborn heart of yours that is so inclined to make destructive choices, and you will run to me. In its place, I will give you a soft, warm heart of flesh that is surrounded by my Spirit. And guess what else? I'm going to give you that joyful intimate relationship with me that you long for. The one in which we can use possessive pronouns with one another. You will be *mine*, and I will be *yours*. And I will make it feel natural for you to follow my way. In those days, you will walk into life and love as naturally and as easily as you currently walk into failure and defeat. I promise!"

The Messiah's coming was not just to satisfy God's wrath, it was to finally make possible a rich belonging with our Father – our hearts with his heart!

When God speaks to us again about this joyful future in Jeremiah, he pulls out all the stops.

> Behold, the days are coming, declares Yahweh, when I will make a new covenant with the house of Israel and the house of Judah, not like the covenant that I made with their fathers on the day when I took them by the hand to bring them out of the land of Egypt, my covenant that they broke, though I was a husband to them, declares Yahweh. For this is the covenant that I will make with the house of

> Israel after those days:
> I will put my law within them, and I will write it on their hearts. And I will be their God, and they will be my people. And no longer will each one teach his neighbor and each his brother, saying, 'Know Yahweh,' for they shall all know me, from the least of them to the greatest, declares Yahweh. For I will forgive their iniquity, and I will remember their sin no more.
>
> – Jerimiah 31:31-34

Do you want closeness with God? God promises that as he begins to write his name on our hearts, we will no longer have to say to one another "know Yahweh" because everyone will know him – in that deep Hebrew sense of knowing that we keep talking about. God promises that in his future kingdom, everyone will have that kind of intimacy with him. In fact, in Isaiah, God makes this treasure even more extensive. He says that, in that day "the earth shall be full of the *knowledge* of Yahweh as the waters cover the sea." (Isa. 11:9)

That's *a lot* of knowing!

Rejoice in what awaits you because of this King, this Servant, this Sufferer. God promises in the prophets a belonging and connection with him that is as deep and wide as the very oceans themselves. And you can swim as long and as hard as you might in any and every direction and you will never find the end of it.

And who is it who promises these things to you?

Thus says **Yahweh**,
who gives the sun for light by day,
and the fixed order of the moon and
the stars for light by night,
Who stirs up the sea so that its waves roar.

Yahweh of hosts is his name.
– Jeremiah 31:35

Indeed, it is!

He is the God who is aggressively at work to find his people. He began at Eden and has been growing this promise ever since. In the prophets, he shares with us his heart and his promise of the Redeemer, and he will never stop until he and his people are reunited.

And next, we will finally get to meet this Promised One!!

Chapter Twelve

The Teller of all Stories

> *God, after he spoke long ago to the fathers in the prophets in many portions and in many ways, in these last days he has spoken to us in his Son, whom he appointed heir of all things, through whom also he made the world.*
> *– Hebrews 1:1-2*

The prophets have filled our hearts with images of the coming Messiah, and our story now moves to the richness and wonder of actually seeing him arrive on earth. But before we explore all of the work and glory of Jesus the Seed, come take a little walk with me.

This book has been my attempt to tell you the One Story of Jesus as he is promised and unfolded throughout the Bible. As rich as that journey may have been, imagine what would it be like to have heard *Jesus himself* walk us through the One Story; for him to teach us the ways that the Bible has been the story of his coming.

I can think of at least two people who actually got that privilege.

My father-in-law was a real lover of history. A game he liked to play was to ask, "If you could visit any time or event in history, where would you go?" (I think he always wanted to visit Versailles during the reign of Louis XIV. He also wanted to meet Marlena Dietrich.) Now that you have read eleven chapters of this book, perhaps you can guess where I would like to be.

The time: Around 33 A.D.

The place: Walking along a dusty road about seven miles from Jerusalem with my friend Cleopas.

As we traveled that road together, we saw a stranger ahead. As we got closer, he asked if he could join us, "I'm headed to Emmaus, boys. Mind if I tag along?"

Despite the fact that we were still heartbroken and confused by the events of the last few days, we welcomed him. He noticed how disturbed we both were and inquired as to what had happened. Cleopas looked at him with amazement and said something like, "Are you the only person in the world who hasn't heard what has happened this week in Jerusalem?" Our new friend's silence invited us to explain.

Cleopas continued. "It's all about Jesus of Nazareth. He was a prophet, great in word and deed, but the chief priests and rulers delivered him up to be executed like a common criminal. This is so devastating to us because we had hoped he was the One who had been promised throughout the whole of scripture. We had hoped he was going to be the Christ (the Messiah). But since he was killed three days ago, we have been without hope. Furthermore, we just heard that some of the women who followed Jesus went to honor him at his tomb and found that he was gone! And not only did they not find *him* in his tomb, they found *angels*! We went to see ourselves, and indeed his body was gone. Now we don't know what to think."

Then this stranger spoke to us. He said, "O foolish ones, and slow of heart to believe all that the prophets have spoken! Was it not necessary that the Christ should suffer these things and enter into his glory? *And beginning with Moses and all the prophets, he interpreted to us in all the scriptures the things concerning the Messiah."* (Luke 24: 25-27)

He told us everything!

He explained how everything we read in Moses (our Torah), as well as the prophets – all spoke of him! Our hearts burned within us as he spoke.

And here is my best recollection of what he said:

In the beginning, I was God. In fact, even now as I walk with you, *I AM*. I was also *with* God. My dear apostle, John, will get this quite correct when he writes his gospel a few years from now. The word that John will use to describe our oneness together will be the Greek word *pros*, speaking of an intimacy beyond imagination – a face-to-face, breath to breath belonging. The Father, the Spirit, and I swirled in this joy for eternity.

Then we created. Why? That's not the right question. The correct question is how could we *not*? Beauty and wonder, intricacy and life are as intrinsic to us as "wetness" is to water. You would expect water to make you wet. Likewise, you would expect a God who is *Life itself* to spin out a universe that brims with dazzling beauty and love.

All that was good and elegant and alive in us just flowed forth during that season. As the Father began to speak the universe into existence and the Spirit brooded over the waters, I was the "craftsman at his side," the one that Solomon talks about in Proverbs 8. I was his delight (the word literally refers to a frolic and a playfulness) day after day, rejoicing always in his presence, overflowing with joy in the world we were making, and even more so at man in our image. It was wonderful! (Aside from a minor glitch in which we realized that the man was alone – a problem we quickly remedied. I mean, we were never alone, so how could it be good for someone in our image to be?)

And it was all "very good."

But it was here that things began to get painful. Our precious children turned from us. We gave them everything, but they wanted to take more. And not only did this shatter their lives, it shattered our relationship with them as well. It also created an enormous problem for us.

We wanted mankind with all of our heart, but Adam and Eve's betrayal and rebellion created death for them – separation from us and from each other. So what were we supposed to do? If we brought righteous judgment against their rejection of us, then justice could be restored to the universe, but we would lose our beloved children – they would be destroyed. We wanted our children back, but the death penalty for their destruction had to be satisfied somehow.

It was then that we began to unfold our plan. It went something like this: Death would come, but not on that day and not to our children. Instead, the Father and I made a choice that would shatter our hearts. He would bring his just wrath down upon *me*, his most beloved son. I would die in their place.

We decided that we would develop this plan over the centuries. God would not allow our children's betrayal to ultimately destroy the wonderful relationship with them that we had created. We would start rebuilding it. Small at first, but ever-growing, always building toward the day in which we would have our beloved ones back in our arms. But in doing so, we were also building toward the day upon which my own Father would turn his back on me.

Throughout what you know as "history," the Father has been hinting, predicting, and foreshadowing my coming. He immediately told our rebellious children about me in the garden. He called me the "seed of the woman," and talked about how I would be bruised, but he also declared that I would destroy the Destroyer.

Years later, when the earth was filled with people, their evil became so destructive that the Father had to act. His heart so rejoiced in life and purity that he could not permit man's cruelty and hatred to go unchecked – and his solution was eminently destructive. But I was the Ark that carried God's people safe within, protecting them from the death that surrounded them on every side. When the destruction had ended, God promised that from then on, his approach to our children would no longer be this kind of ultimate, consuming judgment. In fact, he hung his "battle bow" in the sky as a promise to no longer use it against mankind. And there it hung for centuries – until just last week, when he picked up his bow again and brought it to bear against *my* heart, piercing me for the judgment that was due our people; crushing me with the same vengeance that had destroyed the world. We worked so hard to protect our treasured children.

The next big step in our plan involved a man name Abram. We decided that it would be through him that we would build our new family. We made a solemn vow, a covenant with Abram, pledging the very life of God that we would never betray our people. We kept our promise completely. Nevertheless, I was still to be killed, not because we broke our promise, but because Abram and his children broke theirs. It was I alone who walked the covenant pieces. And it was I alone who was slain.

Abraham (we changed Abram's name) and Sarah were unable to have children, which was a problem if they were to be the beginning of an entire family/nation. God promised them that a very special son would be given to them. And when the Father made good on his promise, the boy Isaac, brought laughter to us all. I was the Son who would ultimately bring the greatest joy. As I told the Pharisees a couple of years ago, 'Your father Abraham rejoiced to see my day. And he saw it and was glad." (John 8:56) Abraham's belief that this son would somehow be *the* Son was what reckoned him as righteous and pure in our eyes. His faith in me is what healed his relationship with us.

And when God called Abraham to sacrifice that firstborn son in obeisance to him, Yahweh "saw to it." He saw to it that I was there, the ram in the bushes who was killed instead of Isaac. And last Friday, the true Father sacrificed his Son, his only Son, the one whom he loved, on one of those same hills. I was the Son not spared, so that you, like Isaac, might always be safe and loved.

We kept our promises to Abraham, and to his sons, grandsons, and great grandsons. But even our chosen people were often faithless and cruel. At one point, Joseph's brothers sold him into slavery in Egypt, but what they meant for evil, we meant for good. Famine struck and the whole family ended up moving to Egypt and staying there. As a result, they lived surrounded and protected by an invincible world power while they grew into a great nation.

About 400 years later, things turned ugly for our people in Egypt. The Israelites were no longer immigrants; they became prisoners and slaves. This was intolerable to us, so God sent a man named Moses to deliver the people from bondage. I am the new Moses, the one who "draws out." Our whole story is about freeing our people from slavery. Israel was enslaved to Egypt, you are enslaved to sin and to death. And I am the liberator of my people!

We delivered the people by bringing upon the Egyptians the hand of death to take the lives of every firstborn. But the firstborn of Israel was spared because I was also the Lamb who was sacrificed in their stead. Yahweh's hand of judgment and death saw *my* blood on the lintels and door posts of the Hebrew homes – and they were passed over, spared, because I was not.

After we freed our people from Egypt, as they wandered in the wilderness, I was the Bread of Life, new every morning. I was the stone which poured forth water for their thirst. I was the bronze serpent, lifted up to heal my people. And as the Law was given to Israel for the first time, it pointed to me. Our desire has always been for our people to share our image. With the Law, we wanted to begin forming them again into our likeness. Our Law showed them how. However, we knew they would chronically fail at keeping it. That's why I had to come and keep it perfectly. If you want to really understand the Law, look at how I live. When you fail at perfectly keeping the Law, know that I have already done it for you.

I was every lamb, every goat, and every bull that was later slain in the temple for the forgiveness of sin. We created a way of *substitution*, wherein someone else could die to pay for your sins. I am that Substitute. I "offered one sacrifice for sin for all time and will sit down at the right hand of God." (Heb. 10:12) I will soon ascend to that throne and *sit down* – because my work is "finished."

When David pursued God, he was a reflection of how I love the Father. I am the one who lives most deeply "after God's own heart." (1 Sam 13:14) I am also the royal fulfillment of God's promise to David; I will reign on the throne of David forever! And when David sang, he often sang of me. I am the king's Lord in Psalm 110, my enemies and those of my beloved people, will be my "footstool." I am the bridegroom king in Psalm 45. I am the resurrected one in Psalm 16.

To the prophets I was not just a king; I was "Wonderful, Counselor, mighty God, eternal Father, Prince of Peace." But I am also the Servant of Yahweh who alone obeys him fully. I was despised and forsaken, pierced and crushed. I took your suffering and will always suffer at your side, until every bit of pain, sorrow and death has been crushed under my feet. And one day I will be enthroned to rule with a rod of iron (unyielding, protective lordship), and of my Kingdom there will be no end.

When the days of my coming to earth had finally arrived, Zechariah, the father of John the Baptist, understood who I was. Once he got his voice back, he spoke about me, and he knew I was the fulfillment of our promises to Abraham, Moses, David, and the prophets. He said things like, "Blessed be the Lord God of *Israel* (*Jacob*), for he has visited us and accomplished redemption for his people, and has raised up a horn of salvation for us in the house of *David* his servant… as he spoke by the mouth of his holy *prophets* from of old … to show mercy toward our fathers, and to remember his holy covenant, the oath which he swore to *Abraham* our father." (Luke 1:68-73) He knew our story from beginning to end!

And when our angel Gabriel told my mother that she would bear the Messiah, her words (that later will be called the Magnificat) spoke of this wonderful story that the Father and I had been writing. She said, "My soul exalts the Lord, and my spirit has rejoiced in God my Savior. ...He has given help to *Israel* his servant, in remembrance of his mercy, as he spoke to our *fathers*, to *Abraham* and his *offspring forever.*" (Luke 1:46-55)

I was not a surprise, not even to my mother. I had been promised to our people all along.

That's why, nine months later, the angels could appear to shepherds who were abiding in the fields, keeping watch over their flocks by night. And the angels didn't say to them "Surprise! A Savior is coming!" Instead, they said to them, "Fear not: for, behold, I bring you good tidings of great joy, which shall be to all people. For unto you is born *this day* in the city of David a Savior, which is Christ *(the Messiah, the One)* the Lord." (Luke 2: 10-11)

The angels were saying, "You know that Seed that the people of God have looked for since Genesis 3:15? Well, he is finally here! You need wait no longer."

And when I was a little baby, an old man named Simeon held me in his arms at the temple and knew exactly who I was. So much so that he could say, "Lord, now let your bondservant depart in peace, according to your word; for my eyes have seen your salvation that you have prepared in the presence of all peoples, a light for revelation to the Gentiles and for the glory to your people Israel." (Luke 2:29-32)

I am that salvation! I am that light! I am that glory!

Like I told the Pharisees a while back, "You search the scriptures because you think that in them you have eternal life; and it is they that bear witness about me." (John 5:39)

And then, just last week, a day arrived that was so painful to me that even anticipating it made me sweat great drops of blood. I begged the Father to somehow find another way, a way that would not cast me out of his presence. But I honored his will, and just like the ram or the lamb or the temple sacrifices that foreshadowed me, my blood was shed. I was bruised. I died a slow, humiliating, torturous death, nailed to wood that my own pierced hands had once created. But on that day, I went to ruthless war against the Serpent. Though my hands and feet were nailed to a cross, I took his head in my hands and crushed it under my heel.

I won! And the death penalty for my people was satisfied.

Do you know how you can be sure of that? Because I was resurrected. If you ever doubt the safety that you have in me, my Father declared to all the universe that he was satisfied when he glorified his bruised sacrifice and resurrected me. When he destroyed the hold that death had over me, he also destroyed the hold that death has over you. I call him Father, and now so can you! As I said to Mary Magdalene this past Sunday morning, "Go tell my brothers: I am returning to my father and *your* father, to my God and to *your* God." (John 20:17)

I am the Alpha and the Omega, the bright and morning star, and of my kingdom there will be no end.

And I want you to be at my side, as I have continually desired since Eden.

This is my story. Tell it to everyone. It is the hope of all mankind.

We were overwhelmed with wonder at his words. This glorious stranger was the Savior himself, the One who was the focal point of every story!

And we knew that we were now his forever.

Chapter Thirteen

The Redeemer of the World

As you have indulged me in my dream of how our Lord might have told his own story, I hope that you have heard him tying together all the tales told in scripture. In him, they are all brought into One Story, his story. It is the story of how God created everything the way he wanted it to be and of how he has worked for centuries to restore his Way again.

Now the Promised One has arrived. The prophecies have been fulfilled, the characters in our story have played their roles. As we join God's history in this chapter, the Messiah is no longer a shadowy prediction, he now lives in Judea. He wakes up in the morning and talks and preaches and heals. He eats and drinks. He has conversations with people. He now walks upon the earth he created and looks up at the stars that were his handiwork. He is Jesus of Nazareth.

So...now what? We have been anticipating his arrival, but once the Seed of the Woman lands on earth, what does he actually do? This One has a mission. He has a universe to redeem. He is going to go about rebuilding what has been broken. Let's spend this chapter going beyond merely celebrating that the Christ has come. Let's look at the mission, passion, and work of our Jesus while he was on earth.

The Maker of the Kingdom of God

Christ's arrival is a "D-day" event, a storming of the beach, in which God begins to occupy his stolen territory. And as Jesus makes landfall, he gets right to work. But what is he doing? What is on his mind when he wakes up and begins each new day? Certainly, he has come to die that we might live. He has come to pay for our sins and bring us into peace with God. But if we actually listen to Jesus during his time on earth, we hear him talking about much more than just our salvation. If we set our camera lens at its widest focus, we see that there is one thing that Christ spoke about more than anything else, something that was his deepest passion.

He talked about something he called the *Kingdom of God*.

Whether he was preaching, healing, or even dying, Jesus had one goal – to restore the world that he, his Father, and the Spirit had created, to restore their relationship with their people. Everything Jesus does on earth can be seen as moving toward this new redeemed way. If we are to understand the heart of Christ and his work here on earth, (as well as where we are destined to live forever) we must understand the *Kingdom of God* that Christ so loved and pursued.

When Jesus begins his ministry in the book of Mark, his first words are "The time is fulfilled, and the *kingdom of God* is at hand; repent and believe the good news."(Mark 1:15) When he teaches us to pray, his second request after pondering the holiness of God, is a prayer that God's *kingdom* would come. (Matt. 6:9) He tells us that those who are poor or persecuted are blessed, because to them will belong the *kingdom of God*. (Matt. 5:3) When talking to Nicodemus, he tells him that we must be "born again." Why? Because without it, we will not see the *kingdom of God*. (John 3:3)

For Jesus, the kingdom of God is the epicenter of all restoration and life. In fact, he tells us that it is *everything!*

People have speculated about what Christ meant when he talked about the kingdom. I believe that we can only understand its meaning if we understand the One Story. Simply put, the kingdom of God is that restored world that Yahweh has been working toward – the one we've been talking about! *The kingdom of God is what God has been rebuilding since the beginning of scripture, the new "Eden" that Jesus comes like a warrior to reclaim.*

When Jesus tells the people in Mark 9 that "There are some standing here who will not taste death until they see the kingdom of God after it has come with power," he means it literally. (Mark 9:1) The general of the army of God, the king who possesses David's throne, has arrived to take back that which was stolen. And he is bringing with him the establishment of the new kingdom.

We will talk in the next chapter about the ultimate fulfillment of that kingdom, but before we speculate about the nature of God's final restoration, let's treat ourselves to a peek at what earth looked like when the *Mashiach*, the Messiah, the Anointed One walked upon it. Let's look at how he went about recreating his world and creating his kingdom. If you want to understand the kingdom of God, let's follow along behind the one who embodies it.

Let's look at **six ways** in which Christ builds his renewed kingdom:

- He begins restoring the broken world.
- He helps us learn to be small again.
- He shows us how big he is.
- He calls us to be re-born into his image.
- He dies to ransom his people.
- He makes us all fully alive with him, at last.

The Brokenness is Restored

Let me ask you a question: Why does Jesus spend so much of his time in the gospels healing people? More than two thirds of his miracles involve his healing of the sick and the broken. Why?

I grew up going to church. In fact, I tell people that I had a drug problem as a child: I was "drug" to Sunday school, "drug" to church! I've heard stories of Jesus's miracles my whole life and, sadly, we can get used to them, even used to Jesus. Jesus heals people; that's kinda what he does, right? But why? Was it to demonstrate his divinity? Partially, yes. The Old Testament makes it clear that the veracity of a prophet was demonstrated by his signs and wonders. In John's gospel, he makes that point overtly, saying that he wrote about Jesus's miracles "so that we may believe that Jesus is the Christ, the Son of God." (John 20:31)

So of course, Jesus's miracles point to his divinity, but my real question is not why does he perform miracles. My question is why does he bring healing, sustenance, restoration? He heals the sick; he casts out demons; he raises the dead. Why these *particular* miracles? I mean, to miraculously prove his divinity, he could have made animals talk or the sun stop in the sky (like Yahweh does in the Old Testament). Why healing and bringing life?

Well, remember who he is. Remember what he has come to do. He is the Seed. He is the One who "will bring us rest from the curse." (Gen. 5:29) He is the Savior who has come to establish God's restoration, a world in which there will be no more crying or sorrow or pain. (Rev. 21:4) He is making all things new.

So why the miracles of healing in the New Testament?

His miracles are foreshadowing! They are a foretaste of the full restoration that God has been working toward throughout the One Story. Just as every Old Testament story has pointed forward to the restoration of God's rich life with his people, so do Christ's miracles!

The King comes to earth to establish his future reign, but while here, he begins to scatter previews of the wholeness that will one day fill our lives. When that day comes, the kind of healing that Jesus brings to earth will no longer be called "miracles." Miracles are by definition things that are *unusual.* In that future kingdom, the kind of healing that Christ brought to Judea as he walked its dusty roads will be the norm. In the new heaven and the new earth, Christ's healing of his people will not be called miracles; it will be called *life everlasting*, an eternal celebration!

Here's the real message of the One Story: Jesus didn't come into the world just to "save you from your sins." If you believe that, you're thinking too small. Jesus comes, not just to make everything right between you and God; Jesus comes to make everything *right*! To restore the world he's always wanted. To bring a new life, a new us, and new hearts! He is the bringer of Life. And he starts bringing that life the moment he begins his ministry.

Let's watch him at work.

Images of Life

He begins his relationship with his disciples by surprising them in a manner I find delightful. James, John, and Simon (Peter) are fishermen. They have been fishing all night and are exhausted, frustrated, and ready to hang it up. Suddenly a stranger (who is clearly not a fisherman) shows up and tells them that all they need to do is to row out into deeper water and cast their nets in yet another time. These professional fishermen should be complimented for their restraint at what I'm sure felt to them like an absurd recommendation. Nevertheless, they comply.

Imagine the amusement in Jesus's face as he watches these guys discovering that their boats are practically sinking from the schools of fish that are tumbling out of their overflowing nets. He even punctuates the event with a playful pun. "From now on, you will fish for people!" (Luke 5:1-11) Out of their futile work, the one who brings rest from the curse shows these men what true work and richness can look like.

The immediate result of his miracle, however, is that the event floods the fishermen with fear. They know that what they are seeing is not luck or magic. They are in the presence of the one whose voice created the world. In fact, Simon Peter sees what Jesus does and immediately says, "Go away from me, Lord; I am a sinful man!" (Luke 5:1-11)

No, sinful Simon. He will not go away. He is here to stay.

One day while visiting his own village, Jesus is preaching at someone's house, and there are so many people in attendance that the home is overflowing. (Mark 2:1-12) Suddenly, something shocking happens: men begin breaking through the roof of the house, tearing open a hole in the ceiling! Everything is interrupted as Jesus and the crowd look up to see men lowering a crippled fellow down to Jesus by ropes. We are told that the man is paralyzed, and his desperate friends are going beyond the call of duty to get him to the healer as quickly as possible.

Despite the fact that their desire is obviously for Christ to heal their friend, Jesus's reply to the paralytic speaks to something else entirely. He says to this man, "You don't need to be afraid, my son, your sins are forgiven." (Matt 9:2)

While all of this is going on, there are some Jewish scribes and chief priests in attendance who silently take issue with this statement, knowing (correctly) that it is only God who has the authority to forgive sins. Jesus reads their thoughts, and responds to them with the following statement, a statement I find fascinating for many reasons, not the least of which is that it gives us a peek into the subjective experience of what it was like to be Jesus on earth.

Momentarily ignoring the man, his friends, and the hole in the ceiling, Jesus addresses the thoughts of the scribes and priests directly, saying, "Which do you think is easier, to say to the paralytic, 'Your sins are forgiven' or to say, 'Rise, take up your bed and walk?'" (Mark 2:9)

THE REDEEMER OF THE WORLD

Which is easier?

Do you ever think that some things were harder or easier for Jesus?

Of course, *we* know that experience. It's easy to cook scrambled eggs. It's hard to cook eggs benedict. It's easy to play tennis at the club. It's hard to play Roger Federer at the U.S. Open. And for Jesus, it is easy to heal paralyzed legs and enable a man to walk. That's easy!

It is hard for him to forgive sins!

The cost for Jesus was deeply hard. It came at a huge cost to him. Apparently, he knew this and he thought about it. Don't miss this! This is the person who is our Anointed One. He is alive. He hurt. He felt pain and fear, just like we do. And he still chose to give his life for you. And it was hard!

Then Jesus says to the paralytic, (and in response to the Pharisees' doubt) "But, that you may know that the Son of Man has authority on earth to forgive sins…I say to you, rise, pick up your bed, and go home." The man's frozen, withered legs suddenly fill with strength and movement. Shockingly, the man finds himself able to obey the Master's command, and walk! He rose, picked up his bed and went out before them all. "And the people were all amazed and glorified God, saying, 'We never saw anything like this!'" (Mark 2:10-12)

You are correct; we have not. The Son of Man has arrived!

The One Story is about a God who reaches down into the hearts of his people. In fact he comes down to *be* one of us. And surely he wishes to heal our "broken legs," but moreso, he longs to mend our broken, fearful hearts. This Jesus walks his shattered earth and causes men's hearts to learn to love and makes their legs finally able to run to him.

The Son of God speaks to a storm.

He spits on a blind man's eyes and makes him see.

When he is told that he no longer needs to come help a sick

little girl because she has died, the Lord of Life and Death mocks her "death," saying, "She's not dead; she's just asleep." (Luke 8:52)

And when an unclean woman with internal bleeding secretly touches him, he feels the power leave his body, whirls around, and he finds her. He speaks to her. He reaches out and touches the untouchable one. And he calls her "daughter." (Mark 5:25-34)

The question the disciples ask after Jesus calms the storm is perfect: "What manner of man is this?" (Matt. 8:27) He is the Seed. He is the New Adam. He is the new manner of man. And he has come to make us all alive to God and alive to the world as he intended it to be.

As this Jesus's hands touch the broken, we are witnessing the dawning of the Kingdom of God. As the Christmas carol says, "He comes to make his blessings flow, far as the curse is found." [6]

But first we have to be small

Now the bad news:

It is glorious to follow Jesus through his healing ministry as he causes the blind to see and the lame to walk. But he also comes to heal our *hearts*. We humans have a very deep problem; one that the "surgeon of the cosmos" must excise if he is going to bring us into his kingdom. In order to be the most alive and the most his, we will need to give up our desires to be good, strong, right, and powerful. We will have to learn how to be "small."

Remember God's message to his children at Eden, "If you want all the blessings of being one of my *creatures*, you have to stay a *creature?*" In other words, "You have to be small and needful (i.e. obey me)." Well, I don't know if you have been keeping up with current events, but we humans hate this. We want to be *Superfly TNT; The Guns of Navarone!* We like thinking that we are in control. And for religiously-minded people, that usually means that we also want to believe that we are "good" and "righteous," at least better than those "other people."

When I'm cruising along, engaged on my most self-deluded autopilot, I can sometimes convince myself that I'm a spiritual "steely-eyed missile man." I've got it all together. After all, I heal the heartbroken in my office; I do conferences that benefit the multitudes. Heck, I even write books about God! Surely, I'm a better Christian than most. (And I'm certain that my wife wholeheartedly agrees with me on this point!)

Problem is, when I feel this way, I am proudly living out of the most narcissistic parts of me. I'm living a self-righteous fantasy that I am "rich and powerful and have need of nothing." (Rev 3:17) And if there's any hope of Jesus establishing his new Kingdom of God on earth (much less in my heart), he's going to have to deal with obnoxious, self-righteous people like me. He's going to need to bring me back to Eden, back to the place where his people were small and knew that they needed help. Only then will we see that we need someone else who is bigger than us; someone to save us. Only then will God's Eden Plan be restored – the one in which God is God, and we are not.

I told you it was bad news.

Seeing that we need him

Part of Jesus's work on earth is to teach us that we are lost people, people who are humble and need a savior. He begins this project as he preaches the Sermon on the Mount. (Matt. chapters 5, 6 and 7) Just as Moses brought the Law down from a mountain, Jesus, the new Moses, brings *his Law* from a mountain as well. Only his Law is impossible, and he wants to make sure that we see that.

His message in the Sermon on the Mount goes something like this: "You say you haven't killed anyone, and you feel like that makes you pretty good. Well, my question is about your heart. Have you hated your brother? How are you doing at will-powering that?"

See what's he's doing here?

Then he says, "How about adultery? You haven't actually betrayed your marriage, eh? Good for you. But have you had any impure thoughts? And just in case I missed anybody, be perfect as your Father in heaven is perfect!"

How do you feel now? Concerned? Frightened? Guilty?

Excellent!

Now you are ready to hear his ultimate question, the implication that rises like the dawn in the background of the Sermon on the Mount:

"Do you see now that you cannot be 'good'? Does anyone need a savior yet? The Redeemer has come!"

Jesus is devastatingly skilled at undermining any fantasy we might have that we can be good enough to please God. He knows that our self-righteousness is a cancer that will prevent us from ever being close to him.

Jesus drove this point downtown in his interaction with the man we call "the rich young ruler." (Mark 10:17-22) The young man runs up to Jesus and asks him a very important question. He says, "Good Teacher, what must I do to inherit eternal life?"

Jesus is about to nail the answer to his question. He will pinpoint and address the exact problem that this fellow has. The rich young ruler doesn't realize it yet, but his problem is about to be surgically engaged.

Jesus's surgery is to say this: "Why do you call me *good*? No one is good except God alone."

Now at this point, we could all stand for the benediction. As we will soon see, the rich young ruler's problem has been perfectly diagnosed and the solution prescribed. More on that later, but for now, Jesus plays along and answers his question.

"Obey the law and the prophets," the Savior says.

Now here's where the rich young ruler shows his hand. He is about to reveal the dangerous belief that hides in his soul. He responds to Jesus by saying, "Teacher, all these things I have kept since my youth."

In other words, this guy actually believes that he is good!

The passage tells us that Jesus hears this preposterous statement, and in response, looks at this man and feels *love* for him. Jesus feels a love that moves him to give this young man the most wonderful gift; a gift designed to help him at the point of his greatest need; a gift to cut through his frightened self-righteousness; a gift designed to help this "rich" young ruler see that maybe he isn't so rich after all.

Jesus says to him in essence, "You think you've kept all the commandments? Well then, let's start with the *first one*, the one that says, 'You shall have no other God's before me.'"

With the first commandment in the back of his mind, Jesus continues, "So, there is one thing you lack." *(He's not going to tell him what it is he lacks; he's going to show him!)* "Go and sell all you possess and give it to the poor, and you shall have treasure in heaven and come and follow me."

Now, why? Why does Jesus say this? Is Jesus trying to test this guy's commitment? "Are you faithful enough to sell your possessions?" Do we believe that giving money will get us into heaven? Does our faith tell us that if you go and sell everything, you will be saved? Is this a new gospel?

No. Jesus tells him this because he wants to save him from the *Lie*, the *Illusion*. Jesus says in essence, "Your true sin (the lie you tell yourself) is that you think you are *good*, and that will kill you. Let me help you see the truth about yourself. Let me help you die to that self-righteousness. Let me help you feel the most important feeling you could ever feel. Let me help you walk away 'grieved.' Not because you're not 'committed enough' to sell everything; not because I'm asking you do something and you don't want to do it. But grieved because now you *know that you can't do it*. You can't sell everything; you are too in love with your money. You are *not good!* Only our Father is heaven is good.

Need a savior yet, young man?"

Jesus makes it patently clear to the rich young ruler that he is *not* obedient, that he hasn't kept *jack* since his youth.

Now this guy stands a chance!

Call me crazy, but I don't think that this is a story of a failed conversion. This is Jesus giving this young fellow (and us) the only thing that might ever help him to "get it;" to finally see that he needs this Jesus he is talking to. He doesn't need a way to earn eternal life; he needs a Redeemer!

I have always wondered, what would have happened had the rich young ruler responded differently. (And I can't help but wonder if one day he did.) What if he had heard Jesus say, "Obey the commandments," and he had fallen on his face, and said, "Son of Man, I can never obey you like you demand and deserve. My heart is too hard. I love money more than I love anything. But you help the blind men see by healing their eyes, and you help the lame to walk by healing their legs. Could you help me by making my money-loving, greedy heart soft and faithful and submissive to you? Because I have *not* obeyed since my youth. And I need you. I need someone to save me."

What do you think Jesus would have done?

I think that the resurrected Christ answers this question in Revelation 3. He says, to those who believe themselves spiritually well off, "You say, I am rich, I have prospered, and I need nothing, not realizing that you are wretched, pitiful, poor, blind, and naked. I counsel you to buy from *me* gold refined by fire, so that you may be *rich*, and white garments so that you may clothe yourselves and the shame of your nakedness may not be seen, and salve to anoint your eyes, so that you may see." (Rev 3:17-18)

The rich young ruler simply sought the wrong kind of gold.

But Jesus says, "Once you see that you are lost and helpless and poor, you are a perfect fit for my arms." This is why he says that we must receive the kingdom "like a child." (Mark 10:15) And the Greek word Jesus uses here refers to the youngest and most helpless of children.

The Eden Design was about God's small children running to him in the cool of the day, needing their God, relying on him, knowing him, enjoying him. At last, our Jesus beautifully comes to make us small again. Our "inability" is his love language. Run to him!

And we get to see how big he is

There's nothing more beautiful and comforting than the mercy (even the "severe mercy") of our Savior toward his needful, broken children. But there is much more to him than his meekness and gentleness. He certainly saw himself as more than that.

One way he brings the kingdom is by showing us who *we* are. Now, let's hear more about who *he is*. We have looked for the heart of God in all our stories; let's now take a look at the heart of Christ. How did Jesus think about himself? When he looked inside, whom did he see himself to be?

His favorite name

Jesus has many names throughout the Bible. I took a class on Jesus in seminary. It was called "Christology," and R. C. Sproul was again my teacher. For our first assignment, he told us to collect every name for Christ that we could find in the whole of scripture. Of course, there are the easy ones like "Christ" and the "Son of God." And then there are the more esoteric ones like the "Rose of Sharon," the "Bright and Morning star," or the "Chief Cornerstone." Up most of the night, I found thirty-five. I got a C. I think there are almost 200 names of Christ in scripture, (so maybe Sproul was generous with my grade). Personally, my favorite name for Jesus is "friend of sinners." (Luke 7:34) I know I need a friend. How 'bout you?

Interestingly, of all the names and titles given to him, one stood out as the personal favorite of Jesus himself. That name was the "Son of Man." He used it constantly as a self-designation.

He would say things like,

> "The foxes have holes, and the birds of the sky have nests, but the Son of Man has nowhere to lay his head." (Luke 9:58)

> "For the Son of Man came to seek and to save the lost." (Luke 19:10)

> "The Son of Man must suffer many things and be rejected by the elders, chief priests and teachers of the law, and he must be killed, and after three days rise again." (Mark 8:31)

I find it fascinating that as Jesus walked the earth, his self-image was that of the "Son of Man." Contrary to a lot of our contemporary Christian zeitgeist, it is not an identity of gentleness. It's actually a self-designation that is a bit frightening.

The name is derived from one of Daniel's visions in chapter 7 of his book. Initially, Daniel sees someone who is called "the Ancient of Days," an individual enthroned above all the universe. Then, another person is brought before him and Daniel says, "Behold, with the clouds of heaven there came one like *a son of man*, and he came to the Ancient of Days and was presented before him. And to him was given dominion and glory and a kingdom, that all peoples, nations, and languages should serve him; his dominion is an everlasting dominion which shall not pass away, and his kingdom is one that shall never be destroyed." (Dan. 7:13-14) The Apostle John will echo this image after first beholding the reigning Christ in the book of Revelation. He witnesses this glorious figure, shining with light. In his hand he holds stars, and the power of the sword came forth from his mouth. John says, he was like "the Son of Man." (Rev. 1:13)

Jesus related in different ways to different people. Sometimes he was overwhelmingly tender. With the faithless or the self-righteous, he could be downright insulting. But in the back of his mind, whatever he was doing, he saw himself as the one to whom all kingdoms will be given; whose reign will be forever. The one whom, even when brought before the very Ancient of Days, *remains standing*. This is who he is.

Daniel says that after beholding him, he was "anxious" and "alarmed." (Dan. 7:15) I bet he was.

His true identity

Perhaps the most radical thing that Jesus ever says is in response to a challenge by the Pharisees. Their interaction went like this: Jesus says to them, "Your father Abraham rejoiced that he would see my day. He saw it and was glad." The leaders challenge him by responding, "You are not yet fifty years old, and have you seen Abraham?" And Jesus replies, "Truly, truly, I say to you, before Abraham was, *I am*." (John 8:56-58)

Sound familiar?

Many people want to recognize Jesus as simply another a wise teacher, but here he identifies himself with Yahweh of Hosts, with the God of the burning bush, I AM THAT I AM, the Sovereign who thunders from Sinai. People have different opinions about who Jesus is. Yahweh God is who *he* says he is.

As C.S. Lewis says in, *Mere Christianity*, "You can shut him up for a fool, you can spit at him and kill him as a demon, or you can fall at his feet and call him Lord and God, but let us not come with any patronizing nonsense about his being a great human teacher. He has not left that open to us. He did not intend to." [7]

His glory

There is one moment in Jesus's life on earth at which his true identity as holy God became frighteningly apparent. Traditionally, this event is called the Mount of Transfiguration, but I think it could also be called the Mount of *Revelation*, because upon it, the true nature of Jesus is unveiled.

Jesus, Peter, James, and John go up to the mountain, and while there, something unprecedented happens. For a moment, the veil of humanity is drawn back from the Second Person of the Trinity, and the true nature of the incarnate Son of God is revealed. As the disciples watch, Jesus's appearance is transformed. His face begins to shine bright like the sun, and his clothes become as white as light. (Matt: 17:2) The mighty ruler of the universe whom John later witnesses in Revelation begins to be revealed. After Moses met with God on Sinai, his face shone in a reflected glory. What the disciples see in Christ on the mountain is not a glory that is *reflected*. They see the *actual glory* of God himself in the person of Jesus.

On that mountain, Jesus meets with Moses and Elijah. The Son of Man is met with the embodiment of the full weight of the Law and the prophets; almost as if their presence is a validation that he is their true fulfillment. As Augustine says about this moment, "the grace of the Gospel receives witness from the Law and the Prophets." [8]

See this Christ. The man who walks the hot dusty roads of Galilee lives containing the blistering white light of ultimate holiness and glory. Somehow within his human frame lives one who is incarnate God! He is one whom, when John later sees him in Revelation, causes the apostle to fall at his feet as though dead. (Rev. 1:17) This is who he is.

As Jesus meets with Moses and Elijah on the mountain, a cloud appears, the same cloud of glory that we have seen throughout the Old Testament, the Glory Presence of God himself. God speaks to us all from the cloud and says, "This is my Son, whom I love; with him I am well pleased. Listen to him!" (Matt. 17:1-5)

Let's talk about what it would mean for us to do so.

Being back in his Image

We have a real problem: if we actually *do* listen to all that Christ has to say, things get complicated.

Jesus's heart that welcomes our brokenness and frailty is shockingly beautiful. He has a lot to say about his own humility and welcoming gentleness, and throughout his stories, he pledges his love for sinners. Yet, he also pledges something else: somehow, he also makes it very clear that he demands our *obedience* to him as well. He says it again and again. He calls us to be righteous and to forsake our sin.

I don't know about you, but, knowing my own heart, this worries me.

Listen to him. One of the last things that he says to his eleven beloved disciples the night before he dies for their sins; the night in which he washes their feet and institutes his New Covenant is this: he looks at them and says, "If you love me, you will keep my commandments." (John 14:15)

I'm not sure what to do with that. Are you?

I would tell Jesus that I do love him. I also know very well that I do a terrible job of actually keeping his commandments. But, he says that we must, and that if we love him we will! And, he says stuff like this all the time.

In John 8, some Pharisees use a woman to try to trap Jesus. She had been caught in adultery and they were challenging him as to whether he would enforce the Mosaic Law that required that she be stoned to death. We all know Jesus's somewhat mysterious first response to this: he begins writing something in the dirt at the feet of the Pharisees, and says, "Let he among you who is without sin be the first to throw a stone at her." (John 8:7) (I've always imagined that he was just quietly writing the names of women these guys had committed adultery with: "Sally... Betty... Mary Sue... Penelope... ")

Anyway, one by one, these guys shuffle away with their tails between their legs, and Jesus is left alone with the girl. Intriguingly, there actually *does* happen to be someone in this group who is without sin, but his response is not to throw a stone.

His response is heartbreakingly gentle.

He looks at this poor, scared girl and says, "Neither do I condemn you."

All good, right? Great gospel moment, right?

But then he adds, "Go, and from now on sin no more."

What!? Is that even possible!? Can anyone go and sin no more? I know that I cannot. I wonder if that scared girl could. Are you scared yet?

Throughout my years studying theology and the Bible, I have read countless explanations of this quandary, the classic dilemma: how do we make sense of *grace* in the context of God's call to *obedience*. This is not a new question. But I would like to offer a slightly different way of answering it; an answer I think we must engage if we are to follow Jesus.

What if obedience is actually wonderful?

I think the reason that Jesus's call to obedience gives us pause is because our hearts still think in the concrete legalistic categories of *rules and law*. It's part of what was broken in us when we ate of the Tree of the Knowledge of Good and Evil, way back at Eden.

Since that deadly choice, instead of understanding "righteousness" as the most blessed and "right" way for our hearts to live, we turn obedience into a dreadful chore. When someone says "obey," we immediately associate that with some dreadful list of "do's and don't's." Most of which we probably don't want to do. I believe the reason we all puzzle at Christ's call to obedience is because something in our gut has this visceral reaction that obedience would be *unpleasant*. (Right? Tell me I'm not the only one here!) As we have said before, this is one of the greatest lies of the universe, a lie we all believe; a lie we all *live*.

Let me pose a different way of looking at Jesus's call for us to keep his commandments. Let me do so by asking you this: have you enjoyed the Jesus we've looked at in this chapter? Do you find him compelling? Do you look at his grace and wit and power and feel drawn to him? He's gentle with those who are small. He doesn't put up with bullies. He is charmingly clever. He makes wine at parties. He is not afraid to stand up to a Roman governor. He's sarcastic with self-righteous church people. And he is willing to die because he loves you so much.

Do you like what he is like?

Would you like to be like that, too?

Here's how I believe we make sense of Christ's call to obedience: Moses went up on the mountain and came down with laws written on stone tablets, and the people were called to *obey* those laws. Jesus, the new Moses, went up on the mountain and also declared the Law. He said he came to *fulfill* it.

But, then he came down from the mountain *without stone tablets*. What came down from Jesus's mountain was not rules of law. What came down from this mountain was *Jesus of Nazareth*, the embodiment of righteousness itself!

Do you want to understand the commandments and obedience? Stop defaulting to thinking that righteousness means you have to act like a good boy. If you want to understand what Jesus means by "obedience," watch how he lives and loves, and ask yourself, "Would I like to be like this man?" He *is* the commandments.

His message to the girl to "go and sin no more" was a command for her to walk away from this moment of overwhelming forgiveness and be forever imprinted by the power of who Jesus is. Once you see and experience his heart, you will fall madly in love with wanting to be like him. How could you not? That shocking encounter with who he is, is what changes us. It is the kindness of God that leads us to repentance. (Rom. 2:4)

One day, one of my clients came to a shocking realization about the depth at which Christ loved her. She saw a love that pulled all of her brokenness and sin into the arms of her savior. As this beautiful, welcoming grace flooded over her, she started sobbing. She then looked up at me through her tears and said, "I would wash his feet with my hair for that kind of love!" (Luke 7:36-38) Now that she had seen him, she longed to honor him, to serve him. She wanted to be like him.

And now can you see that the woman caught in adultery was *absolutely* able to "go and sin no more." Because certainly her heart would never ever forget this encounter with the Son of Man. Her heart would always remember his power and his wisdom and his tenderness. She would never forget the look in his eyes when he said, "Neither do

I condemn you." She would spend the rest of her life wanting to be like him. And even in the times in which she would certainly fail him, her heart was his.

This is what obedience is, and this is what happens when we see him – my heart can finally stop wanting to be like John Cox and start wanting to be like Jesus of Nazareth.

This is one of the reasons I've wanted to devote this entire book to showing you who God is and what he is like. Because real obedience and real Christlikeness is subsumed in this statement:

If you see who he is, you cannot help but love him and want to be like him. Or as he put it, "If you love me, you will keep my commandments."

And now the only thing that doesn't make sense would be someone who *didn't* feel this way. Someone who could look at Jesus's heart and say, "I love you, but I don't care about any of the things that you care about. When I see someone hurting, it doesn't bother me. When I see someone mock the heart of God, I don't mind. I just love whatever brings me immediate pleasure, and don't care that I don't long more deeply for you.

But I love you."

That is what doesn't make sense.

But it still hurts

Of course, another problem is that there is an aspect of this Jesus that most of us find quite *unappealing*. One that we do not wish to emulate at all: *he dies*. His heart so desires and values the beauty of God's Way, that he is willing to suffer the loss of something precious (his life), in order to achieve it. Most of us don't like this part of the plan.

We have talked about how God's Law is good; how it is the

instruction manual for the human heart; how following it gives us the best life. But for some reason, following his Way also hurts. As we said, the human heart "runs downhill," and we like our sins. Deceit, pride, and revenge are actually quite enjoyable in the moment. Hoarding my money keeps me feeling safe. Gossiping about other people makes me feel like I'm better than they. Lust gives me that little "rush." Anger keeps me from feeling small. Most sins are fun for the moment. (Curiously, covetousness and envy are popular sins, despite the fact that, the more we engage in them, the *less* happy we are. Explain that one to me!)

If you talk to most Christians, they will tell you that they long to let go of their selfishness and be more obedient to Christ. But the problem is that, when it gets right down to it, doing so *hurts*. The bottom-line problem is that if we attempt to "keep his commandments," we will have to face lots of painful feelings: sorrow, deprivation, going without. And that stuff feels terrible! I'm sure the rich young ruler would have felt enormous loss in his life if he had obeyed Jesus and let go of the pleasures and security of his money. But he didn't want to have to suffer like that.

Neither do we. If I set limits on my anger, I'm going to feel weak or sad. If I tithe to his kingdom, I'm going to have to give up some of the security I find in my money. If I don't snap back at my spouse, I will have to actually engage my sadness and hurt. If I forgive you, I will need to absorb the injury you gave me without retaliating.

The psychology of obedience

Let's get honest here. Lots of church people call us to be more obedient. But they don't usually talk about how much we will have to hurt in order to actually pull that off. And I know as a therapist, that unless we remain really honest and proactive about that how much it hurts to obey, we will not be able to face it; we will run away, and we will find ourselves right back in the middle of our sinful choices again. We will never be able to serve our Jesus well until we acknowledge together that if we do obey him, we are choosing to face pain we don't want to face. That's what "dying to self" means – *turning from sin requires turning toward pain.* That's the bad news.

But there's good news too. "Hurting" is as bad as it gets.

The sadness of obeying Christ will rarely kill you (like it did him). In fact, it is a hurt that will actually help you. We all have categories for that kind of "helpful hurt" – a trip to the dentist, a tough workout, investing money instead of spending it. We all have a category for choosing pain because it will reap us something we desire more than comfort. Well, obedience to Christ is the biggest, brightest, most wonderful example of that.

If we are willing to engage the pain of denying ourselves, taking up our cross and following him, we will find hiding right behind that loss and "death," a freedom, peace, and joy that we were created for. If we will push through the pain (which we can all do if we help each other), we get Life! If we follow our Jesus into suffering, we get to follow him to Easter!

On the other side of how much it hurts to obey him is a life that feels free and alive and whole. Don't forget that we were *created* to follow his way, to bend the knee to him. It is our original, natural state. And though it often hurts to push against the downward pull of our "bentness" and sin, when we do, something "right" happens: the string becomes properly tuned. That "flat chord" of our twisted ways of living sharpens and begins to resonate with the creator and savior of the universe. Obedience can often feel to us like a step down, when in actuality, it is a step up. Don't insult your "obedience" by just seeing it as good behavior. When you follow him, you are vibrating in tune with the Creator of the cosmos, the Redeemer of Israel, the Bright and Morning Star. Feel him alive within you as you follow him!

The fellowship of obedience

In the midst of that call to suffer with him, Jesus also promises us that he is only calling us to go somewhere he has already been. He is not pointing down a lonely, painful road and telling us to walk it. He is grabbing us by the shoulder as *he* starts walking, saying, "Come on! Be like me, my brother, my child! It hurts, but we will be together. And guess what?! At the end of this road is a richness and a freedom that we will delight in together! It's worth it. I'm worth it. And you will never do this alone."

Sin is fun for a little while.

And dying is not fun, for a little while.

But, on the other side of the veil of the sadness and loss of not taking what we want, stands this Jesus at whom we've been marveling. And he promises that if you are with him in death, you will be with him forever.

So worship him with me. But let's suffer with him, too – and with each other.

What if we don't have to be afraid to fail?

Christ's call to follow him is daunting. I don't know about you, but I constantly fail him. I guess that's the scariest part, isn't it? He is resolute in his command for us to obey him, but if you are like me, you chronically don't; sometimes through failure, sometimes through direct disobedience. At that point my heart often cowers, wondering what he thinks about John, the sinner? Is he angry at me? Is he deducing that I must not love him since I don't "keep his commandments?"

Would he turn his back on me because of my failure or rebellion? Wondering what he thinks about my sin sometimes scares me. Does it ever scare you?

This book has been about listening for the true heart of God. I keep saying "this is who he is." To those of us who feel vulnerability and fear about displeasing him, I want to comfort us by reminding again us of who he is.

First, let's remember that he only calls us to obey him *after* he has adopted us as his own children. We walk into the boxing ring of growth and obedience already washed pure in his blood. He would no more "unadopt" you because of your sin than you would evict your child for disobeying you. He is in it for the long haul. He knew what he was getting into when he met you. Your failure doesn't surprise him. For him, it was part of the package.

Secondly, let me ask you this: do you *care* about your sin? Do you wish you were different? Do you have that same experience that Paul describes in Romans 7, the one we talked about in the Eden chapter, the one in which you wish you could do good and yet find yourself doing the very thing you hate?

If so, then take comfort. *If you hate your struggle and failure, that is your built-in reminder that you are truly his.* Unrepentant rebels who hate God don't care that they harm him; only his children do. In other words, the fact that you are asking this question can remind you daily that you deeply belong to him. I want the conviction you feel about your sin to stop being an accusing voice that exiles you into the loneliness of fear and shame. I want it to become a warm blanket that reminds you that, if you struggle with your sin, he is alive and at work inside of you – because he is your savior and your friend, the friend of sinners.

One day our Lord witnessed a widow who dropped only a penny in the coffers of the church. Then he turned and saw the "righteous" pouring in gallons of false wealth in a showy service to God. Our Jesus treasured the tiny amount that the poor widow offered. It was all she had.

I often feel as though I barely have a penny's worth of true obedience to offer God, and a dirty, old, smelly penny at that. Does he still want it? Does he still want me? I believe that he does, and I believe that he cherishes the tiny widow's mite of our heartfelt love for him more than he values the "riches" of the self-righteous. He knows our frame. He is mindful that we are but dust. (Ps. 103:14) And I believe that as we overcome our anger or our passivity or our pride, even just another penny's worth, that the whole host of heaven rejoices! You are in a growth process that lasts a lifetime, and you are part of a renewal that he promises he will complete one day, despite our frustrations and fear. He is astronomically bigger than we are, and bigger than our sin. And one day, he will complete his good work in your heart, throw your brokenness on the trash heap, and you may dazzle us all with how beautifully you love him.

His death to ransom us

Happy hopelessness

The "Good News" behind all of this is the fact that Jesus knows that none of us can do anything he asks. In other words, he says two things at once about our obedience, two messages about our righteousness:

You must do it, and you can't do it.

At the same time he compels us to look just like him, he brings us to hopeless despair that we could ever do so.

Gratefully, we have his gentle grace to fall into.

As we've said, Paul calls the Law a "schoolmaster" to teach us that we are doomed without Christ. (Gal. 3:24) And if we hear God's commands to us with any level of clarity, we discover that the Law does its schoolmaster job brutally well. Hopefully we are left frightened and looking for hope.

And that hope comes on a hill called Golgotha.

Despite the fact that Jesus calls us all to obey him in the upper room, his next act demonstrates that he already knows we will fail. He calls us to obedience and then immediately walks out to Gethsemane and surrenders himself to a death that is necessary because he knows that we can never obey him like he wishes.

One of the things that I find most compelling about Christianity is that it is a system based on our *failure* (at last I have found something I am quite adept at). It's also one of the reasons I believe it. Think about it; no one would ever make up a religion like this, one that is predicated on failure, one that is based on the total inability of the penitent to ever please the god. It's crazy! Every other religion (including funky versions of Christianity) provides all sorts of duties and rituals, which, if properly done, will appease the deities. You cannot appease Yahweh.

I was reading the work of a noted atheist the other day, and he was scoffing at the "primitive" notion of "some angry, thundering, legalistic god in the sky." He didn't read far enough. Surely God is thundering and absolutely demanding, but he didn't need some atheist to tell him that was a problem. He already knew it was. So he created another solution: to inflict all of that thundering vengeance on himself so that he could have his children, *even as* they are constantly failing him! Only in the context of this overwhelming love does he call us to be like him. Only in the context of such love would being more like him even be possible. And after seeing this love, how could we not long to be his righteous children – set apart for him.

But Jesus has to die

In order to provide this stunning rescue from our infinite problem, however, something horrible has to happen: Jesus has to die. Since you've been reading the whole One Story, you understand something vital. You know now that a death sentence has been hanging over the world since Adam and Eve's betrayal of God at Eden. This death sentence is very old, but God is very patient. And the bottom line is that if we are ever to live again, the promised Seed will have to be bruised. And pierced. And crushed.

We've reflected on who Jesus saw himself to be, what it was like to be him. Well, know this: he walked his 33 years on earth knowing that his ultimate destination was to be brutally tortured to death for us. As he says, "the Son of Man came not to be served but to serve, and to *give his life* as a ransom for many." (Matt 20: 28) He walked among the people of Israel, seeing their faces, and knowing he would be their Lamb. He came to die.

Remember how God tells Adam in the Garden, "The day you eat of [the tree] you will surely die"? Have you ever wondered why Adam and Eve didn't drop dead on that day? Certainly, there was a "death" in a sense. In the Bible, death doesn't so much refer to the *cessation* of life as it does a *separation* from life – and Adam and Eve are immediately "separated." They are separated from each other, and they are separated from God. God's desire to be "with" his people was destroyed. God could not be close to us. And that is the kind of "death" that Yahweh is most concerned about.

But we still have our question: why did Adam and Eve not just keel over? Was this all just metaphorical? Was God bluffing? Is he really not just and faithful in his response to the destructiveness of sin?

Paul answers our question in Romans 3:24-25. He says, "God presented Christ as a sacrifice of atonement, through the shedding of his blood – to be received by faith. *He did this to demonstrate his righteousness, because in his forbearance he had left the sins committed beforehand unpunished.*" Paul is telling us that God didn't *neglect* the death that Adam and Eve owed, he just *postponed* it!

The life-debt that mankind owned to Yahweh hung over the universe for centuries. God saw the sin of man and felt the just retribution that it deserved. But he waited. He withdrew his battle bow with Noah. He began a new family with Abraham. He brought his nation of people to himself in the wilderness, and then established them in the land that he had promised – all the while providing sacrifices that pointed to the cosmic debt he was owed. Yahweh was patient. He waited. He delayed the payment of death until thousands of years after Eden, long after his vow to Abraham to provide a son. He waited millennia for a hill called The Skull. And there he finally called in the debt of death that was owed him. There, the Seed of the Woman finally paid that penalty on a cross. In Jesus's death, the patient, gracious God who "passed over the sins previously committed," became the King to whom a death sentence was owned. Truly he is the God of ultimate holiness and justice.

In the cross, God essentially says, "Look at the vengeance that my justice requires. I have not forgotten those who have been harmed. I have not forgotten how my own holiness has been violated. I have not forgotten that you constantly fail to obey me as you were created to. But instead of harming you, I will harm my only Son. He will be your substitute, and in the cross, you will see his greatest humiliation, and you will also see his greatest glory! You will see my justice satisfied through the most brutal act of infinite love."

The glory of the Rejected One

Within ancient Jewish worship, on the Day of Atonement, animals were sacrificed on behalf of the sins of the people. But, something else happened as well. Another animal, a goat, was taken to the city gate and then rejected. It was sent out into the darkness of the wilderness. Alone and forsaken, it was called a "scapegoat," and all the curses due the people were laid upon its back. It was sent out, accursed, and alienated from everyone.

In his death, Jesus is our scapegoat. The true brutality of the cross is not the nails or the spear. The ultimate "death on the cross" is that moment in which the sinless Seed cries out to his Father, "My God, my God, why have you forsaken me?" In that moment, the death that we have all been living since Eden, that separation from God, is poured out on Christ. The One who was nearest to God is cast out as the scapegoat for our betrayal. The ruthless wrath we saw destroy Noah's world is piled on him. He is rejected, expelled, and forsaken; all so he could have his beloved children back.

The Seed comes. The Seed is killed.

And because of him, we can never die.

Who would possibly do something like this? What kind of person would give up everything, brutally die, and lose the heart of his Father – all because he loved ungrateful, selfish, angry, self-righteous people like us?

What kind of person would act this way? A person who is bold and wild and more courageous than we can ever imagine. Let's quit pretending that Jesus is only easy and safe and tender. No one who is just sweet and kind allows their hands to be pushed down against a beam of wood and a nail to be driven through them. That requires somebody who is frighteningly bold. Someone who is terrifyingly powerful. Someone who makes demands that feel impossible. And someone who is so loving that it should scare us to death.

This person came to repair the breach, to cover the sin of all of his children – for Adam and Noah and Abraham and Moses; for the prophets, and for David the king. And he came and died to pay the penalty for us, too; all of his broken, angry, hurtful children – the ones who see their desperate need for a champion and a big brother and a king, those who call upon his name. He gave up everything to get us back.

As a result, we are brought near again to God. The separation caused by death is over. *Christ's rejection makes our rejection go away!* Christ's death makes our life possible. And because of him, God's song of the Covenant can rise in chorus forever: "I will be your God, and you will be my people, and I will dwell among you." (Rev. 21:3)

And then we all live

A very long time ago, God made a promise to a serpent. He promised that one day that serpent would die. He vowed that a special seed would come and would crush the Serpent's head under his heel. To be a champion for his people, this Seed would have to be bruised, pierced, and forsaken. That Seed finally came. His name is Jesus. And he submitted to being bruised – even unto death on a cross. And the Serpent was destroyed.

Then, sometime between the Friday of the cross, and Easter Sunday, something happened, something initially hidden and secret. The dead body of Jesus was visited. The same blinding light of creation that the Father had wielded to speak the universe into existence, entered into a tiny cave near Jerusalem – and Jesus's dead body inhaled breath! His eyes opened, and the cloth wrappings of death fell away. He lives! And when God makes him alive again, he is trumpeting to the universe that the Seed has come; that the Serpent has been defeated; that all of the danger that has hung over the world throughout the One Story has now been conquered. Christ is raised! He is alive forevermore! God's justice is satisfied! And the days of walking with him in the Garden can be restored.

And in Him, we are *all* restored. You see, in the resurrection of Jesus, God is not only bringing his Only Begotten Son back into his arms, he is bringing all of us into his arms as well. In other words, the reason that we celebrate Easter is not just to rejoice that Christ is raised. We celebrate Easter because it promises that *we* will be raised as well! Just as he is brought back into the deepest life; his resurrection proclaims to the universe that our future is bright. We have no idea how bright.

Because of him, it is finished.

The veil is ripped; the cherubim at Eden's gate are driven away.

And his people are his again.

    He has wanted this for so long.

And because of this precious One, this "Seed of the Woman," Yahweh will one day be able to wander through his garden again, and call to his children, "Where are you?"

And then we can all respond at last, "Here we are, Abba. We are right here. We haven't gone anywhere at all! Can we please go for a walk?"

This is who he is.
This is why he came.
And this is his Story.

Chapter Fourteen

Heaven and the Beginning of the Always Story

This is *our* story

Jesus is the bright point of our One Story, the center of the turning world... but his work on earth is not the end of God's plan. God has always been working toward rebuilding his "Eden," and though much has been accomplished, this story is not yet over. There is an ultimate fulfillment yet to come, something more that we look toward and long for. In that sense, we are just like Abraham, Moses, David, and Isaiah. Like the Old Testament believers who looked for *some* fulfillment, we still look for the *ultimate* fulfillment. So welcome to the lineage of God's One Story! We are part of God's people throughout history, waiting and wondering how he will finally fulfill all of his promises. Because by this point in our journey through the One Story, we know he will.

I love those passages in Deuteronomy where Moses speaks to the second generation of the wilderness nation. He says in essence, "You know how God made all those promises to your forefathers? Well, he was also making those promises to *you* – you who hadn't even been born yet – *you* who are alive today. God spoke to *you* from Horeb. God made a covenant with *you* on that day." (Deut. 5:1-5)

In other words, Moses is telling them (*and us*) that when God was making covenants and promises to his patriarchs, he wasn't just committing himself to them. He was committing himself to us as well! God gives Noah's rainbow to us. God walks the cut animals in a promise to Abraham *and* us. God saves us with a Passover Lamb. *All of this story is ours. We get to live it!* We are the family of God for this age, and we look toward a fulfillment just as the figures in the Bible did. We are just farther down the historical road of this One Story than they. Perhaps even today, we might see the bright coming of our risen Christ and be able to say like Simeon, "Now, let thy bondservant depart in peace, for my eyes have seen thy salvation." (Luke 2:29)

So what is God's ultimate fulfillment going to look like? Remember this One Story is a restoration project of something that was destroyed. Where is this story going? What will God's world look like when his restoration and redemption is fully completed? Play with me here. This chapter is going to be joyful fancy. *Let's imagine heaven together!* What is the ending of the One Story? And what is the beginning of the *Always Story* that we will share with him forever!

You're going to live forever

Sometimes it feels like we've forgotten about heaven. People rarely talk about it as if it were real, and those who don't know God often disdain the mention of heaven, seeing it as some kind of 'pie in the sky' naivete. But throughout history, Christians have lived their lives oriented with a hope toward their eternal life with God. Technically speaking, we are eternal beings. Our lives will continue forever. But do we live that way? It seems to me that many of us have lost this vision, and I believe that losing sight of our eternal destiny can leave us with a sadly narrow picture of our current lives.

I was speaking with a client once who was contemplating betraying and leaving her family. She said, "I just can't imagine living the rest of my life like this." Though I initially responded to her pain, I also added, "By the way, what if *this* is not the rest of your life? I believe that our lives right now are just a minuscule blip. Real life hasn't even begun yet. What our 'life' is, is *eternal*. And I'm not so sure that living in godly suffering during this 'blip' would actually qualify as 'wasting that life.' Within the One Story, our lifetimes are immeasurable, and God's heart pours out to his dear ones who are in pain. He suffers with us now, and promises a life forever that will make this one never feel like a waste."

It is my joy to reflect with you about where God's covenant promises may be leading us eternally, but I also feel like it is my duty to remind us that *real life has not even started yet.* Speaker and writer, Damon Gray calls this way of thinking "long-view living," living our lives aware that the 80 years (if we're lucky) that we have on this earth are but a vapor. I want to invite you to begin living life with the knowledge that whatever pain, growth, circumstances, or joys we experience here on earth are just "school days," leading us on to something bigger, wilder, and more alive than we can imagine.

I was talking to a curious skeptic recently who said to me, "I'm not even sure that there *is* anything after death. How do you know that there is an afterlife?" My first response was an involuntary smile. I replied, "I'm not sure exactly how I can prove it to you, but your statement feels to me like someone who is asleep and dreaming, wondering if anything would exist were he to wake up."

Let's wake up to the truth of our eternal life, and begin orienting our hearts toward the forever-adventure that awaits us!

A caveat

Everything that I have spoken about so far in this book has come from what I believe the Bible really says, at least my best interpretation based on my study of it. Certainly, I have used my imagination and read between the lines in places, but my attempt has been to communicate what I think God has wanted to tell us in his story.

This chapter will not be like that. Compared to other things the Bible describes to us, we know very little about heaven. We can't be certain about what our days will look like when God finally completes his project of re-creating his world and the Kingdom of God finally fills the earth. But I do believe that we can make some suppositions based on what he does tell us. And that's what this chapter will be – suppositions. In other words, I'm guessing.

This chapter will be the musings and wonderings of someone who has enjoyed reflecting on what God has wanted all along – with this confidence: *if we understand what he has always wanted, we can make some educated guesses about what he might want in the future.* God is a very consistent fellow. What he loves, he tends to always love. What he wants, he tends to always want. Let's end our One Story journey together by imagining the future God might have in store for us. So place your seat backs and tray tables in their upright and locked positions, and hold on. We are going outside the box!

The Architecture of Eternity

To imagine what God might want in our future with him, I'm going to assume that he still wants what he originally desired when he made everything in the first place. Remember the Eden Design? When God could have made things any way that he wanted, he made them according to a specific form. He wanted a physical earth. He wanted a people who were in his image. He wanted us abiding in deep, safe relationships with him and each other. He wanted rich work and an even richer rest. The One Story has been about God's work to restore that Eden Design. So I believe we can make some projections about what heaven will be like by remembering the architecture that God originally wanted.

Christ has come. The debt has been paid. The Kingdom of God is at hand. What will that world be like when it is fully restored?

He wanted spiritual and physical

A physical earth

Usually when people imagine heaven, they picture some sort of spiritualized place with disembodied saints floating in heavenly bliss. But remember, when God could have made things any way he wanted, he made them both spiritual *and* physical. Certainly, he made us with souls that will never die, but he also gave us physical bodies. He made a planet that was made of dirt, stone, and water – carbon, hydrogen, oxygen, and silicon. He likes physical reality. He invented it! Christians can often live with a strange sense that the "spiritual" is somehow better than the physical – higher, more lofty. And we forget that God has always loved physical reality.

Our sense that the spiritual is somehow more holy than the physical was originated by groups like the Ascetics in the 2nd and 3rd centuries, men who were influenced by the thinking of Plato. They declared that everything that wasn't spiritual, ephemeral, or heavenly was somehow evil and to be avoided. My personal favorite Ascetic monk, (doesn't everyone have a favorite Ascetic monk?) was a guy named Simeon Stylites. He achieved notoriety by living for 37 years perched atop a tall pillar near Allepo, Syria. While there, he ate only beans. His goal was not acclaim, of course; he was trying to live out his belief that it was godly to purge oneself of all earthly pleasure. In other words, "spiritual was good; physical was bad."

We can find that silly, but let me ask you this: when you think of heaven, haven't you been taught to imagine some sort of cloudy spiritual realm where souls are joyfully drifting around singing hymns and playing harps? In other words, don't we often make heaven into some kind of non-physical, ethereal place? Something in us can feel like God's ultimate goal is for us to finally be "spiritual."

I speculate that in the fulfillment of the Kingdom of God, heaven will be *physical,* just as Eden was. Physical life is what God has always wanted for us, and I believe he still wants it. The Bible implies that when everything is renewed, we will live forever in something incarnational and physical – like earth. After all, we are told that at the final day, we don't go up to heaven, heaven will come down to us! Revelation 21 says, "I saw the new Jerusalem *coming down out of heaven* from God." We are told of a new heaven and a new *earth.*

In Romans 8:22, Paul talks about how the whole *creation* groans for redemption. When it is finally redeemed, I believe that the earth will be new. I'm not sure whether God will repair this planet or create a new one. Will we get to watch this time as the Trinity broods and dances their words of creation, spinning a perfect new earth into existence? Either way, I am certain that it will be a physical place with mountains and rivers and oceans, and those lovely sounds that thunderstorms make.

Doesn't this feel right to you? We were created to crave the beauty of earth. It's not accidental that we will travel across the world to visit a range of mountains or a Caribbean island. Why is it a selling point for a house to say that it has "a great view?" Everything in our deepest hearts is made to delight in the physical world that God delights in. He has always promised a *land* to his people. At Eden, that land was a garden. For Israel, it was the Promised Land. And for us all one day, it will be the New Earth. This has always been his plan. In fact, I believe that one of the things you will find most surprising about heaven will be how natural it feels. It will feel "right." You were made for this place (literally).

Physical bodies

It is not just the creation that groans to be redeemed. Paul tells us that the saints do as well, "… waiting eagerly for our adoption as sons, the redemption of our *bodies*." (Rom. 8:23)

When God could have made us any way he wanted, he made us with physical bodies. We're not just spiritual beings; we are physical *and* spiritual.

You know those condescending aliens you find in silly science fiction movies who say stuff like, "We have evolved beyond the need for your puny physical bodies. We are now beings of pure energy." Or as Yoda says so inaccurately, "Luminous beings are we, not this crude matter." Wrong, Master Yoda. Matter isn't crude. God made it. He likes it. God made humans to be physical *and* spiritual.

When Jesus came to earth, he had a body. In his resurrected state, he has a body still. Remember how he ate fish on the beach? Thomas touched the scars in his hands. I believe that when the full redemption is accomplished, we will have physical bodies as well. You declare that you believe this as well every time you recite the Apostle's Creed: "I believe in the resurrection of the *body*, the life everlasting."

Glorified bodies

But our bodies will be better.

I remember hearing Tim Keller speculate about the nature of a glorified human body, unharmed by the fallen world and made like Christ's. What might that body be like? He says it will be glorious, "having about as much in common with your body today as your present body has in common with a tomato."

Our current bodies are profoundly limited and fragile. What might a glorified body be like? Let's take our sense of *sight* for example. If you think about the electromagnetic spectrum (of which visible light is a portion), it is extraordinarily broad. It ranges from gamma rays, which have a tiny frequency of 0.1 nanometers, to long radio waves which have a frequency of 1000 *meters*. That's a range of 10e10 nanometers. (That's a 1 with 11 zeros following it!)

For those of you who stink at math like me, here's the bottom line: it's a *very* broad spectrum. And the punchline is this: the visible spectrum of light that humans can see occupies only *400* of those nanometers. That's right, 400 nm out of 100,000,000,000 nm.

In other words, we look at the universe through a pinhole!

What would the universe look like if we could see the whole spectrum of light? Birds already see in infrared as well as visible light. Those glorious photographs of the galaxy that we get from telescopes like Chandra or Webb, are so magnificent because they are showing us more of the vast spectra of the electromagnetic range. What would a sunset look like if you could see *all of it*? And that's just sight! What about how we encounter the rest of our physical world? What does "run and not get weary" mean? What does "mount up on wings like eagles" look like? I don't know but dream of it with me.

I do know this: heaven will not be *less* real than our current lives; it will be *more*. We haven't even gotten to *real* life yet. I love the imagery in C. S. Lewis's *The Great Divorce*. Lewis portrays heaven as being *more* physically real than earthly life, so much so that the frail visitors from earth are unable to walk on the pointed grass because the blades won't bend under their insubstantial feet. When they try to lift an apple from the ground it is so infinitely real and heavy that they are unable to budge it.

When this vapor melts away and we stand in the massive gravity of real life, I wonder what a real apple will taste like.

So as we begin anticipating God's future fulfillment, remember that he has always loved physical reality. I believe heaven will be weighty with the glory of taste, touch, sound, smell, and sight. You won't believe your eyes!

He Wanted Work

Another thing that God wanted when he originally made everything was for his people to be involved in meaningful, powerful work. The first commandment in scripture was not about obeying some set of rules or laws. The first commandment was God's call for Adam to subdue the earth, be fruitful and multiply, to name the animals.

Remember what we've said about the significance of naming within Hebrew culture. God was telling Adam, "Yes, I have created all of this, but I want you to be in authority over it. You will be the one who names the animals, my lieutenant in charge of running this place." Likewise, we talked about the weighty meaning of David's moving the Ark of the Covenant to Jerusalem. As he did so, David was fulfilling this directive from God to rule. In other words, David was ruler over his kingdom, but acting as God's man.

God has always wanted us to have the blessing of meaningful work, and I believe that there will be rich, exciting work on the New Earth. There will be creativity and growth and learning and lordship. Get the image out of your head of saints, beatifically sitting around on clouds. God's restored kingdom won't be about spending all day reciting catechism. He wants people who are workers, stewards, rulers, and vice-regents. We will engage our eternal lives with craftsmanship and creativity!

Does that sound strange to you? Maybe you're thinking heaven should feel more like summer vacation. Work is a bummer, right? How could there be work in heaven?

I believe that kind of thinking is our natural reflex because the only work we know of happens here in our lives on earth, and that work is cursed. Remember how one of the costs of Adam and Eve's betrayal of God was that God said that work would now become painful? There would be a "sweat of the brow" futility to it. Since then, we don't have very much experience with work that feels the way God created it to feel. So, let's try to reimagine it.

When we first talked about the Eden Design, we said that the best way to understand lifegiving, redeemed work would be to imagine your favorite sport or hobby. Think about your favorite recreational thing to do: travel, golf, cooking, sailing, painting, playing music. And you *kill it!* You play your best round of golf. You cook a steak, you cut into it, and it's perfect. You try to capture an image in a painting, and it pops into life on the canvas!

I've always loved sailing. A few years back I got the opportunity to sail on *Stars and Stripes,* the 12 Metre yacht that won the America's Cup back from Australia in 1987. The race was in the Virgin Islands, and we were set to confront another 12 Metre in a "friendly" competition: a two-boat match-race, just like the real America's Cup. The skipper allowed me to take the position of mainsail trimmer and tactician (essentially, second in command). The race started and we battled the other boat around the triangular course. We used strategy, the massive sails, and ultimately a cleverly played wind shift to win the race! Afterwards, I was exhausted. Sailing that race was *work*, the hardest work. But it felt life-changingly wonderful! That is what Godly labor is supposed to feel like: mastery; wonder; the hardest thing you've ever done, but you *score*!

I believe we will learn new abilities and greater mastery in heaven, too. (There'll be plenty of time!) Personally, I have always wanted to be skilled at music. I'm currently quite inept, but I hope to learn music in the new life (jazz piano, to be specific). And given my current lack of musical ability, (combined with the principle that, in heaven, "the last shall be first") I expect to be a veritable Dave Brubeck and Thelonious Monk combined!

If this kind of thinking sounds strange to you, remember you're used to the "clouds and harps" fluff. Shake that off and look forward to being with our very busy, creative creator, and plan on doing a little creating of your own while you're at it. God has always treasured mastery and skill in his creations and our own. He wants us to be masters of our craft and to delight in our work as he always has in his. In Genesis 1, when he looks at his creation and says, "…and it was good," the Hebrew word alludes to the kind of satisfaction and joy that an artist takes in stepping back, looking at his work and thinking, "Yeah! I got it! That's it! Boom!!" God wants us to join him in that kind of wonderful, skillful work, and in heaven we surely will.

This kind of work is *worship*, by the way. We often envision worship as just being about long prayers and church songs, but in God's economy, worship also involves his people living under his lordship and doing everything he created us to do – and doing it in celebration of him. Adam worshiped God by obeying him, naming the animals, and subduing the earth. In the kingdom of God, we will certainly glory in the presence of our Maker, but we will also rejoice in exercising our best talents and gifts.

He wanted Rest

I saw a client recently who was a medical student. She was overwhelmed with her workload and filled with a sense of shame about a recent failure. But, her real burden lay deeper. As she spoke, she began to unfold a life-story filled with driven perfectionism. When her friends were goofing off in high school or playing around in college, she was constantly working. She took the MCAT over and over again, trying to get a better score. And now that she was in medical school, she was miserable. She finally collapsed in tears in the session and said, "I just need *rest!*"

I was moved at the poignancy of her pain, especially since I was literally working on this part of the book at the time. God created us to need rest. In her case, she longed for relief from the constant demands of her life. Don't all of our hearts live with a level of exhaustion at how difficult life is? We long for spiritual, emotional, physical, *rest*.

As we mentioned earlier when we were discussing the Eden Design, the notion of *shalom* was woven into the fabric of Hebrew culture, an ultimate peace that God promised. When he could have made things any way he wanted, he invented rest – even for himself. He apparently saw the blessing of that kind of peace, even in a perfect Garden. And if he saw the necessity of rest for Adam and Eve at Eden, how much more do we need it now in our world that so is deeply broken? Our hearts long for relief. One day, we will finally find that fullness of rest in his arms.

Real rest

I imagine that of all my suppositions about the nature of heaven, this one is the least surprising to you. All of God's children look forward to everlasting life with God and expect that it will be peaceful. We even speak of the deceased and say, "Rest in Peace."

But I think it goes even deeper than that.

Revelation 21 begins with an intriguing statement. John says, "Then I saw a new heaven and a new earth; for the first heaven and the first earth had passed away, *and there is no longer any sea.*" (Rev. 21:1)

As a lover of the ocean and a lifelong sailor, I've always found this announcement to be somewhat disappointing. I mean, what's more wonderful than the ocean? Why would God get rid of it? Well, like other things in the book of Revelation, this passage is speaking to us in metaphorical imagery. Within Hebrew culture, the sea was a symbol of chaos and danger, as well as judgment (don't forget the Noah flood or the Egyptians and the Red Sea!). The announcement that the sea would be no more is a promise that we need never fear condemnation or judgment again, and that the awful, chaotic unpredictability of our daily lives will be abolished. What awaits instead will be a life free of turmoil and fear, in which all that is left will be grace. All that will remain will be that which is life-giving and life-flourishing – a haven of rest and richness.

Jesus spoke warmly of this kind of security and peace. I love his assurances to his disciples that, though he would be taken from them, he was going to prepare a "place" for them. (John 14:1-4) He promised that in his Father's house were many "dwelling places." The Greek word he uses here is *mone*, and what it means speaks to our deepest longing. *Mone* means "home." The word only appears twice in the whole of the New Testament – both times in this fourteenth chapter of John. The other occurrence is likewise comforting, "Anyone who loves me will obey my teaching. My Father will love them, and we will come to them and make our home [our *mone*] with them." (John 14:23)

What other word better conjures images of safety and rest for our hearts than the word *home*? Perhaps you've been on a wonderful vacation, but it's still such a relief to get home. Maybe you've been in the hospital. Then the doctor comes in and tells you that you have been cleared to go home. Even people who describe home as having been painful do so with the understanding that home should *not* be lonely or full of fear and sorrow. Home should be the place of deepest warmth.

In the midst of the wonder and adventure that I expect we will find in the new earth, we will also be Home. Our hearts will settle in. We will finally know true belonging, and as T.S. Eliot says, we will "know the place for the first time." [9]

In Psalm 90, Moses says, "Lord, you have been our dwelling place (our home) in all generations." And he will continue to be our home forever. Demands gone. Dangers eliminated. Stress and striving ceased.

Rest. Feel relief. Welcome home.

He wanted us to be like him

From the beginning, God has wanted a people who were like him – in his image. As we have said repeatedly, our fundamental human moral error is to think of such godliness as being some sort of a "Dudley Do-Right," "don't drink, smoke, or chew" kind of stiffness. I hope to have broadened your thinking on this matter. It is my prayer that by now, you are understanding "Godliness" as a dynamic, free, powerful gift. Holiness and righteousness are not about rule following, they are about living at last in the ways a human being was intended to live.

People come to me, a psychologist, because something in their lives is not working. What they are seeking from me is a way of living that stops life from being painful; a way of relating that brings fulfillment and joy. What they want is *wholeness*.

Think about yourself for a moment. What are you like? Do you ever wish you were less angry or insecure? Are you tired of being fearful, controlling, depressed, or anxiety ridden? One of the things I see in my work, as people grow in their character (in their hearts), is that humans can be unbelievably strong, beautiful, loving, powerful beings – once they get what they need to be whole and complete.

Imagine what it will be like to be *complete* in God's image, fully human, so to speak: to see yourself automatically react with compassion (or power, if necessary). To reach inside and feel the courage to risk, yet to know warm comfort if you fail; to find creativity and cleverness waiting for you to draw upon them; to delight in goodness; to love

love. This is what God is like. And so shall his image-bearers be!

I believe one of the best things about life in heaven will be that our hearts will at last be "right." The "piano" will finally play in tune. Our hearts will look like his! We just need to scratch the surface of what God wants in our lives to see that he is seeking the richest kind of completion and wholeness in us. Remember he is involved in a restoration project here, and he intends to finish it. He wants to finally melt away your fear and anger and self-centeredness and let you live whole and free.

The Completer of Persons

Hebrews 13:21 is a 'prayer promise' that God will ultimately "make you *complete* in every good work to do his will, working in you what is well pleasing in his sight." The Greek word that the writer uses in this passage for "complete" is *katartizo*, which refers to a rebuilding, a re-fitting, a process of restoring something that has been damaged. This is what God's promise of wholeness is about: not squeaky-clean docility, but an adventurous, free life. Our broken, painful lives get a wheels-up restoration!

Of course, I love this word *katartizo*, because it's what I seek to do every day at my office. When I see my people grow, (get "*katartizorized,*") I'm often shocked at the strength and power that pours forth from a human being. We call that "good psychological health." But what it really is, is a human beginning to realize the rich wholeness that God created us to reflect. They are living "accurately" as we said before.

One of the intriguing results of such growth in wholeness is that people begin to "accidentally" act more like Christ. They're not white-knuckling their way to obedience anymore. Love, humility, and boldness just flow out of them as naturally as their paranoia and resentment did before. They are reflecting the true image of God. They are being "Christ-like."

In *The Weight of Glory*, C.S. Lewis imagines encountering a fully-realized human. He says, "the dullest most uninteresting person you can talk to may one day be a creature which, if you saw them now, you would be strongly tempted to worship." [10] This is what God is talking about when he promises that we will be "glorified" in heaven. (Rom 8:17) He means that we will at last be complete and whole, like our elder brother, Jesus.

And how will this transformation happen? The Apostle John tells us that this dazzling transformation of our very souls will take place simply because we will *see* Christ. "Beloved, now we are children of God; and it has not yet been revealed what we shall be, but we know that *when he is revealed, we shall be like him, for we shall see him as he is.*" (1 John 3:2)

Try that on. You will *see him as he is!*

Think about what keeps you from being whole? What are you seeking so desperately? What is your wounded heart thirsty for? Well, Paul tells us that upon seeing the face of the enthroned Christ, all of the majesty, beauty, peace, wonder, and loveliness of the Son of God will flood into your battered, selfish, frightened heart. Nothing broken in you will be able to resist the awakening healing of his wondrous gaze. You will finally be made whole. Because as he steps down from that throne to touch you, you will find the wholeness you've always been missing, the drink you've always been wanting, and the balm you've so badly needed. You will be complete. You will finally be satisfied. You will be like him. (And even the Apostle John admits he's not sure exactly what that means.)

And I imagine that the sight of his face will also be the sweetest part of heaven as well. (Perhaps it *is* heaven!) We will get to see our

Jesus! Not in vague symbols, not in stories from the Bible, but *as he really is!* The Beloved One of Yahweh – we will see him! I imagine it will take 10,000 years for us to even consider doing anything else.

He wanted relationships

Belonging with each other

The bedrock of emotional health is relational connection. Humans are created to belong and be seen and safely known by other people, something that is tragically absent in our broken world. This is actually the cause of most psychological symptoms. Parts of us that are disconnected from relationships grow more and more unhealthy. In fact, a primary reason that psychotherapy works is that it creates an opportunity for those disconnected parts of us to finally be known again, emotionally naked and not ashamed. Unfortunately, this kind of safety is rare in our day-to-day existence.

In the background of most of our lives is a loneliness. We don't feel known. We feel misunderstood or not seen. What is it that we say in our marriage conflicts? "No! That's not it at all! You don't understand!" We fight to be understood, to be "gotten."

In our daily lives, we often obsess about being liked. We put on a good face or spin ourselves so that people will think we are cool. Then we get home and wonder why we feel empty. My wife teases me sometimes saying, "You psychologist types have all those sophisticated diagnoses and such. The truth is that everyone is just *insecure*." She's got a point. It's rare that I meet someone who feels safe enough to let themselves be known. We are frightened and lonely.

Think about how much you live listening for the rejection or scorn of other people. Think about how much it hooks you when you feel criticized. Well, no one would live that obsessed with rejection or insecurity if there wasn't something inside of us that was absolutely desperate for its opposite: love and acceptance. The longing to be warmly known and loved is the epicenter of the human heart. So much so that we can literally obsess about losing it.

Can you imagine never having to worry about that again?

If God is about restoring the Eden Design, I believe that the wonder of being "naked and not ashamed" again will be fundamentally woven into our lives in the New Earth.

As we have said, "naked and not ashamed" describes a relational status, and know it or not, it's what we all most deeply long for. Naked and not ashamed means that when I am truly seen by another person, the result is greater closeness. I express a longing, and you let that need matter to you. You see my weakness or failure, but you still respect me and want to draw me closer. (Anybody interested? We'll pass a signup sheet around...and we would all sign!) I believe that one of the most beautiful (and relieving) aspects of heaven will be that we will be able to finally be safe with each other, fully known, and not afraid.

Try that on. What it would be like for it to never cross your mind again whether you will be loved or not; to never second-guess something you said, fearing someone's scorn. To never wake up in the morning with that feeling that accuses: "Oh, I can't believe I said *that!*" Shame will be gone – *dead!* We will belong! We will be in the family of God. We were created for this.

Images of intimacy

What can we project about what those relationships in heaven will be like? I've heard Christians sometimes lament Jesus's comment that there will be no marriage in heaven. (Luke 20:34-36) Their conclusion is that we will therefore somehow be deprived of the wonder and richness of (a good) marriage. But remember, God never replaces something good with something less. His gifts always increase in octave, deepen in richness. If we remember who this God is, then we can conclude that there will be no marriage in heaven because there will be a closeness that is of even greater wonder!

When we worry about the absence of marriage in heaven, we are like a child asking his father if, when he grows up, he can still ride his tricycle. "No," his father responds, "there are no tricycles in adult life." What the little boy doesn't know, however, is that though there are no tricycles, there are Ferraris and sailboats and jet planes. No, there will not be marriage. Instead, we will share something of unimaginable beauty and intimacy that will show us what real human connection was supposed to be. If marriage was intended to reflect oneness, then God will give us a better kind of oneness together, one that will overflow our imaginations. If marriage was created to be the playground for fun and belonging and togetherness, then somehow, he has something in store for us all that will knock our socks off!

Will we know each other in heaven? I'm convinced we will! I will still be John. You will still be Mark or Janie. We will still be who we are now, just more so. Someone once asked a wise man if we would know each other in heaven. He said, "We won't know each other *until* we get to heaven." At last, you will be fully you.

I think we will remember our old lives here on earth, as well. Yet our memories will only make us more richly grateful for the relief and freedom that we finally share together. I imagine stories and laughter ("How foolish it was how little we trusted him!") Maybe even sweet sorrow at the ways we hurt Christ and each other. (But he will be there to wipe away every tear.) And then we will be drawn even closer to the One who has redeemed us, and also each to other. We can even talk about this book if you want, because we will remember it. (I'm sure it is unforgettable!) You can say, "Remember back in 2022 when you speculated about heaven? You were way off, man! It's even better than you said!"

Lastly, I can't help but imagine the kinds of conversations we will have there, even with some of our wonderful friends who lived this One Story we've been telling. I want to ask Abraham what it was like when the "smoking fire pot and flaming torch" passed between the hacked-up animals. "Moses, was it strange to return to your old palace in Egypt as the liberator of Israel? Did you see any of your old friends? Did they make fun of you for becoming a Midianite shepherd?" "King David, be honest here…were you scared when you faced Goliath?"

Finally, and most unimaginably, we will be able to have those conversations with Christ himself! One of the most tantalizing passages to me in the New Testament is John 21:25. The apostle almost teases us with this statement: "Now there are also many other things that Jesus did. Were every one of them to be written, I suppose that the world itself could not contain the books that would be written." I don't know about you, but I want to sit for centuries and hear our Jesus tell the rest of his stories!

We were created to live in a warm family, and in heaven, that family will be quite large! God promises that it will be the safest and the most loving family we've ever known. We will never be lonely again.

Belonging with God

In Proverbs 8, the second person of the Trinity (who is defined as Wisdom), speaks and describes what it was like as the Godhead created the world. But as Wisdom speaks, "she" also gives us a glimpse into something even richer: a literal peek into what it was like to be alive in the warmth and wonder of the Trinity!

Wisdom personified says things like, "I was the craftsman at his side. I was filled with delight day after day, rejoicing in his presence, rejoicing in the whole world, delighting in mankind." (Prov. 8:30-31)

The speaker is actually a picture of Christ, who has swirled with the Father and the Spirit through all eternity, living in the deepest abiding. The Trinity is the embodiment of precious, wonderous love. And God longs to welcome us into the dance.

We are told in John chapter 1, that Jesus abided at the *bosom* of the Father. (v. 18) Think about it, in what sorts of relationships might we lay our head upon the bosom of another? Only in the most intimate, safe, tender connections. That's the Trinity.

And the reason God has created us is so he might invite us into that kind of belonging with him.

I love how the Apostle John describes himself in John 13, as "leaning back on Jesus's bosom" at the Last Supper. (v. 25) We will get to be right there next to John, at the bosom of our savior – our big brother and king. God has always wanted that kind of abiding with us. One day all his wishes will come true. And so will ours!

When people imagine heaven, their speculations are often replete with images of wealth and reward: streets of gold, mansions, stars in their proverbial crowns. But I promise you that there will be no richness greater than the wonder of finally being able to be wrapped in his love. Every dream you've ever had, every fantasy or wish, will feel like cotton candy compared with the richness of his heart next to yours.

Remember Jeremiah 31, where God promises a world of belonging? He said, "And no longer shall each one teach his neighbor and say to his brother, 'Know Yahweh,' for they shall all know me, from the least of them to the greatest." (Jer. 31:34) Remember what "knowing" means to the Hebrews? God is telling us that in that day, we will never need to remind one another to be deeply entwined in tender closeness with the God of the universe. There will be no need to say that. There will be no more need for that than for a fish to tell another fish to be wet. There will be no need because we will all already *know* him. The deepest belonging with him will fill us to overflowing. "The *knowledge* of Yahweh will cover the earth, as the waters cover the sea." (Isa. 11:9)

Healing from God

The Bible promises that the pain, brokenness, and sorrow of our lives will be healed in heaven. I believe that our *belonging with our Yahweh* will be the agent of that healing. It will be through his *love* that he will "wipe away every tear." (Rev. 21:4)

A fascinating thing about therapy is that when an individual can access the injuries of the past in the presence of current-day love, somehow that ancient sorrow begins to heal. I've been doing it for 40 years and it still amazes me when I see it happen. Time is relative for our emotional parts (that's why you can smell a turkey roasting and be immediately emotionally transported to your grandmother's house on a Thanksgiving Day, 30 years ago). And when our past pain encounters current love and healing, it has a strange retroactive effect. Today's love rolls back through time and repairs our wounds.

If a fallen image-bearer like a therapist can bring such healing in a paltry therapy office, what would an encounter with the risen Christ do to our broken hearts? I believe that his eyes of love will send shockwaves of warmth, healing, and restoration flooding back through time into the most lost and alone parts of our hearts. The pain will mend. The past will be "changed." Simply engaging his heart will do this for us. And I believe that his wash of love will bring us the deepest tears of healing and relief. Then he will wipe those tears away one final time.

Our new name

One of the most beautiful images of our true and ultimate intimacy with God is given to us early in the book of Revelation. There we are told about a special white stone that each of us will receive from God (a symbol in ancient times of a "not guilty" verdict in a court of law). (Rev. 2:17) And on that stone will be a special name by which only he will call you, a name that is known only to you and your heavenly Father. It will be y'all's secret. And the first time that you hear it, it will be spoken from his own lips, calling you by your real name. Our God is a God of personal knowing. He calls you by your name, and on that day, he will run to you when you call his. This is the kind of belonging he eagerly anticipates with you. Even with Moses on Horeb, he was "the God of the Name." He gave us his; one day he will give your yours. You will call him Yahweh. What will he call you?

This kind of safety and closeness is God's passion. Remember his covenant song throughout the One Story. "I will be your God, and you will be my people, and I will dwell among you." This is something he has wanted throughout history. And in the final shout at the end of the world he will say it again, his heart filled with a tone of victory and relief! With thundering joy, he will proclaim from the throne, "Behold, the dwelling place of God is with man. He will dwell with them, and they will be his people, and God himself will be with them as their God." (Rev. 21:3) At last!

The wonder of God himself

As you can tell, I am deeply excited about the richness of being with him! But should I be? In our culture, our gut sense about God is often that he is some kind of big supreme being who lives at church.

He's into righteousness and justice and things that are "holy." Would hanging out with him really be that much fun?

As we draw toward the end of our One Story, let's reflect again on what he is like. And let's do it the easy way. No big biblical exegesis or expository preaching, I'm going to remind you who he is in the same way *he* often does: by inviting us to look at what he has made. When the Bible tells us that the heavens declare the glory of God, it's not just whistling Dixie. (Ps. 19:1) If you want to understand something of what being with God will be like, open your eyes. Look around!

Think about it (and this is the last time I'm going to say that phrase, I promise): the only reason creation could be good, the only reason there could be anything we enjoy about God's world, is that he has decided to make it to reflect a piece of *who he is*. It's good because *he* is good. Life can be delightful because the person who made it is delightful. If his world has such wonder, then what must he be like?

What does his world show us about him?

Think about the things that bring you joy: that deep, creaky-gigantic-staircase sound that an oak tree makes in the windy woods. The explosion in your mouth of a perfect Georgia peach in mid-June. The way a puppy gnaws on your finger with its needle-sharp little teeth. Watching the shadow of clouds move across a mountain on a windy day. Placing your hand on the top of your infant grandson's little head and feeling his soft fuzzy hair as he sleeps. The feeling you get when someone you love really loves you back. The smell of rain. And how every spring, sometime around Easter, everything that's dead starts to live again. (I think he's trying to tell us something.)

We get Miles Davis, Vincent Van Gogh, Annie Dillard, and the Beatles. He gives us chocolate, a confection that somehow melts at a temperature just a couple of degrees lower than that of your mouth.

That's why it feels so unctuous and smooth as you not only taste it but inhale its fragrance.

We get Enceladus, a moon of Saturn that is covered in snow, making it the second brightest object in the solar system, next to the sun. Why is it so bright? Because it's hollow and filled with water and carbon dioxide (i.e. club soda). As mighty Saturn's gravity pummels the little moon, it agitates the interior liquid. Consequently, Enceladus is constantly spewing "seltzer" into space through surface vents like a shaken up can of 7-Up. The fizz sprays into space, freezes, and then rains back down on the planet as snow. The result: a brilliant celestial "snow globe" circles the ringed planet of Saturn!

Yeah, God made that up!

He made it all up!

I love to cook, and my buddies and I have always marveled at how wonderful food can be. (As Dizzy Dean said, "It ain't braggin' if you can do it!") One night, one of my friends said the following as a blessing before our meal: "You know he didn't have to make food taste good. Certainly, we need it for nourishment, but why did he decide to make it wonderful? He didn't have to. He could have made everything 'taste like chicken.' But for some reason, he created this complex richness in food. So why did he make a trillion wonderful flavors for us? Why? Because he longs to bring his people joy. This is who he is! Amen."

Glasses clink. A toast: "To the King!"

So, here's my point – Don't taste the goodness in God's *creation* and miss the fact that the only reason our world is good, the only reason art is beautiful, or that a breeze feels refreshing, or that Saturday mornings are awesome – is because *he* is good, and he lets his creation share a fragment of the goodness that overflows from him eternally.

And if delighting in his world is as wonderful as it is, then what will it be like to be with the source of that wonder. He *is* beauty. He *is* wonder. He *is* creativity. He is the reason you love anything that you love!

I believe that one of the reasons that we will need glorified bodies in heaven is so that we can even tolerate the power of his love and beauty. I believe if we were to truly experience the gravity of his richness and love today, we would literally die – our current fragile bodies would not be able to tolerate it. I've seen clients literally collapse, shake, and sob when they even brush the fringes of real love. They later tell me that they went home and slept the rest of the afternoon from exhaustion. I believe to fully experience the wonder of God literally requires more "substance" than we currently have. In other words, God shields Moses from fully beholding him on the mountain for Moses's own protection! (Ex. 33:20) God invites us to heaven, but right now, I don't think either you or I could handle it. He is too wonderful for us to currently survive!

Until we get to be with him, I invite you to let the joys that he creates for us here on earth lift your heart to his. When you step outside on a perfect spring morning, or downshift into a turn in a convertible, or finally pay off your home mortgage, let that joy remind you of the Maker of all Joy. Let the anticipation of his wildness and love fill your heart. And think, "If the knowledge of this person will cover me like the ocean one day, then drown me, baby!"

The End and the Beginning

This is the purpose of the One Story, gang. Yahweh's goal has always been to take the pain, suffering, loneliness, and isolation of our lives, and throw them into the darkness forever. The point is for us to walk again at his side. At the end of J.R.R. Tolkien's *The Lord of the*

Rings, after all the enemies have been defeated, Sam Gamgee looks up at Gandalf and says "Is everything sad going to come untrue? What's happened to the world?" [11] What has happened is the One Story, Sam. And the answer to your question is "Yes!" God has been working on this happy ending for centuries. It is *Our Story* now, and it is the story that will ultimately lead to our deepest union with him.

My brother, Mark, died 32 years ago at the age of 26. I was 29. As we made sense of his loss, his friends and I routinely had dreams about him. We stayed in touch and shared what we called "Mark dreams" with one another. One of his best friends, Claude, had a dream that I've never forgotten because it speaks so clearly to the reality of our future. In the dream, Claude was at a party, and all of Mark's friends and family were there in attendance. We were told that the guest of honor, Mark, would be arriving soon on a brief vacation from heaven. There was a knock at the door and to our great joy, Mark had come. His face shone with joy as we all embraced him in tears.

Claude said to him, "Mark! You look so happy!"

Mark replied, "I am, Claude. I'm so excited. I'm getting married!"

"Getting married?!" Claude replied. "To whom? Who's the lucky girl? Someone you've met in heaven?"

"No, Claude." Mark replied with a tone of tolerant patience. "The Lamb, Claude. I'm marrying the Lamb!"

This story is not about religion, my friends. It is about love eternal. It is about finally living the richest life imaginable, wedded to the most wonderful person imaginable.

This is how the Apostle John describes it (my paraphrase of his words) in Revelation 21:1-6. Hear him and let your heart lift in anticipation of this day.

"I looked up and saw the renewed world at last. The old broken one had finally been pushed so far away. All of the fear and chaos was gone. In its place, I saw God's own city. The one he fills with his glory; bright and beautiful and pure and lovely, coming down to finally belong to his people. It was their wedding day!

And he spoke with a voice of thunder and joy from his throne, saying, "Look! Never stop seeing this. The restored world that God has always wanted – the one he's given everything to rebuild – is finally here! It will be filled with his precious people. And he will be with them. And they will be together at last!

And your pain? It will be gone. Your tears? I will personally wipe them away. All the sorrow and loneliness and brokenness has disappeared, melted away in my blood. Behold, I am making all things new and alive and right!

All of the Story and all of the work is done. I am everything! I am the beginning of this Story, and I am the ending that will never end! All of you who have been thirsting for so many years can now richly drink from my water, which never runs dry. And the best part is, when you look up from drinking the deepest draughts of my goodness, you will see my eyes, and you will hear me call you, *my son.*"

Then, as he wraps us into his arms, he promises in the passage that he will protect us from all those who would seek to destroy the goodness that he has created. This fallen, broken, hurtful place where we now live will never happen again. And he welcomes us into the rest of our lives, into the marriage supper that will last forever; into the New Life that never ends.

This is the *end and the beginning* of our One Story. This is what it's all been for: Eden, Noah, Abraham, Moses, David, the prophets and Jesus; everything we've talked about has been to at last restore this hope: The One Story of life with Him – the story that will never end. And in a manner that almost bookends the whole of His Story, one of our last sights as John closes his vision of the end of this "old time," is a image of the Tree of Life. The one that was taken from us by God and his cherubim at Eden. Now it appears again at the end of this odyssey of love and hope. Now it sits by the river that flows from Yahweh and the Lamb. (Rev. 22:1-2) And is offered freely to his children.

As Aslan says at the end/beginning of Narnia,

> "'The [school] term is over: the holidays have begun. The dream is ended: this is the morning.' And as He spoke, He no longer looked to them like a lion; but the things that began to happen after that were so great and beautiful that I cannot write them. And for us, this is the end of all the stories, and we can most truly say they lived happily ever after. But for them it was only the beginning of the real story. All their life in this world and all their adventures in Narnia had only been the cover and the title page; now at last they were beginning Chapter One of the Great Story which no one on earth has read; which goes on forever: in which every chapter is better than the one before." [12]

And that is not fiction. It is true.

It is true only because of the One, the precious Seed who was promised by this story and provided by God's covenant; the One whom we have gotten the privilege of beholding. The One who came and obeyed and suffered and died for us: his beloved, sought-for children. He is the "Offspring of David, the bright and morning star." (Rev. 22:16)

This is all about him – because he wanted us.

And that is why the rest of our *Always Story* will be about rejoicing in him, and with him. Forever.

Endnotes

[1] Lewis, C. S. 1960. *Mere Christianity.* New York: Macmillan.

[2] Lewis, C. S., 1994. *The Lion, the witch, and the wardrobe.* New York, NY: HarperTrophy.

[3] Shakespeare, William, 2002. *King Henry V. Cambridge,* UK: Cambridge University Press. Act 4, Scene 8.

[4] Lewis, C. S. 1946. *The great divorce.* London : HarperCollins, 2002.

[5] Lewis, C. S. (Clive Staples), 1898-1963. *The Magician's Nephew.* New York: HarperCollins, 1994.

[6] Watts, Isaac 'Joy to the World' first published in "The Psalms of David" 1719.

[7] Lewis, C. S. 1960. *Mere Christianity.* New York: Macmillan.

[8] Augustine: Sermon on the Mount, Harmony of the Gospels, Homilies on the Gospels Sermons on Selected Lessons of the New Testament.

[9] T.S. Eliot, from "Little Gidding," Four Quartets (Gardners Books; Main edition, April 30, 2001) Originally published 1943."

[10] Lewis, C. S. *The Weight of Glory and Other Addresses.* 1st HarperCollins ed. [San Francisco]: HarperSanFrancisco, 2001.

[11] Tolkien, J. R. R. 1991. *The Lord of the Rings.* London, England: HarperCollins.

[12] Lewis, C.S *The Last Battle Chronicles of Narnia.* Volume 7.

Appendix 1.a.

There is a lovely little inside joke later in scripture that plays on the protoevangelium's promise that the Seed will crush the serpent.

It happens centuries after the Fall in the garden, when the Seed and the Serpent first meet on earth. It is when Jesus is in the wilderness and the Serpent comes to tempt him. In one of those temptations, Satan takes Jesus to the highest point of the temple and invites him to prove that he is God's son by jumping off the temple spire. He then quotes Psalm 91:11,12 (a Psalm of Moses) to make his point. "He will give his angels charge concerning you, to guard you in all your ways. They will bear you up in their hands, lest you strike your foot against a stone." (Matt. 4:5-6)

Jesus responds by quoting Deuteronomy, but he could have responded in another way (if he were as sarcastic as I). He could have said, "That's an excellent point, Serpent. But you only quoted Psalm 91: 11,12. Would you be willing to quote verse 13 for me as well? It speaks of another encounter that we will have one day. And since you seem so well versed in scripture, I know that you know what that meeting will entail."

Verse 13 says, "You will then tread on the Lion and the Cobra, the lion and the serpent you will trample down."

Satan conveniently omits the rest of Moses's promise, the one that describes how the Seed will ultimately crush this Serpent who only wishes to destroy. What a perfect example of how the Serpent operates. Praise be to God that the Seed indeed did his work and crushed this Serpent for us!

Appendix 8.a.

Righteous Biscuits
Makes about 6-8 Biscuits

2 cups self-rising flour
2 nice pinches of kosher salt
1/2 teaspoon sugar
4 tablespoons cold butter, cut in ½ inch pieces.
4 tablespoons margarine or shortening, also cut in pieces.
Scant 1 cup buttermilk

1. Preheat oven 450° (With "grandma's black skillet" (or a cookie sheet if you're not a *real* Southerner), already inside. We want 'em hot!)
2. Combine the flour, salt, and sugar, and cut the butter and margarine/shortening into the mix until grainy and incorporated, the size of peas.
3. Incorporate buttermilk. Biscuit dough should be somewhat sticky.
4. Pat out dough on floured surface and fold over 3 or 4 times to create layers, using just enough flour to manage the dough. (This is key!)
5. Cut with a round cutter, only pushing down, not twisting.
6. Take the skillet out of the oven and melt some butter in the bottom (it will sizzle, etc). (Or just use the hot cookie sheet.) Carefully place biscuits inside skillet and dribble the tops with buttermilk.
7. Bake at 450° in the lower third of the oven for 20 min.
8. Serve to a grateful world.

By the way, Chefs are the most "legalistic" people in the world. Why? Because there is a *way* that makes food taste good, and there is a *way* that makes food tastes bad. We don't get to make up those rules. We just eat bad food if we break them – just like the Law. (There's a sermon in that.)

Appendix 8.b.

Why does the forgiveness of sin require a sacrifice of *death*? The Bible never really explains exactly why. There's just always this background truth that if you have violated God, you deserve to die. But why?

Answer number one: I don't know. I'm not sure we can ever fully understand why death is required of those who turn from God. I think until we meet God and encounter who he really is, we will never really comprehend why a violation of his holiness and justice would require the ultimate sacrifice. So, if you have this question, my first answer is, "Wait and see." I believe when we finally do see, it will be overwhelming. And perhaps unpleasant.

Answer number two: the Bible engages several different analogies to help us wrap our minds around this lofty question. One portrays being a sinner as something like being a debtor who could never pay his debt. Yet, someone else, totally innocent of the debt, comes and pays that which is owed – and the debtor is freed! As Colossians 2 says, "And you, who were dead in your trespasses and the uncircumcision of your flesh, God made alive together with him, having forgiven us all our trespasses, by canceling the record of debt that stood against us with its legal demands. This he set aside, nailing it to the cross." (Col. 2:14-15)

Another analogy compares it to a criminal on death row who is somehow spared because another dies in his place. This theme of course, has become a favorite in literature, the hero who dies to save others (think Sydney Carton in *A Tale of Two Cities* or Spock in *The Wrath of Khan*). Deep in the human archetype is the image of the sacrificial lamb who dies to save those he loves. Something in us knows this is right.

But why does someone have to *die?*

Answer number three: Think for a moment about how forgiveness works. If you really engage the process of forgiveness, you will very quickly encounter the following fact about it — *someone has to pay* — even with simple practical injuries. If you break my phone, someone has to pay. Either you will pay to buy me a new phone, or I will pay to get mine fixed, or I will use a landline. But someone has to pay. There's no way that someone doesn't pay.

That's easy when you're talking about phones, but what about when our hearts are damaged or our dignity violated? And what if God is the one violated? What is the cost there?

Let me tell you a little story from my parenting book, *Setting Parents Free*, that might give you some clarity about the necessity of payment in the face of an injury, to our hearts or to God's. It's hard to *explain* the necessity of payment, but it's not so hard to *feel it* when you see it happen.

I was hanging out with my young kids one day as they were playing on the floor together. Suddenly, as I looked up, Katherine just reared back and slapped Callie across her face. I saw it happen!

Callie began crying, and I said to Katherine, "Oh my Gosh! You just hammered your sister! Go to timeout, now!"

Katherine immediately softened, looked at me, and said, "But Daddy, can't you just forgive me?"

I paused, wondering perhaps if this could be an opportunity to teach her about grace and forgiveness. After all, I am constantly doing destructive, hurtful things and then turning to God and asking for forgiveness. For a moment, this seemed reasonable.

But then I looked at Callie's face as she saw me considering this option. Her eyes and mouth were open and pleading with a look of betrayal and disbelief flooding over her, as if to say, "She just hit me, and you are going to just let that *not matter?* You're just going to let the fact that she assaulted me cost her *nothing*? Does my heart and my injury matter that little?"

Think about it. What would it have said about Callie's dignity, or the significance of her injury, were I to have just let Katherine "off the hook?" It would have said to Callie that she mattered so little in the universe that someone could assault her and there need be no consequence whatsoever. It would've said that her heart and her dignity were not worth any value at all. Everything *just* in the world would have felt violated to her. And she would have been correct. (Katherine went to timeout, by the way.)

As I have contemplated the problem of a death requirement by God, it hit me that this story about my kids was a small picture of why a violation of God's heart requires such a deeply significant payment. If it would violate Callie for me to not discipline Katherine in any way, imagine what sort of payment it would require to bring satisfaction for an offense against God himself (a slap in his face)? It might require something as grave as the death of the sinner or even the horrifying death of the very Son of God.

Beyond this difficult question is the staggering fact that whether we understand it or not, God understood it. He understood it enough to go ahead and solve this problem for us. Whatever the reason death is required, God loved us enough to do the dying for us. His unending love "cut us out of the loop" of justice, so that we could be his forever.

Why he was willing to do that for us is the question that should really puzzle us.

APPENDICES

Appendix 9.a. The Advocacy of Moses

When Moses stepped into the halls of the pharaoh to free the people, a new era began for God's people. The people now had an *advocate*, someone who spoke on their behalf. Moses was a go-between amongst Yahweh, the people, and the Egyptian king.

Once they are freed from slavery, Moses remains the people's advocate in an even more important way. He will be their advocate before *God himself!* Moses plays many roles in our One Story: he's the recipient of God's holy name at the burning bush. He leads the people in their escape from Egypt. He mediates their disputes among one another, and he brings them God's Law. But as we watch the unfolding of God's redemption, perhaps Moses's most beautiful role is that he is the *first advocate between God and man.*

An advocate is a third party. An advocate has the power to speak to the strong on behalf of the weak. An advocate is someone who is acquainted with both parties. He has the ear of the powerful, and he cares for the needs of the vulnerable. Moses's role as advocate will be a landmark in God's relationship with his people. *From now on, God's relationship with us will be a triangle. A three-way relationship. Until the end of the world, there will be God, his people, and their advocate.*

It is so even today. We live with "an advocate with the Father, Jesus Christ the righteous." (I John 2:1) But Moses was the first. His advocacy for his people foreshadows Christ's advocacy for us.

If we look back through the history of our One Story, we see that before Moses, there had never been an advocate between God and his people. God had historically dealt with individuals or with families, but now, as he's dealing with his people in the wilderness, he has a go-between: Moses. Sometimes Moses will bring God's wonder and glory down from the mountain and shine it upon the people. Sometimes he will work to stay the hand of God's judgment as he pleads on behalf of the people. In the midst of all of their interactions with Yahweh, the people had a friend, an advocate, Moses.

One of the most powerful examples of Moses's intervention for the people occurs in Exodus 32. While Moses was up on the mountain receiving God's Law, the people build and worship the golden calf. (This is sort of like cheating on your fiancé while he is out buying your wedding present!) God's anger burns against the people, and he orders the priests to kill 3,000 of them by the sword. But Moses intercedes for them, and he actually does so by telling God's own One Story back to him. He comes to God and says, "Remember Abraham, Isaac, and Israel, your servants, to whom you swore by your own self (*he's referring to God's covenant walk between the cut pieces here*), and you said to them, 'I will multiply your offspring as the stars of heaven, and all this land that I have promised I will give to your offspring, and they shall inherit it forever.'" (Ex. 32: 11-13)

But then Moses goes a step further. He goes deeper in his advocacy than I think even he imagined at the time. Moses stands before Yahweh and pleads for something unprecedented, something that will actually *occur* centuries later. But not to Moses.

On that mountain, Moses, the advocate for the people of God, looks to God and says, "But now, forgive their sin – and if not, *please blot me out from your book which you have written.*" (Ex. 32: 32)

Here is the deepest advocacy: as he stands in front of the accused and condemned people, their representative before God says, "No, Father, take me instead. Make *me* an outcast; make *me* forsaken, and draw *them* to your heart." Here, Moses most truly points us to the one true Advocate between God and man. The one whose name would *actually* be blotted from God's sight.

We are told in Exodus 32 that, as a result of Moses's intervention, "Yahweh relented from the disaster that he had spoken of bringing on his people." Truly, Yahweh "remembered" his covenant promise to preserve his people, all because of the work of their advocate. In Moses we have yet another picture of the promised Seed who is to come, our advocate, Christ.

Acknowledgments

My deepest gratitude goes to Katie Walker Sikkema. No one has contributed to this book as much as she. She waded through the mire of my awkward early drafts; she confronted my flaws, brightened my thinking, and brought refreshing wisdom to this book. But mostly she has remained a powerful tether, helping to anchor this book to the heart of God. My deepest thanks to you, my friend.

I offer a special dedication of this book to the Reverend Jimmy Turner, who, by personally loving me, taught me that God did too. I had always been to church, but he helped me want to *know* this God. He also taught me I could study psychology and God, and be faithful to both. Few have so powerfully impacted the kingdom at large, and he has always done so simply by pursuing the hearts of his students. I got to be one of them.

To my innumerable Sunday school teachers, who, when I was a child at First Presbyterian Church, Jackson, first told me these stories: Ms. Mary Jane Wilburn, Ms. Lowery, Ms. Stringer, Van Rusling, Harry Fulcher, and, in 6th grade, my dad!

To Donna Dobbs for telling me to learn and teach the covenant, and for putting that book in my hands.

To Steve Rosenblatt for telling me to write this book years ago, and for reassuring me that he would "have my back."

To my seminary professors: Dr. R. C. Sproul, Dr. Reg McClelland, Dr. Knox Chamblin, Dr. Richard DeWitt, Dr. Doug Kelly, Dr. Willem VanGemeren. I give you deepest thanks for showing me what a joy it could be to study, learn about, and draw closer to our Yahweh. And to you guys especially, I beg forgiveness for all the ways in which this book probably goofs up your excellent teaching!

THE ONE STORY

To Intown Church in Atlanta, to whom I preached these stories – for teaching me that God's people could be grateful to hear them.

To Catalina Foothills Church in Tucson, who helped me finally pull the trigger to write them down.

Special thanks to Neil, Lindsay, and Carroll at Nautilus Press in Oxford, who took in some jake-leg shrink and made him sound like a decent writer.

To John Evans and the crew at Lemuria Book Store, who, for both of my books, have inexplicably treated me like someone important.

To Leigh and Abbey at the office, for their wise and ready insights as I wrote.

Deep, warm thanks to my wife, Norma, who for decades has celebrated with me as have I tumbled into rooms breathless or tearful with excitement, proclaiming yet another amazing part of God's story that I had uncovered. She also told me I was a good enough writer to tell this story. Even if it wasn't true, it was helpful to hear.

And to my parents, who, as I sat in a little wooden rocking chair at the age of five, taught me that I would actually live forever because of Jesus.

And I believed.

Made in the USA
Middletown, DE
21 May 2024